The Complete Idiot's Reference Card

Burning Wedge Shot

This shot can be played with a pitching wedge, gap wedge, or sand wedge and is ideal when playing to a hole at the back of a green with the wind in your face. Here are the vital steps to playing this low-trajectory shot that takes two or three small hops when hitting the green, checks hard, and then screeches to a halt next to the hole.

1. Set up open, with the ball back in your stance, just behind the centerline of your body.
2. Stand a little closer to the ball than you would normally when hitting a wedge, so you ensure an upright swing plane.
3. Position your hands ahead of the ball so that the club shaft leans toward the target.
4. Put 70 percent of your weight on your left foot.
5. Grip more firmly with your left hand than with your right hand.
6. When swinging back, keep the takeaway action narrow, your hands close to your body, and the action compact. You should feel as if the club swings a little outside the target line.
7. At the start of the downswing, let the club loop back to the inside on a sharp angle of attack as you feel a distinct pull-down action.
8. Keep the image of squeezing the ball with the clubface clearly in mind and retain the firm pressure in your left hand. That way, you will be encouraged to hit down sharply with your hands leading and the back of your left wrist flat at impact.

Extra-Long, 7 Iron Chip

When the ball lies cleanly in the front fringe, about 60 to 90 feet from a hole that's positioned on the upper level of a two-tier green, hit a chip with a 7 iron instead of a wedge, and follow these steps:

1. Visualize the ball travelling a quarter of the distance to the hole in the air and rolling the remaining three-quarters of the way.
2. Take a slightly open, narrow stance to help you see the hole and target line more clearly, and swing the club freely through on the downswing.
3. Play the ball opposite the midpoint in your stance with your hands slightly ahead.
4. Grip the club more firmly than you would normally when hitting a standard chip shot. This will help you to resist breaking down through the impact area.
5. Swing the club back using the triangle formed by your arms and shoulders. For added feel, you can choose to let the right wrist hinge just slightly to help aid touch and feel.
6. Swing down through the ball with the hands leading the club into impact.
7. Hold your body's triangle until shortly after impact.

alpha books

Plugged-Lie Bunker Shot

No matter where you travel in the world to play golf, you eventually find your ball plugged, meaning that the ball is buried halfway or more in the sand with little or no crater of sand around it. The following are the steps you should take to recover:

1. Play the ball back in your stance. You almost cannot play it too far back. (Just the opposite of a bunker shot from a good lie.)
2. Place your hands well ahead of the ball so that the shaft leans at least 10 degrees forward to the target.
3. Set about 75 percent of your weight on your left foot.
4. Grip the club firmly.
5. Set the face of your sand wedge behind the ball and above the sand slightly with the clubface looking downward slightly. Remember that when you lean the shaft forward, you must carefully check clubface alignment. So close that clubface.
6. Make an abrupt upright backswing.
7. The ball will come out quite fast or hot, so you do not need to swing down all that quickly or extra hard for a normal length shot.
8. Contact the sand about an inch behind the ball, burying the club into the sand.

The Long Putt

Course designers believe that if they make it quite easy for you to reach a green in regulation figures, you will have to earn par by two, putting a long distance from the hole. The following are the steps to take when lagging the ball close to the hole from, say, 40 feet or more, on a level green:

1. Visualize the ball rolling at a particular speed and along a particular line to the hole. See whether you can estimate the actual time the putt will take to reach the hole. Check yourself by timing putts, and then practice real-time visualization.
2. Translate this speed into feel—determine how long and strong a stroke you must make to propel the ball to the hole.
3. Position the ball as you do normally when putting, but stand more erect because this enhances your overall perspective of the line and may help your feel for distance.
4. Take a wider stance than normal to promote a slightly longer stroke.
5. Set your eyes just inside the target line, as this helps promote a slight inside-square-inside path, similar to a full swing.
6. Make a pendulum-type, arms-and-shoulders stroke, but allow your wrists to hinge slightly for added feel.
7. Before you play, make a habit of practicing long putts for at least five minutes. Do this every time.

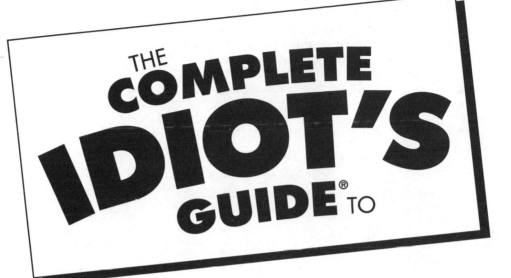

THE COMPLETE IDIOT'S GUIDE® TO

Improving Your Short Game

by Jim McLean

alpha books

Macmillan USA, Inc.
201 West 103rd Street
Indianapolis, IN 46290

A Pearson Education Company

THE COMPLETE IDIOT'S GUIDE TO and Design are registered trademarks of Macmillan USA, Inc.

International Standard Book Number: 0-02-863889-1
Library of Congress Catalog Card Number: Available upon request.

05   8   7

Interpretation of the printing code: The rightmost number of the first series of numbers is the year of the book's printing; the rightmost number of the second series of numbers is the number of the book's printing. For example, a printing code of 00-1 shows that the first printing occurred in 2000.

Printed in the United States of America

Publisher
Marie Butler-Knight

Product Manager
Phil Kitchel

Managing Editor
Cari Luna

Senior Acquisitions Editor
Renee Wilmeth

Development Editor
Tom Stevens

Production Editor
JoAnna Kremer

Copy Editor
Susan Aufheimer

Illustrator
Jody P. Schaeffer

Cover Designers
Mike Freeland
Kevin Spear

Book Designers
Scott Cook and Amy Adams of DesignLab

Indexer
Lisa Wilson

Layout/Proofreading
Svetlana Dominguez
Ayanna Lacey
Heather Hiatt Miller
Stacey Richwine-DeRome

Contents at a Glance

Contents

Foreword

When I was asked to write this foreword, I felt honored, for Jim McLean has had a tremendously positive influence on my golf career. In addition to helping me with my swing, Jim has given me guidance on all aspects of the short game.

Jim and I first started working together in 1990, just after the United States Open was played in June. His knowledge and passion for the game were instantly apparent. I love taking lessons from Jim, knowing that he backs up his own knowledge and theories on proper pitching, chipping, bunker-play, and putting techniques by citing information he has received from numerous legends of golf. In short, when you work with Jim, you receive proven tips.

What I like most about Jim's teaching philosophy is that it is free of any magic tricks or hidden secrets. He is a-meat-and-potatoes type of teacher who believes that hard practice, a positive attitude, and good solid fundamentals will help you evolve more quickly into a top player. I agree.

I feel fortunate that Jim let me get a sneak preview of the manuscript of the book you now hold in your hands. All I can say after reading the manuscript of *The Complete Idiot's Guide to Improving Your Short Game* is that it will inevitably become one of your most valuable instructional tools. This book covers everything. And you are definitely not an idiot for buying it.

Happy golfing!

Brad Faxon

Bradford John Faxon is a former top amateur player and a five-time winner on the PGA Tour. Although Faxon is a fine swinger of the club, he is best known for his short-game talents, particularly his putting prowess. His most prestigious victory on this side of the Atlantic was The International. Overall, his most-prized win was the 1993 Australian Open. Faxon has also represented America as a member of the Ryder Cup Team.

Introduction

I doubt if there is a teaching professional alive who has read more golf books than I have, taken more personal lessons, given more lessons, or played more golf. Further, I bet no golf teacher has worked privately with as many of the greatest short game players, practiced as long and hard on pitching, chipping, bunker play and putting, or observed and conducted as many clinics.

I'm very proud of my experience, for it allows me to speak authoritatively and present to you short game tips that pros and top amateurs depend on every time they play.

We live in and age of mass information. But that's not necessarily a good thing for golfers. In fact, much of what you see and read, via television and the print media, is meaningless garbage. I find this tragic because inaccurate information is far worse than no information. In fact, misinformation is the reason golfers have not improved all that much in the 500 years the game has been played.

I'm happy to report that *The Complete Idiot's Guide to Improving Your Short Game* is packed with original and evergreen tips on everything from the ins and out of establishing the proper pitching set-up to how to best putt indoors. These tips are largely based on my conversations and observations of such legendary players as Gene Sarazen and Ken Venturi, and also the modern giants Tiger Woods, David Duval, Sergio Garcia, and putting great Justin Leonard. I share with you what I learned from other supreme putters, most notably those on my top ten list: Ben Crenshaw, Bobby Locke, Jack Nicklaus, Gary Player, Billy Casper, Bob Charles, Bobby Jones, Tom Watson, Greg Norman, and Brad Faxon.

This book is so special that it even contains a chapter describing what you can learn from the late great Payne Stewart. Payne was a superb short game player, so hopefully the instructional messages you receive will help raise the level of the shots you hit from around and on the green.

Extras

There are some special elements in this book to help you along the way to improving your short game:

Bet You Didn't Know

These sidebars provide bits of history, little-known facts, and the inside scoop on the pros.

Jim's Tips

These tips from the expert provide that little extra advice to help you perfect your short game.

Death Moves

Think of these as warning signs. Here you get the lowdown on what to watch for and avoid.

Swing Lingo

Here you find definitions and explanations for the technical terms that will have you talking like a pro.

Acknowledgments

The planning and creativity involved in the publication of this book could not have been possible had it not been for John Andrisani. Andrisani, a former senior instruction editor at *Golf Magazine*, did a wonderful job of putting my ideas on paper and clearly communicating the instructional message involving the short game.

Additionally, I thank my entire staff of 25 teachers, including Dave Collins, Deborah Doniger, and John Mills. They all did a fine job of allowing me to bounce some ideas off them, when they were not contributing some themselves.

I am also grateful to all the professionals and teachers who I have learned so much from over the years, most notably Jackie Burke, Ken Venturi, Len Mattiace, Tom Kite, Carl Welty, Jimmy Ballard, Jerry Tucker, Bill Davis, Al Mengert, and the late Claude Harmon Sr.

I must also thank my agent Scott Waxman, of the Scott Waxman Agency in New York City, New York, for believing in this idea and presenting it to Marie Butler-Knight of Macmillan USA. Speaking of Macmillan, I owe a great degree of gratitude to Tom Stevens, a very good editor affiliated with that company.

I am grateful, too, to photographers Yasuhiro Tanabe and Phil Sheldon, and to the illustrators.

Last, but by no means least, I thank my family: my wife Justine and my two boys Matt and Jon.

Dedication

To Carl Welty, Jack Burke, Ken Venturi, Claude Harmon, and Johnny Revolta—five short-game stars who shared their knowledge and their friendship.

I also dedicate this book to Doug Sanders, who invented many of the short-game shots now played on the PGA Tour, and my students that I learned so much from.

Photos

Unless otherwise indicated, all photos were provided by Yasuhiro Tanabe, Beyondship.

Trademarks

All terms mentioned in this book that are known to be or are suspected of being trademarks or service marks have been appropriately capitalized. Alpha Books and Macmillan USA, Inc., cannot attest to the accuracy of this information. Use of a term in this book should not be regarded as affecting the validity of any trademark or service mark.

Part 1

Early Short-Game Steps

If you are a newcomer to golf, or have just played it casually up until now, you know that it can be very intimidating. You really know what I mean if you have failed to hit short-game shots well. Pitch shots, chips, and bunker shots look simple because they are played from areas of grass and sand close to the green. Moreover, they don't require much power to propel the ball to the hole. This is precisely why many golfers become so frustrated when they can't get the job done. Maybe you fall into the same category. If so, don't panic. I help you learn how to play these basic shots, plus give you the groundwork necessary for becoming a good putter.

I put you on the right track immediately by providing you with a foundation for building a solid short game. In this part, I define short game shots so that you have a clear picture of them in your head. You learn how to set up and make the right swings. I will also teach you to use mental imagery to your advantage, work on drills to drum the correct actions into your muscle memory, and even give you some tips for honing your pitching, chipping, bunker play, and putting swings at a local pitch-and-putt course.

Chapter 1

What Is the Short Game?

> **In This Chapter**
>
> ➤ Pitching, chipping, and bunker play secrets
>
> ➤ Short game versus long game
>
> ➤ Playing that other game—putting
>
> ➤ Following a routine

The short game consists of the variety of shots played within 75 yards of the hole and encompasses four categories of shots: chipping, pitching, sand play, and putting. All these shots are highly critical to scoring, or "going low" as the pros say, considering that about 70 percent of shots in a round are played from a distance of 75 yards in.

Being able to hit good pitch shots, chips, sand shots, and putts enables you to save par after missing a green. More importantly, mastering the clubs that you play these shots with, such as the sand wedge and putter, puts you in position to save strokes, and beat the course in the process. For this reason, it's vitally important to grasp the elementary material put forth in this chapter, because information on the proper shot-making routine, as well as that relating to proper equipment, will become your foundation for building a solid short game.

There are a number of advantages to learning the short game before the long game, starting with pitching and chipping and moving on to bunker play and putting. The basics to hitting all full shots are hidden within short shots. Good pitching and chipping skills train you to learn the correct path along which to swing the clubhead, as well as the critical elements of impact—the moment when the club meets the ball. Last, but certainly not least, improvement in your short game leads to a speedy reduction of your handicap.

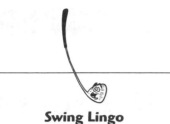

Scoring Shots

The basic pitch, chip, bunker shot, and putt are the shots that you will have to depend on most during a round of golf. The ability to hit the ball close to the hole from near or around the green and then sink the putt is what separates low handicap players from high handicap players. Believe me, you never see a top pro or amateur player possess less than a first-class short game. Make no mistake, even powerful hitters, such as Tiger Woods, depend on the art of getting the ball "up and down" (two strokes to get into the hole from around the green) to shoot low scores. The average Professional Golf Association (PGA) or Ladies Professional Golf Association (LPGA) Tour professional hits only 12 greens per round, in *regulation* figures, on par-three, par-four, and par-five holes, so you can imagine how silly it would be to let the short game take a back seat to the long game.

The Chip Shot

A chip shot spends more time rolling along the ground than flying through the air. A chip can be played with a variety of lofted clubs—anything from a 5 iron to a sand wedge. When chipping, the general rule is to select the club that will carry the ball onto the green and start it rolling as soon as possible. Chips are normally played from the immediate first cut of grass bordering the green, called the fringe.

The Pitch Shot

A pitch shot spends more time in the air than on the ground. The basic pitch is a shot lofted into the air from as far as 75 yards away from the green and from as near as 10 yards off the green. From farther out, the idea is to pitch the ball near to the hole and let it spin up to the hole. From closer in, the idea is to land the ball a few yards short of the hole and let it roll quietly toward the hole. The pitch is normally played with a club called a pitching wedge or sand wedge. Pitches are normally played from the fairway and light rough.

What you see me doing here is chipping the ball cleanly and crisply off the low cut fringe grass with a sand wedge. Although the ball is lifted into the air quickly, it will spend more time rolling than flying (as is the case with all chip types).

Here, my swing is compact, even though I'm playing a shot from 75 yards out from the green, which is the recommended maximum distance for hitting a controlled pitch.

The Bunker Shot

The bunker shot is played from a dug-out area filled with sand. Bunkers are usually located on the sides of greens. The wall of the bunker is called the lip. Using a sand wedge, the idea is to loft the ball out of the bunker so that it carries the lip and lands softly on the green.

What makes the bunker shot so frightening is that you do not hit the ball. Instead, the club must contact the sand several inches behind the ball and dig down under it so the sand actually lifts up the ball and carries it toward the hole. The technique involved takes a little getting used to. However, once you start listening for the splash sound of club to sand and see the shot float softly over the lip, you will start looking forward to the challenge of recovering from these course hazards.

On bunker shots, it's critical that you dig out an area of sand under the ball.

The Putt

Unless you hole out (sink) a pitch, chip, or sand shot, you will finish a particular par-three, par-four, or par-five hole by putting the ball across a very tightly mowed area of grass called a green and then into a hole. The club used to hit a putt is called a putter.

Most professionals and country club golfers play with three basic putter designs—blade, mallet, or flange. The traditional blade is streamlined, low and compact, and designed to transmit feel to your hands. Most blades look thin or compact, when compared to a fat-looking semicircular shaped mallet. The flange putter is a cross between a blade and a mallet, with a small wing behind the front portion of the putter (Jack Nicklaus, among many others, used a flange type putter).

Death Moves

Don't buy a new putter just because it is the hottest thing on the market. An old putter can be a good putter if it is aesthetically pleasing to your eyes, feels good in your hands, features the correct length, lie (club shaft angle), and loft for you and, most of all, helps you hole putts.

Here, I employ the basic short-putt stroke. My goal is to roll the ball smoothly over the green's manicured grass into the hole.

Technical Differences

In order to improve your short-game skills at a rapid rate, it is essential that you understand some very basic technical differences between the long swing and short swing. This information will be of particular importance to those of you who started the game recently and hit only long shots at the range.

Take an Open Stance

Short-game shots are better played from an open stance, because this allows for a free-feeling swing movement and gives you a clearer visual picture of the target line—an imaginary line, running from the ball to the target. You establish an open stance by setting your back foot closer to the target line than your front foot.

This is what an open stance looks like from the front view.

Stand Closer to the Ball

In playing pitches, chip shots, bunker shots, and putts, stand slightly closer to the ball, than you would playing a driver or other longer clubs. One reason is, short-game clubs are much shorter in length. For example, the typical driver is around 44 inches long. By comparison, the sand wedge is usually only 35 inches long, and more upright than the driver. The upright *lie* of the short-game clubs, most notably the wedges, is another reason you should stand closer to the ball when playing short shots, particularly chips and putts. Generally speaking, the closer you stand to the ball, the more control you have.

Swing Lingo

Lie is the angle of the club shaft. (Don't confuse this usage with good or bad lie of the ball.)

Minimize Body Movement

The short shots do not require you to make as full a body turn in order to generate power. Of course, on long pitches, you still need to coil. But, when hitting pitches and chips around the green, minimize your shoulder and hip turns. When putting, let your arms and shoulders do the work.

Swing Up, Not Around

Pitching and bunker-play strokes are more upright in nature, meaning that the club is swung back on a sharper angle, or *plane*, than the driver. Never overdo this, of course. Under normal conditions, you never want your backswing angle to become so steep that it causes you to stab the club into the ground on the downswing. As is putting, chipping is virtually a straight back, straight through stroke. In short, don't swing these clubs along an exaggerated inside path, or you set yourself up for serious errors.

In playing the lofted pitch shot from an open stance, the club should swing up, not around the body.

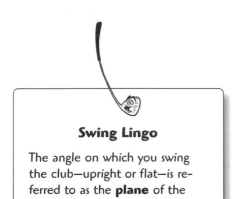

Employ a Brisk and Crisp Swing

In playing short shots from good lies and putts of any length, think controlled acceleration. These two simple words mean that pitch shots, chips, bunker shots, and putts require you to swing the club smoothly, but never at maximum speed. Understand that if the ball is sitting in rough, for example, your pitch swing should be much faster than normal. And, if you have to hit an extra-soft, extra-short pitch from the fringe around the green, the swing should be slower. Nevertheless, in normal conditions, your swing speed should be controlled and brisk.

Swing Lingo

The angle on which you swing the club—upright or flat—is referred to as the **plane** of the swing.

The Game Within a Game

No matter how well you hit your tee shot on a par-three hole, or how good your approach shot is on either a par-four or par-five hole, you still must convert the putt. The baffling thing about golf is that you could hit a long drive and an on-target approach two feet from the hole and then take two putts to hole out. What will drive you crazy is realizing that a 300-yard drive and a 1-inch putt each count as one stroke. This is why golfers become so frustrated when missing short putts, or taking three putts from say 20 feet away from the hole.

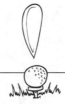

Bet You Didn't Know

It is common for professionals to refer to putting as "the ground game," because all other shots are hit into the air. The great professional Ben Hogan, known as the most solid and accurate ball striker of all time, became so frustrated with putting that he called it "another game." And another legendary player, Gene Sarazen, campaigned for the hole to be made bigger.

Because most golfers think that their fellow players expect them to sink short putts, particularly those in the three-foot range, he or she feels added pressure. Putting can be so intense that CEOs of top companies have told me that they would gladly conduct a tough board meeting rather than stand over a short putt and think about the fear of missing the hole.

Frankly, putting is another game, namely because it is played totally on the ground and is so unpredictable. Most golfers can usually predict how well they are going to play from tee to green, after finishing their preround warm-up session and hitting the opening drive of the day. In contrast, most golfers can never tell how well they are going to putt. There have been days when I have holed out all or nearly all putts in practice and then putted terribly on the course. Other times, I putt badly in practice before the round and then make everything out on the course. It is this aspect of the game that causes players to throw their putter in a lake, break it over their knee, or retire it and buy a new one. Some players become so frustrated with putting that they develop a nervous type *yip* stroke, while others give up golf altogether.

The formula for good putting is very simple. All you need is a putter, a setup, and a stroke that works for you. Sure, there are many basics to good putting, which all the masters share. Having said that, it's amazing how many players putt well by using an unorthodox putter or an unorthodox putting style.

The sundry styles of good and great putters is proof that putting is the most idiosyncratic part of the game. Although, good putters usually share some fundamentals, and it's advisable that you include them in your method. By the same token, never be afraid to listen to your instincts and develop individual stroke traits of your own. Only then will you ever feel truly comfortable and confident on the greens.

If, after developing a good style of putting, you suddenly have a bad day on the greens, avoid being quick to start immediately tinkering with your stroke, and ignore the urge to switch putters. Missing putts is not always the fault of your putter or putting stroke. Dave Pelz, *Golf Magazine*'s technical and short-game consultant, proved that even when a robot strokes putts exactly the same way, on exactly the

Swing Lingo

A **yip** is a nervous twitch or involuntary jerk of the hands during the stroke causing the putter to jab at the ball and, thus, badly missing a putt. A yip usually occurs on fairly close putts but can occur at any distance. Yips usually become worse and almost never get better without a dramatic change in style.

Jim's Tips

The next time you watch golf on television, pay close attention to the differences and similarities of putting styles among the players. You'll see, for example, that some players take a wide stance while others keep their feet close together. You'll also see that on short putts nearly all players keep their eyes directly over the ball. Look and learn, and then go experiment.

same line, and on tournament class greens, some do not drop into the hole, due to tiny imperfections in the surface of the green. These imperfections include shoe marks or poorly repaired ball marks.

Regardless of what Pelz discovered, remember one thing: The more technically sound your putting setup and stroke are and the more repetitive you can become, the better you will putt.

It's Routine

One thing that all the finest short-game players on all pro tours do is stick to the same preshot routine. Whether or not the typical professional is playing a pitch, chip, or bunker shot, he or she goes through a set procedure that involves analyzing the lie, picking the right club, visualizing the shot, and rehearsing the same swing he or she intends to employ when taking the shot.

Death Moves

Don't ever hit any short-game shot without first seeing the shot come to life in your mind's eye. When you rush your preshot routine, and fail to see the shot play out in your head, the tendency is to hit a bad shot. Good swings and good shots start with good visual imagery.

Going through a set preshot routine, around and on the greens, makes you so prepared that you give yourself the best possible chance of hitting the best possible shot. A set preshot routine raises your confidence level, and relaxes your muscles too, which in turn enables you to physically perform to the best of your ability.

To provide you with a clearer understanding of the intricate details of the preshot process, I am now going to share with you further details on what works best when preparing to play a pitch, chip, bunker shot, and putt. My knowledge is based on first-hand experiences in practice and play, as well as observations I made while watching the great players in action, on film, and live at tournaments.

The Pitching Routine

In preparing to play a pitch, take note of the wind direction and the pin (flagstick) placement before you even get to the ball. This early planning helps you to decide what type of pitch you will hit. Obviously, the distance of the shot and the lie also have a bearing on whether you will play a low pitch, high pitch, or some other kind of imaginative shot. You may even play a running pitch, should the pin be located on the top level of an undulated green with no bunker in front of it. If the lie is bad, this tells you that you must employ a steeper backswing action and a sharper angle of attack on the downswing, because these two technical elements are secrets to recovering. Once you determine the type of swing you need to make, visualize it and then physically make a practice swing to the side of the ball.

Ken Venturi, a great player and close friend, uses his right arm to rehearse the motions involved in hitting a very high and very low pitch. Before hitting a high pitch, Venturi often swings his right arm back, down, and then up as if throwing a ball skyward. To prepare for hitting a low pitch, he follows the same routine, except that he points his right arm directly at the target. These same preswing tips may help you hit creative pitch shots.

The Chipping Routine

In preparing to play a chip, do not automatically grab your favorite club out of the bag. Good club selection depends on your ability to take into account the nature of the lie, the distance to the flag, and the slope and speed of the green. More importantly, you must also try to determine how the ball will react in the air and on the ground. The general rule is as follows: The farther the ball is from the green, or the closer the pin is cut to the green's edge, the greater the *loft* of the club you play should be.

After assessing the situation, if you still have a problem determining what club to hit and how best to play the shot, look again at the terrain and the line to the hole while simultaneously swinging your right arm back and through at different speeds. This is a motion that many great short-game experts use to match the tempo of the swing to the distance of the shot.

Let's say you choose a sand wedge. Figure out where you want to land the ball on the green. That's your prime target. The secondary target is the hole. Once you have your prime target in focus, stare at it. Last, practice your chipping technique a couple of times, concentrating on swing-

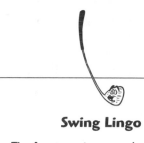

Swing Lingo

The **loft** of the club is the angle of the clubface as it lies flat on the ground.

Swing Lingo

The **bounce** is a rounded area of flange, below the club's leading edge, that allows the club to slide through the sand more easily.

ing smoothly and correctly before stepping into the shot. Sometimes, as you make your practice stroke, something won't feel quite correct. You may detect that the shot will require a little more or less force. If that's the case, take the time to get the technique right. That way, you'll be more apt to hit a good chip shot.

The Bunker-Play Routine

It is against the rules to touch the sand with the club before you actually swing and make contact at impact. For this reason, in preparing to hit the standard bunker shot, it is advisable that you first practice slapping an area of grass with the *bounce* of the club at least a couple of times, before even stepping into the bunker.

In making your practice swings, imagine a ball on the ground, and try to contact an area of grass a few inches behind it with the bounce of the club. This is the same basic technique you will use in a bunker, except that the club will hit sand instead of grass.

Bet You Didn't Know

In 1931, Gene Sarazen invented the modern sand wedge that featured bounce. The bounce feature of the club head helps loft the ball in the air. Sarazen's idea came to him while taking a flying lesson. He noticed that during take off the pilot lowered, rather than raised, the plane's flaps. The plane glided in like a duck landing in a pond. Sarazen considered how a duck would make a soft glide landing with its wings angled back. Using this image, Sarazen soldered metal to the back of his 9 iron, which immediately produced the results he had hoped for. The club no longer dug into the sand. Instead, it skidded and took a shallow swath of sand.

Once in the bunker, wriggle your feet into the sand to determine whether it is soft or firm. If the sand is soft, you must swing a trifle faster; if it's firm, swing a trifle slower.

Next, as always in preparing to hit a short shot, focus your eyes on the target to get a feel for the type of shot you are going to play.

The Putting Routine

The preshot putting routine should never be underestimated simply because you are hitting off a smooth surface. I learned a lot about the elements involved in a well-planned putting routine from watching Seve Ballesteros, the legendary Spanish professional. Although Seve is older now, he is still one of the all-time great putters.

Your putting routine should start before you get to the green. It's easier to see the undulations from this distance out, especially in the late afternoon.

Once on the green, glance at the line between your ball and the hole to get a preliminary feel for what you'll need to do. Next, mark the position of the ball, and then lift it. Mark the ball by putting a small coin behind it.

Next, walk around and check the line from both ends and sides, to be certain that you detect the subtle variations in ground contour you have to deal with. To get a true bird's-eye view of the breaks in the putting surface, look back to the ball and make your final conclusions about break, grain, and speed. Next, replace your ball on the green so that the letters in its logo run along the target line, not across it. This serves as a good alignment aid. Next, make two practice swings, concentrating on keeping the putter head low to the ground on the way back and on the forward swing. Concentrate, too, on keeping the putter square (perpendicular) to the hole, especially when rehearsing a short putt.

In working toward the completion of your pre-shot routine, take a couple of long breaths. The Japanese call these *zazen* breaths. Inhale through the nose and exhale through the mouth. Breath control puts the nerves at peace and triggers intense concentration. During these breaths, visualize the ball rolling toward the hole at perfect speed and then falling into the cup. The mind must focus on the read, which is the line pictured by the golfer before the putt is hit. A good read is picking the proper line, and a bad read is a mistake in your putting line image. (An example of a bad read is expecting a putt to break left when it actually breaks to the right.) When the mind fixes on the read, the putter, the golfer, the ball, and the hole all become one, and a precise stroke operates essentially on automatic pilot.

In this chapter we looked at the importance of your short game. In the next chapter, we'll look at what you need to get started.

Death Moves

During your preshot putting routine, don't let your mind wander. The last thing you want to think about is how well or how poorly you are scoring. Ironically, if you are scoring well, and focus too much on this fact, you will begin to put pressure on yourself. As a result, you will rush your routine, make a faulty stroke, and miss the putt.

Jim's Tips

Pro golfer Jack Burke gave me this tip: To determine the speed of the putt, focus your eyes on the line and imagine the ball rolling in real time toward the cup. A shiny look to the grass means the grain is with you, thus the putt will roll more quickly. A dull look means the grain is against you, thus the ball will roll more slowly. Visualize the exact speed before you putt.

The Least You Need to Know

➤ Respect the importance of the short game.

➤ Trust the bounce of the club to splash the ball from sand.

➤ Play your short shots from a stance that enables you to see a clear line to the cup to help you make a free and solid stroke.

➤ Develop a personalized putting style that you can repeat time after time. Remember to get into a comfortable stance that enables you to be relaxed and confident.

➤ Stick to your preshot routine when preparing to hit a pitch, chip, sand shot, or putt.

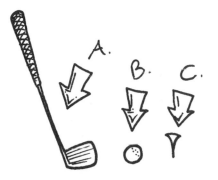

Chapter 2

How to Get Started

In This Chapter

➤ Buying customized wedges

➤ The scoop on the perfect putter

➤ Setting yourself up for short-game shots

➤ Succeeding with the help of mental images

Two chief reasons the majority of professionals on the PGA, LPGA, and Senior PGA Tours play better short-game shots than the average amateur is that they take time to customize their equipment and setup to the ball properly.

The "smart shopper" and "shop until you drop" philosophies definitely apply here. I say that because I want you to be prepared to study a detailed list of club-fitting guidelines so that when you go shopping at your local pro shop you'll know what to look for.

Be prepared, too, to learn how to set up to the ball to play all types of pitches, chips, sand shots, and putts. You have already learned the importance of the preshot routine in playing short-game shots. Now I'm going to educate you on the starting position—or address, as it's called by teachers—and show you how to have fun learning about this and other basic fundamentals.

Custom Fit Wedges

Knowing you have the right club in your hand, one perfectly suited to you and only you makes you feel more confident standing over a shot. You're like a good advertising salesman who feels more secure at a presentation meeting, knowing he's got a nice suit on, the right pen in his pocket, and an attractive briefcase in his hand.

I'm not suggesting for one second that looks are everything or that you can buy a good golf game. Of course, you need to know what you are doing. In fact, without the knowledge of the right technique, even solid gold golf clubs and golf balls couldn't help you. However, without question, the right equipment puts the percentages for hitting good shots highly in your favor. Playing with customized wedges helps enhance your feel for shots and is a sure way to chop strokes off your score.

Bet You Didn't Know

Nowadays, on professional tours, some players are carrying four wedges in their bag: a pitching wedge, at approximately 48 degrees, a gap wedge at 52 degrees, a sand wedge at 56 degrees, and a lob wedge at 60 degrees. Often, too, these clubs are of a different brand from their matched 3 to 9 iron set makeup. Note that there is a 4-inch gap between each wedge. This equal spacing should coincide with the rest of your golf clubs. If you carry only a 48-degree pitching wedge and a 56-degree sand wedge, you have a huge 8-degree spread between your two main scoring clubs.

Before buying the right wedges, you should first understand the basic components of the clubs. Let's review those elements that include proper grip type, grip size, lie, length, loft, shaft flex, shaft type, swing weight, and aesthetic appeal.

Grip Type

The two most common grips are rubber and leather. Although most tour professionals now prefer rubber, your choice should be personal. Go with what feels comfortable and enables you to swing without any slippage. Hard or slick grips will force you to hold tight, which is, of course, a death move in golf.

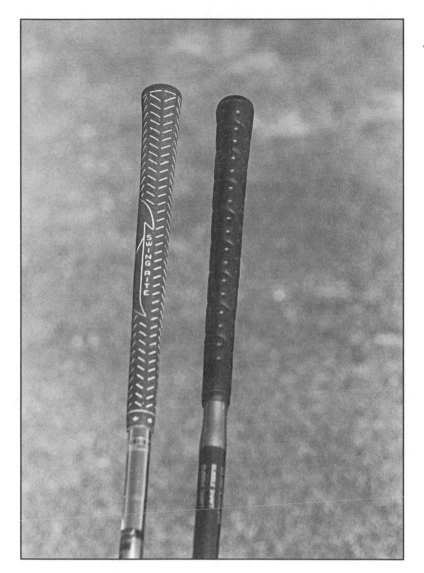

The two most common grip types: rubber (left) and leather (right).

Grip Size

For better control of the club head, players with a large glove size (9) should be fitted with a built-up grip. Those with a small glove size (7) should have thin grips, while those with a standard size (8) are best fitted with the standard stock grip. Certainly there are exceptions, such as the great Scottish player Tommy Armour who had very large hands but preferred a thin grip. Why? Because of what we all strive for—feel.

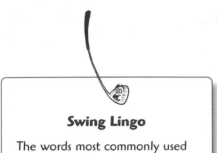

So often players compensate for an improper grip size. Don't you. If the grip is too thick on your pitching wedge, for example, it decreases club head feel and doesn't allow the your wrists to work correctly. This causes you to be late in swinging the club-head back to the ball, resulting in a push shot that veers right of target. When the grip is too thin, the club-head often turns over dramatically through impact. The result is usually a shot that veers left of target. Players with skinny grips try to adjust by squeezing the handle tightly, which leads to other shot-making problems. Avoid making the same mistakes by seeking help on correct grip size from your local PGA golf professional.

Lie

Lie is simply the angle of the club shaft at *address* or *setup*. Except for players with extremely short or long arms, very often a need for a correction in club length can be corrected by adjusting the lie. For example, if your wedges feel too short, sometimes this problem can be corrected by having them made one or two degrees more upright. If, on the other hand, your wedges feel too long, you can have the lies flattened by 1 or 2 degrees.

The key to being properly fitted is the position of your hands and the way the bottom of the club, or *sole*, sits at address. The club should sit virtually flat on the ground. If the lie is not suited to your needs, you will have problems with direction. The only way you'll have a chance of hitting an accurate shot is by trying to make compensations during the swing. That, my friends, is not a good idea.

Length

A player's height has very little to do with being fitted for the proper length wedges. When being fitted, the distance of your hands from the ground is the variable to be considered. Generally speaking, players with short arms need longer clubs while players with long arms need shorter clubs. However, there are exceptions. In the end, personal comfort and results are your priorities. Remember that the wedges are the scoring clubs so they must feel good in your hands.

Loft

Once again, when considering this club variable, you should be guided by your tendencies. If, for example, you determine that your sand wedge shots fly too low and that you want less *roll*, less distance, and more backspin, you should be fitted with a club of increased loft. If you find your shots fly too high and you want more distance and less backspin, you should have the lofts on your sand wedge decreased slightly. When you make changes, just make certain that the degree gaps between your wedges are mathematically correct. Again, check with your local golf pro.

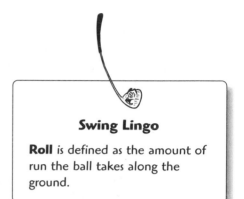

Swing Lingo

Roll is defined as the amount of run the ball takes along the ground.

It's easy to see from this photograph of a sand wedge the added loft, or "scoop," built into the club's face.

Shaft Flex

When choosing the correct shaft for your wedges, you should be guided by your strength, the tempo of your swing, and your ball flight. Generally, if you are strong and your tempo upbeat, you should use stiff shafts. If you are a senior player and not as strong as you used to be, or a female player and you prefer to swing rather than hit the ball, I suggest you go with a medium flex shaft, or maybe even a whippy shaft. The best way to determine what's right for you is to hit shots with clubs featuring different shafts and come to a conclusion on what type of flex feels and performs best.

Shaft Type

Because of the varying shaft types available—namely lightweight steel, graphite, and titanium—I again advise you to experiment on the practice range to see which shaft provides you with the best feel and yields the best shots. If a steel shaft feels better in your pitching wedge, and graphite shafts in your other wedges, don't think that you have to match them up. The choice is yours. You are the only one playing the clubs and turning in a score at the end of the round.

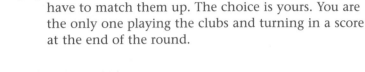

Jim's Tips

Your pro will be able to provide you with keen insights into why a thick grip may be good for one club and a thinner grip better for another. For example, your pro may tell you to put a thin grip on your sand wedge because bunker shots require the hands and wrists to be quite loose and more active.

Swing Weight

This is an element of club fitting that you rarely hear mentioned anymore. However, it is still important. When you grip the club, swing weight is actually the weight that you feel in your hands. Many golfers believe that wedges with heavy heads cause the ball to go a greater distance. However, this is a fallacy because of the difficulty in getting the club back square to the ball. Remember that the secret formula to hitting the ball solidly is club-head speed applied correctly.

If you are in the market for, say, a new sand wedge or lob wedge, let your professional match up your favorite clubs with new ones that have the same swing weight. Also, be sure that the pro is certain the bounce feature is the same as before, or else you will feel lost when it comes to playing one of your bread-and-butter short-game shots.

Most clubs for men measure in the D-0 to D-4 swing-weight range, while clubs for most women measure in the C-8 to C-9 range. Most sand wedges, however, have a slightly higher swing weight for both men and women—usually D-4 to D-8. The extra head weight makes sand shots easier.

Death Moves

If the shafts in your wedges are too stiff, you experience a dead-ened feeling at impact, hit extra low shots, and push shots. If the shafts in your clubs are too soft, you tend to hit the ball too high and lose distance.

Choosing the Right Putter

There are numbers of putters, from the traditional types to the more way-out looking models, available in pro shops. Consequently, choosing the right putter can be as difficult as choosing a gift for the person who has everything.

When selecting a putter, you must pay close attention to the same variables I mentioned when discussing shopping for custom-fit wedges. Proper grip size, lie, length, loft, shaft flex, and grip type are equally important considerations. Yet, other critical guidelines come to into play, namely the material the putter head is made of and the position of the alignment-aid marking. Understanding them makes your choice a whole lot easier.

Putter-Head Material

There are many putter-head materials available on the market, including brass, beryllium, copper, cobalt, zinc, manganese bronze, and titanium, including putters with these materials as face inserts. Experts agree that the harder metals— namely cobalt and stainless steel—roll the ball a little more quickly across the putting surface than the softer metals, such as forged steel and titanium. Most good putters love a putter with a good feel. When you stroke a putt and it feels like you are cutting butter, you've found a putter that will enhance touch. Putters with a hard composition make distance control more difficult. That's why many newer putters have soft face inserts.

Alignment Markings

The next time you go into a golf shop, walk over to the putter rack and look at about a half-dozen putters. When you set the putter down, you will notice that some putters feature a dot, arrow, thin line, or some other marking. The mark is there to designate the sweet spot, or part of the clubface that imparts the best contact with the ball. Some players I know like these markings, while others are thrown off by them. Some of these markings are off because they are not opposite the center point of the putter face; and as I discovered, the sweet spot is often closer to the heel of the club.

Jim's Tips

When shopping for new wedges, remember to carefully check the bounce angle. Generally speaking, more bounce is better than less. More bounce greatly decreases your chances of sticking the club head into the ground and helps to glide the club off the turf.

Death Moves

Don't buy a putter with a marking designating its sweet spot until you have tested it for accuracy. Hold the putter in front of you, gripping the handle lightly with your thumb and forefinger. Tap the area of the face below the sweet-spot marking. If the putter rebounds straight back, the putter is fine. If it twists, move on.

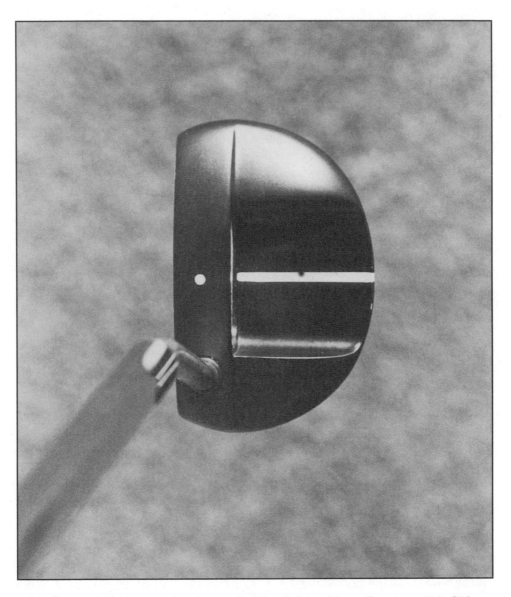

The alignment markings (white line and white dot) on this mallet type putter designate the sweet spot of the club's face.

Because the putting game is so important to scoring, you should not let yourself be impatient when picking out a putter. Try out several before you make your choice. And, just like when you buy shoes, make sure the fit is right. If there are any doubts in your mind that something is not right, hold off making the purchase until you seek the advice of a qualified professional.

Short-Game Setup Positions

The starting position for playing a basic pitch, chip, bunker shot, or putt is the most critical of all because to a large degree it determines the nature of the swinging action you will employ. Professionals and top amateur players know that if they set up to the ball correctly, there is a fairly good chance they will make a technically sound swing and hit their target. You will too, provided you smoothly coordinate the tempo of the swinging club with that of your body.

To get you on track, please read carefully the following instructions for setting up to play each of the four basic short-game shots, because if you start right, you'll probably finish right.

Basic Pitching Address

Start with a stance that is narrower than your normal stance. Your feet should be about 6 to 12 inches apart from the heel of one shoe to the heel of the other. Stand open by pulling your left foot back a few inches farther from the target line than your back foot. Play the ball opposite the midpoint in your stance. Be sure to keep your shoulders fairly parallel (or square) to your foot line in a slightly open position.

When hitting pitch shots, particularly those from a bad lie, it's critical that you direct the club into impact on a descending path, and hit the ball before the ground. To help you accomplish this, put approximately 60 percent of your body weight on your front foot and lean the shaft somewhat toward the target putting your hands slightly ahead of the ball.

Basic Chipping Address

Set your feet a little bit closer together than you did when preparing to pitch. A slightly open stance helps you to see the hole and target line more clearly and to avoid taking the club head low and inside. Be sure to set your shoulders pretty much parallel to the target line, or you run the risk of pulling the club across the ball through impact and hitting the shot left of target. Play the ball closer to your back foot with your hands a few inches ahead of the ball to encourage a slight descending hit. Also, keep the ball close to your body. Arch your wrists slightly. This setup adjustment seems incidental, but it is very important because it minimizes wrist action. Moreover, this address key helps raise the club's heel (the end of the club head closest to you) off the ground, which helps you to swing through with less resistance from the grass.

In setting up to play a standard pitch, it's critical that the ball be positioned virtually opposite the midpoint in a slightly open stance.

The chipping stance is narrower than the pitching stance, and the ball is positioned closer to the right foot.

Bet You Didn't Know

When setting up to play low chips, tour pros grip more firmly and position the ball farther back in their stance. When hitting high chips, they grip down slightly and hold the club more lightly with the ball positioned more forward. This adjustment automatically adds loft to the clubface.

Basic Bunker-Play Address

Get your center of gravity forward by leaning toward the target, putting about 60 percent of your weight on your left foot. Wriggle your feet into the sand to feel the texture and depth and so that you are firmly anchored. Push your hips toward the target slightly because this makes it easier to adjust to the position of the ball, which should be a bit ahead of the center point in your stance. Let your arms hang down limp, as if they were spaghetti. This relieves tension and promotes a more fluid swing. Open the clubface (more when the lip is high and the pin close to you) by leaning the shaft away from the target or by turning it into an open position before you've assumed your grip. Incidentally, because the bunker swing should be loose and free, hold the club using a pressure of around three (one being superlight and 10 being superfirm on the Jim McLean–designed grip-pressure scale). Also be sure to keep the club head above the sand behind the ball. It's against the rules to touch the sand. It is a severe two-stroke penalty or loss of hole in match play.

Basic Putting Address

Putting is the most personalized department of the game, with many good putters looking different at address. Some start from a wide stance, others from a narrow stance position. Some players let their arms hang straight down, while others bend their arms at the elbow. Some good putters stand erect, while others crouch over. Ben Crenshaw and Brad Faxon, for example, who have been great putters all their lives, stand erect; while golfing great Jack Nicklaus crouches over when addressing a putt. You get the idea: There is a lot of leeway in establishing a putting setup. Still, there are certain fundamentals I encourage you to adopt.

The basic bunker-play address shows the feet open and the hips tilted toward the target slightly.

Set up with your shoulders square, or slightly open (pointing slightly left). Play the ball slightly inside your left heel, with your eyes directly over it, and parallel to the target line. Keep your hands in line with the ball. Set the putter face at right angles to the hole, using the top line of the putter head to help you aim. On breaking putts, aim at the point where the ball will start curving right or left. This means all putts can then be thought of as straight putts. I also recommend the reverse overlap grip used by most male and female tour professionals.

The reverse overlap grip is formed by laying the club across the palm of the left hand, with the handle running diagonally from the base of the forefinger along the heel pad or lifeline. The V formed by the thumb and forefinger of the left hand points to the left shoulder. All four fingers and the thumb of the right hand go on the handle, the V pointing to the right shoulder. The forefinger of the left hand overlaps the finger of the right and acts as a guide when you stroke the putt.

Whatever grip you choose to adopt—the interlock, standard overlap, baseball grip, split grip, and so on—the secret is to find a position that stabilizes the hands and wrists and promotes an arms-and-shoulders–controlled pendulum stroke.

Putting is the most personalized department of the game. However, here you can see me in a classic address position, with my hands in line with the ball and my shoulders parallel to the target line.

Bet You Didn't Know

During golf telecasts, you are bound to hear a commentator refer to a player's grip as cross-handed or left-hand-low. This just means that the right-handed golfer is gripping opposite to normal, using a cross-handed hold that sees the left hand closer to the ball. Jim Furyk, one of the finest putters on the PGA Tour, uses this grip, as does Se Ri Pak on the LPGA Tour. So, who is to say it won't work wonders for you?

Mind Games

Now that you have learned the proper address keys for hitting the four basic types of short-game shots, realize that, before you swing, it's important to use mental imagery because that helps you hit better pitches, chips, bunker shots, and putts. Let me review one of these visual aids for each department of the game so that you have a clear understanding of what I'm talking about.

Pitching Mind Trick

A common fault among average amateur golfers is hitting wedge shots short of the flag. The next time you face a pitch, say in the 60- to 75-yard range, particularly one over water, imagine a flagstick five yards behind the actual hole. This will encourage you to make a freer swing, land the ball beyond the hole, and spin it back toward it.

Chipping Mind Trick

The secret to good chipping is landing the ball on a particular spot on the green between you and the hole and letting it roll the rest of the way. Before you swing, imagine a 6-foot circle in the area of the landing spot you picked out. This will give you that "can't miss" attitude.

Bunker-Play Mind Trick

A mental key to help you blast the ball out of a bunker is to imagine the ball as the yolk of an egg, with an imaginary circle around it as the white. Before you swing, think about removing the entire egg and you will likely hit a super recovery shot.

Bet You Didn't Know

Jack Nicklaus's bunker play improved dramatically when his teacher Jack Grout had him imagine that he was removing a shallow slice of sand and that the ball was floating atop it, as if on some sandy magic carpet. This image enabled Jack to take a long but shallow cut of sand instead of a swing that would dig deeper and require more sand to be removed. It is a much easier and more consistent method.

Putting Mind Trick

To ensure that you do not hit weak short putts that often miss either right or left, imagine a backstop behind the hole. This mental image will help you make an accelerated controlled stroke and knock the ball firmly into the back of the cup.

The Least You Need to Know

➤ Be sure your wedges fit you to the letter.

➤ Choose a putter that suits your stroke.

➤ Be meticulous about the way you set up to hit a short-game shot.

➤ Use mental images to put your short-game swings on track and mind at ease.

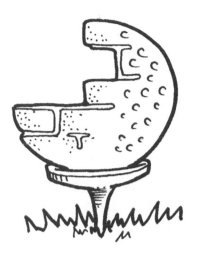

Chapter 3

Building Blocks

In This Chapter

➤ Learning the basic short-game swing

➤ Drills for fast improvement

➤ The importance of good eyesight

➤ Playing pitch-and-putt courses

Surely, many of you will agree that, after just reading the first two chapters of this book, you have learned more about the short game than you ever thought possible. Well, to be up front with you, there is still more preparatory work to be done before I teach you the more sophisticated side to pitching, chipping, bunker play, and putting.

Please keep the patience you have had so far. I realize you're anxious to go out on a championship course and try everything you were taught. I assure you that day will come, but first I want you to complete the learning process regarding the basic strokes involved in all those short-game departments that you are, by now, familiar with.

I start by teaching you how to swing back and through when playing short shots. Next, I provide you with basic drills to help you ingrain the proper technical movements into your muscle memory. I then teach you how to test out your skills and hone them through the pitch-and-putt golf course experience.

Basic Strokes

Now that you have learned the all-important address positions for playing pitch shots, chip shots, bunker shots, and putts, you are a step closer to becoming a good short-game player. To reach the next level, you must first understand how to employ the proper backswing and downswing actions.

Basic Pitch Stroke

The first backswing key to playing the basic pitch stroke is to make the most minimal weight shift onto your right foot and leg. Actually, there's really no true shift action at all. Keeping most of your weight on your left foot helps you hit the ball on the descent when coming down. The second vital swing key is allowing the wrists to hinge almost immediately, so you set the club upward into a position where it can come down on the ball at the proper angle.

In the early stage of the pitch stroke, allow the wrists to hinge slightly so that you are better able to swing the club upward on the correct plane.

When coming down, you should make a slight forward shift and rotate your hips. When making actual contact with the ball, you want to have that feeling of hitting and holding back (resisting) with the *left wrist flat,* especially on shorter shots. Finish with your belt buckle and the club pointing at the sky.

Basic Chip Stroke

When hitting the basic chip stroke, allow your right wrist to hinge just a little. Many golfers are taught to use zero wrist action, which I feel is a mistake. It makes the chip action too mechanical, and you lose feel. So be sure you let the wrist cock slightly. This allows you to lift the club only slightly so that you are poised to crisply contact the ball on the downswing, using a fluid brushing action.

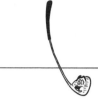

Swing Lingo

Having your **left wrist flat** (flat left wrist position) means that the left wrist remains stable and lined up with the top of the left forearm. There is no indentation between the wrist and forearm. This flat wrist position is critical to hitting a well-struck and accurate basic pitch stroke.

When playing the basic pitch from the fairway, I recommend that you concentrate on finishing with your belly button pointing at the target. This mental key will help you accelerate the club through the ball.

When chipping, it's important that the club swings up slightly, so that you are poised to make crisp contact with the ball on the descent.

The secrets of the downswing are keeping the handle of the club ahead of the club head, the left wrist solid through impact, and letting your eyes follow the ball in the follow through. Again, many amateurs are taught to keep their heads and eyes down. Forget that and look to the target immediately after contact.

To hit a solid accurate chip like this, keep your left wrist firm through impact.

Basic Bunker Shot

To play a basic bunker shot, make a longer backswing, allowing the wrists to fully cock, the arms to swing the club freely upward, and the shoulders to turn quite fully.

Even at this early stage of the bunker-play swing, the wrists have hinged freely and the shoulders have turned quite a bit.

When coming down, concentrate on releasing the club in front of the body and thump a general area of sand a few inches behind the ball with the bottom of the club. Forget about trying to hit precisely an inch behind the ball. That is too precise and not necessary for excellent results. You must release the club fully with your right arm so that it passes underneath the ball and exits on the other side.

In swinging through, focus on keeping the club in front of the body and releasing it with your right arm.

Basic Putting Stroke

When playing the basic putting stroke in the 10- to 15-foot range, make a pendulum-type back-swing, controlling the action with the triangle formed by your arms and shoulders. On this length putt and anything closer, the putter face should stay square to the target. On longer putts, the putter face should swing slightly inside the target line on a natural arc.

On the downswing particularly, you should feel that one hand has more control than the other. Jack Nicklaus uses his right hand to push the put-ter head directly along the target line, keeping it low to the ground well past impact. This tip was given to Nicklaus when he first joined the tour in 1962, from 1956 Masters Champion Jack Burke. I believe it, since I have learned so much from Jackie over the years.

Jim's Tips

To hit a very short bunker shot to a close and tight pin (a pin located near the edge of a green), you must alter your tech-nique slightly. Make a full back-swing, but hold the clubface open through impact, with the finish being extra short. The short finish ensures a short shot as long as you do not contact the ball first. Remember that this is the only shot in golf in which you don't hit the ball. You hit the sand behind the ball.

In hitting a basic putt, the putter's head swings back along the target line.

Basic Stroke Drills

I have learned a lot from my many amateur and professional students. One thing is that the quickest way to get a student from point A to point B (especially, with respect to teaching him or her a basic pitching, chipping, bunker play, or putting stroke movement) is by having the student perform practice drills.

The following are my favorite drills for grooving the basic strokes I just taught you. If you work on at least some of them, some of the time, you will be very surprised how quickly the individual movements involved in each of the various short-game techniques flow together and become second nature.

When swinging the putter through, low to the ground, feel that one hand has more control than the other.

Buddy-System Drill: For Pitching

One of the most agonizing things for a golfer is employing a good pitching swing and hitting the ball solidly but off target. Faulty foot alignment is often to blame, so work on this drill with the help of a buddy.

Pick out a target to aim for, and then set up to the ball. Now, have your buddy visualize both an imaginary target line and a line across your feet and check to see to it that the line across your feet is only slightly to the left of the target line. If a friend is not available, analyze your pitching setup in front of a mirror. Another way to check your pitching address is to lay two clubs down—one along the target line and one across your foot line—and then step away to see how your are aiming.

Pillow Drill: For Pitching

The key to hitting good short pitches is coming into impact with a flat left wrist and feeling the sensation of resistance. Place a pillow or impact bag against a wall. To groove (make automatic) the proper impact position, make left-handed swings, accelerating the club head into the back of a fat pillow or impact bag. Hold your finish for two or three seconds. Memorize this solid resistance and practice it often.

Bet You Didn't Know

Three-time British Open Champion Henry Cotton, who was also one of the best-ever low-trajectory wedge players, invented the pillow drill, except that he used an old tire to make certain that he did not bend his left wrist at impact. Cotton would have his students hold the clubface squarely against the tire. The student would repeatedly swing, hit the tire, and hold this position.

Target Drill: For Pitching

Good distance control is a common trait among tour professionals and top-notch amateur players. One sure way to develop this skill is to hit pitch shots to various targets—one 75 yards, one 50 yards, and one 25 yards away. Hit shots from different lies and with all wedges. (Many amateurs find that they cannot hit the lob wedge 75 yards.) Note exactly how far you hit a full lob wedge.

During practice, make sure to aim at a specific target when hitting pitch shots. If you aim at nothing you will hit it every time.

Plank Drill: For Pitching

To learn the right hinge action for hitting short-pitch shots, lay a plank down perpendicular to your targetline approximately 10 inches behind the ball you are addressing. Swing back with an effort to miss the plank. If you hit it, you made a faulty drag action rather than a slight upward hinging action of the club head. You must miss the plank on both the backswing and downswing.

Death Moves

If you employ a robotic, firm-wristed action on short-pitch shots, you lose the feel for the club head and have such problems with distance control that you are likely to miss your landing spot. A no-hands pitch action is extremely artificial and extremely hard to use effectively.

Shaft Drill: For Pitching

In order to feel and groove the correct upright backswing plane for hitting short-pitch shots, lay a shaft on the grass so that it extends straight back and away from the midpoint of the outside of your right shoe. If you lay it down correctly, it will be parallel to the target line. Swing the club back to the first horizontal point on the backswing (thigh level) so that it is directly in line and parallel with the shaft placed on the ground. When you do this be sure to keep your arms down. The club is set more with the hands than it is with the arms. The grip end of the club should be quite close to your back thigh.

Clock Drill: For Pitching

To learn the proper length of backswing and down-swing and to drum it into your muscle memory, imagine that your head is at 12 o'clock and the ball is at 6 o'clock. Now, simply swing the club back to 9 o'clock and then through to 3 o'clock.

Shaft-Grip Drill: For Chipping

To ensure that you make crisp contact on chip shots, your hands must lead the club head into the ball. To promote this type of through-impact action, address a ball with a seven iron. Next, make your normal-length chipping backswing. Have a friend place the grip end of a club in front of the ball. Hit the chip, letting the club held by your friend stop your club head just after impact. The moment your club head is halted by the grip end of your friend's club, freeze this position for several seconds. Feel this hands-leading position so that you can repeat it on the course. By the way, this drill is safe. However, if you would feel more comfortable, use a slightly slower chip-stroke swing.

Eyes-at-Target Drill: For Chipping

Contrary to what you may think, good *eye-hand coordination* is not solely an innate talent. You can develop this skill and become a better chipper by first setting up to a ball with one of the clubs in your chipping arsenal—a sand wedge, for example. Next, turn your head and look toward a hole about 30 feet away. Swing. Make a mental note where the ball lands and how the ball reacts in the air and on the ground.

Hit about 20 chips. Change clubs, hitting the same number of shots with a 7 iron and 9 iron, again watching how the ball reacts but not looking at the ball. Now go through the same procedure while looking down at the ball and noticing how well you judge distance.

Practicing the shaft-grip drill will help you freeze and learn the vital hands-leading position of the downswing.

On-Line Drill: For Chipping

To hit accurate chip shots, you need to swing the club virtually on a straight-back, straight-through path. To groove this action, place a ball between two clubs set down on the ground, parallel to each other, and about 6 inches apart. Now, hit chips with a seven iron, keeping the club head within the boundaries of your homemade trough.

Backyard Chair Drill: For Chipping

Long chip shots should be hit on a low trajectory so that the ball rolls to the hole like a putt. To learn to hit this shot, set down a four-legged chair in your backyard. Now try hitting the ball between the legs without hitting the seat of the chair. If you have trouble, position the ball back in your stance slightly, firm up your grip, and lead the club into the ball with your hands. (You can do the same drill indoors, using plastic golf balls and hitting off carpet.) Strive for solid contact. That means hitting the ball first and then brushing the ground.

Swing Lingo

Eye-hand coordination simply means the ability to look at a target, see a hole, and after judging how far away it is, feel the distance via your hands. According to medical experts, the eyes see the target and the brain processes the data. The brain then tells the hands the right speed to swing the club to propel the ball to the target.

Bet You Didn't Know

Greg Norman, the Australian-born golf sensation, plays all his long chips with a reverse-overlap putting grip. This hold, he feels, gives him a stronger sense of security and, in turn, prevents him from exaggerating hand–wrist action and hitting a high chip shot. It is the same grip he uses for putting.

Footprint Drill: For Bunker Play

Before you go out to the course, you better have the basic bunker-shot technique down, particularly the action of splashing the sand with the bounce of the club. Hitting a ball out of a bunker can be an intimidating experience, especially if you're new at the game. So let me help you learn the proper swinging action by teaching you what pro Al Mengert taught me many years ago.

Make a footprint in the sand. Take your normal bunker-play address, placing the club above a spot toward the heel end of the footprint. Swing back and then down, trying to erase your footprint with the bounce of the club. Imagine that your golf ball is in the center of the footprint.

In practicing the footprint drill, concentrate on removing the imprint behind then in front of the ball. Do that, and the ball will be lifted into the air and propelled toward the hole.

Tee-Time Drill: For Bunker Play

This drill, taught to me by friend and golfing great Ken Venturi, also trains you to splash the ball out of the bunker.

Place a tee deep into the sand and then put the ball atop it. Swing back. Swing through, trying to cut the tee in half. This encourages you to go down after the ball just enough and blast the sand under the ball.

Rope Drill: For Bunker Play

Here's what Gary Player, a phenomenal bunker player, does to make sure he's accelerating the club through impact. Gary sticks two stakes in the sand, with a rope tied loosely from one to the other. Ideally, he wants the rope level with his chest. He places a ball approximately 2 feet behind the stakes, closer to him than the green. He swings the club up and then down and through, with the club shaft hitting the rope. This image will keep you swinging all the way through to the finish.

Death Moves

Claude Harmon, the late 1948 Masters Champion, was a renowned bunker player. I became friendly with Claude when he was teaching at the Winged Foot Golf Club in Mamoroneck, New York. He told me that the worst move that amateurs make in bunkers is swinging too hard. He was right. Just watch the top pros; they accelerate the club, but never swing violently. Don't overuse your body but rather learn to swing and release the golf club.

Spare-Change Drill: For Putting

One excellent way to prepare for putting on the course is to practice hitting to dimes set down at different distances on the green. This type of target is tiny. Consequently, when you putt on the course, the hole will seem so huge you will feel superconfident about sinking everything.

One-Two Drill: For Putting

To groove a rhythmic backstroke and downstroke, such as that employed by my student and former World Putting Champion Len Mattice, swing the putter back on the count of one and through on the count of two.

Dip Test: For Putting

Chi Chi Rodriguez told me about the following test that he uses to find out whether or not the sweet spot (the dead center) of the putter face is meeting the ball.

Dip a ball in a glass of water (or you can use talcum powder) and putt it across the green. Examine the putter face and you'll know exactly where contact was made. If you are off, go for another dip. The contact point should be dead center on the putter face and the ball should be hit on its equator.

Ball-Game Drill: For Putting

To intensify your concentration, go around the putting green of your local club four times or more, using just one ball. The mistake amateurs make is throwing three balls down and casually practicing putts. Alternatively, try to consecutively hole out 10 putts in a row from 2 feet, eight in a row from 4 feet, six in a row from 6 feet, and four in a row from 8 feet.

A good practice drill is to try and sink 10 putts in a row from varying distances, starting at a point 2 feet from the hole.

Windy-Day Drill: For Putting

You will not always play golf in calm conditions. Therefore, one windy day, go to the practice green and practice long and short putts. Experiment with your stroke to see what setup changes you have to make to putt well. One hint: Take a wider stance than normal.

See for Yourself

My long-time friend Carl Welty and, more recently, Dr. Craig Farnsworth explained to me why some students appeared to have good chipping and putting strokes, yet miss the hole again and again. Welty has used his own testing for many years to identify visual perception errors, and Farnsworth, an optometrist, confirmed that many professional and amateur golfers he had tested perceived the hole to be right or left of its actual position, nearer or farther away.

Jim's Tips

Some players own three special putters: two identical putters with different lofts and an extra-long model. You can use the low-lofted putter for bent greens and the higher-lofted putter for coarse Bermuda greens. The long putter is great for regrooving a pure-pendulum type arms-and-shoulders stroke.

Bet You Didn't Know

In testing Nick Faldo's eyes, Farnsworth discovered that this former British Open and Masters Champion perceived the hole to be left and short of its actual location. Farnsworth helped him straighten out his eye and aiming problems prior to the 1996 Masters, which Faldo won.

The next time one of your friends tells you that you have such a great stroke, but you miss putts, pay a visit to an eye doctor or sign up for a visual acuity lesson. Farnsworth has studied much of the research done by Carl Welty, on putting and teaching putting. He has also worked with numerous tour professionals and has designed many special eye-improvement techniques. He can help a lot.

Pitch and Putt

As a novice golfer, your best bet is not to go to a championship course until you feel comfortable hitting all kinds of short-game shots. Having said that, once you get a feel for the basics involved, leave your backyard practice area or range and visit a pitch-and-putt course. There are many of these short-hole courses located around the country, and they are perfect for helping you hone your short game. Most pitch-and-putt facilities are not that crowded, so you can pitch, chip, hit bunker shots, and putt to your heart's content. If you seek total freedom, the ideal time of day to visit one of these courses is early in the morning or late in the afternoon. That way, you can drop a few balls around a green and test out what I've taught you, without worrying about people pressing you to hurry. Additionally, you can experiment with different clubs and shot-making keys of your own. In this game, you just never know what will work magic.

The Least You Need to Know

➤ On standard pitch shots, allow your wrists to hinge on the backswing, and forget rigid, lock-wristed, robotic methods.

➤ When chipping, keep your hands ahead of the clubhead from the start of the swing to its finish.

➤ Spend some time working on drills to help you groove good short-game techniques.

➤ Good eyesight helps your pitching, putting, bunker play, and putting games.

➤ Play pitch-and-putt courses to hone your short-game skills and prepare for your championship course debut.

Part 2

Building a Solid Shot-Making Game

Now it's time to really have some fun and learn the art of shot making. The ability to hit a variety of basic trouble shots and more sophisticated short-game shots allows you to enjoy the challenge of doing battle with the golf course.

You learn how to handle virtually any short game situation on the course. I teach you how to hit longer pitches, chips, bunker shots, and putts, plus common trouble shots and wild shots so that you progress rapidly and steadily lower your handicap. And, as an added bonus, I teach you how to hit wedge shots more powerfully, just in case the conditions call for a stronger pitch. Relax. The formula for setting up and swinging with added acceleration is not complicated. Besides, the drills I give you help accelerate the learning process.

Chapter 4

Different Strokes

In This Chapter

➤ Playing the pitch-and-run

➤ Going long on chip shots

➤ Mastering what maybe the toughest bunker shot of all

➤ Dealing with a "snake" on the greens

Now that you have learned and practiced the most common short game shots required to play at least a respectable game of golf, I want to discuss some more exciting pitches, chips, bunker-play shots, and putts that are, in many ways, offshoots of those I have already discussed.

Don't think for a second that we are in the arena of sophisticated shot making. We are not there yet. However, I will keep my promise to teach you the short game gradually so that you can become more educated and confident as you progress. In this chapter, we take another step forward. Don't panic. The shots I'm about to teach you are ones that are merely longer or only slightly different from their basic counterparts discussed previously, so they don't require you to make an overhaul of your new setup and swing mechanics. Still, there are subtle technical changes that have to be applied. Let's give it a go.

The Pitch-and-Run

Whether you decide to visit St. Andrews, the famous course in Scotland on which golf was first played nearly 500 years ago, or play courses in windy states, such as Florida, Texas, or Oklahoma, don't ever think about leaving home without the long pitch-and-run shot in your bag. From as far out as 75 yards from the hole, this is an ideal shot to play into stiff wind. It is often a better choice than the standard lofted shot, because you don't have to worry about the ball being held up by a headwind or misdirected by a crosswind. When playing downwind, it's a good shot to hit too, especially if the green you're hitting to is firm. The beauty of the pitch-and-run is landing the ball short of the green and letting skip and then check on the green. When hitting a high pitch at such a target, with a wind at your back, you run the risk of carrying over the green or bouncing the ball over it. The spin will be taken off the ball if it is hit high with a strong wind behind it. The low burning pitch will retain more spin and thus more control.

I learned to play the pitch-and-run when I played golf at the University of Houston, in Texas, where the wind sometimes howls.

Throughout the years, there have been great wind players to come out of Texas. Going back, Ben Hogan and Byron Nelson lead the list. Jack Burke's wind game was top shelf, too, as was his famous partner Jimmy Demaret. Then along came a guy named Lee Trevino, who may have been the best wind player of them all. Of the living Texas-born players on tour today, Ben Crenshaw, Tom Kite, and Justin Leonard are three of the best wind players. They are also the best at playing the pitch-and-run. Crenshaw depended on this shot to win his second of two Masters in 1995, played, where it is every year, at the prestigious Augusta National Golf Club in Augusta, Georgia. Tom Kite won the 1992 United States Open championship at the Pebble Beach Golf Links in Pebble Beach, California. This course is located on the lip of the Pacific Ocean and, like the other courses mentioned, requires golfers to play the pitch-and-run shot at least a couple of times during a round. Most recently, Justin Leonard depended on the same long pitch-and-run shot en route to victory in the 1997 British Open.

No matter where you play golf, you are bound to play on a windy day. But, being able to fight the wind is not the only reason you should know how to play the pitch-and-run. Like St. Andrews and other seaside links courses, many modern American courses feature entranceways to the green that are devoid of bunkers, which opens the door to hit one of golf's most useful shots—one that flies low, skips a few times, and then rolls all the way to the hole.

Let me teach you what I learned from some of the great American pitch-and-run players. Let me also share with you the swing secrets I learned from observing Sergio Garcia, the young Spanish superstar golfer, who learned practically everything he knows about playing the long pitch-and-run with a 7 or 8 iron and the short pitch-and-run with a pitching or gap wedge from his fellow countryman Seve Ballesteros.

Bet You Didn't Know

The late Ben Hogan was born in Texas, lived in Texas, and played much of his golf in Texas. He competed in only one British Open championship—the one played at Scotland's Carnoustie Golf Club, in 1953. He won, thanks to his keen ability to hit deft short-game shots, including the pitch-and-run.

The Pitch-and-Run Setup

You can establish the same stance I taught you for playing the basic pitch shot, as long as you are careful not to drop your left foot too far back from the target line. The danger is that opening the stance too much can cause you to pull the club across the target line through impact and hit a pull left of your target. Test your stance, and if you have trouble, work more toward a square stance, with both feet parallel to the target line.

Play the ball back only slightly in your stance. Letting the ball drift too close to your right foot promotes too steep a swing. Stand fairly erect, because bending too much at the knees and hips can also cause an overly upright backswing and steep downswing plane. Like Ballesteros and his protégé Garcia, I prefer that my students not grip down on the club too much, for fear of making an overly steep swing, causing mishits. Instead, hold the club pretty much at the end of the club to ensure a better club head feel, gripping down about only an inch or so. Adjust the clubface from square to slightly open, depending on the height and spin required for individual shots.

Death Moves

Don't open your shoulders too much by aiming them well left of the target, or you are likely to swing the club on an exaggerated out-to-in path and hit your shot left of the target.

The Pitch-and-Run Backswing

You are not looking to generate a lot of power on this shot, so there's no need to make a big upper body coil. Use the arms to swing the club back to about the halfway point. Be sure to let your wrists cock. Don't worry about failing to generate enough

Jim's Tips

If you choose to play the pitch-and-run with a seven or eight iron, rather than a pitching wedge, be sure to maintain a smooth tempo. Failure to do so could cause you to overshoot the green, simply because the seven iron has less loft than the pitching wedge. The ball will go much further than you expect when you hit it solid.

force to hit the ball to the hole. Your arm speed and turn through the shot is what will carry the ball to a landing spot short of the green and roll it to the hole. At the highest point in the backswing, your hands should be at shoulder level.

The Pitch-and-Run Downswing

To promote a good weight shift and swinging action of the arms, push your right knee toward the target, à la Ballesteros and Garcia. The split second you trigger the downswing, you should feel as if you are effortlessly directing the club back to the ball with both your arms and your turn. If you are swinging rhythmically, and letting the arms do the work, the right hand should rotate smoothly over your left through impact.

In hitting the pitch-and-run, it's paramount that you let the right hand rotate over the left through impact.

The Extra-Long Chip

The trend to build courses with an overwhelming number of hazards (a *tough track*) is over. First of all, these courses are even too demanding on the pros. As for amateurs, they cause the typical player so much trouble that he or she takes too much time to complete a round. Furthermore, courses featuring numerous and difficult water hazards and treacherous bunkers guarding the front of the greens are a maintenance nightmare, both logistically and financially. At the Doral Resort and Country Club—my home base in Miami, Florida—our five courses, including the renowned Blue Monster, are tough but fair and fun to play. At one time, the Blue Monster had too many bunkers that caused extra play. That changed, and everybody including the tour players are a lot happier with the course.

One popular feature that makes a course challenging is the big two-tier green. You are bound to play one of these courses. When you do, you better be able to hit a long chip shot from the bottom level of a green to its top level.

When the ball lies cleanly in the fringe and about 60 to 90 feet from a hole that's positioned on the upper level of a steep two-tier green of normal speed, high handicappers often reach for the pitching wedge or even the sand wedge. This makes me cringe, because I know the player is making a grave shot-making error.

The player who attempts to carry the ball onto the green's top tier with a wedge usually either pitches the ball far short of the top level so that it rolls all the way back down to the lower level or hits the ball over the green. It requires tremendous touch and practice to attempt this shot.

The pitching wedge and the sand wedge are great clubs, but not from this lie. In this extra-long chip situation, the percentage play is hitting a seven iron shot. Chip it short to your target area and let the ball roll all the way to the cup. Think of it this way: Would you have a better chance to toss a ball into a bucket 15 feet away or 50 feet away? Of course you would choose the closer bucket. It is the same with chipping. Aim for the closer target by using less loft.

Swing Lingo

When playing a very difficult course, call it a **tough track.** That's the golf speak used by pros and top-notch amateurs.

The Extra-Long Chip Setup

Before even stepping into the shot, remember that you need to apply what I (and my fellow short-game teaching experts, Jeff Warne, Debbie Doniger, and Carl Welty) call the one-quarter ratio. This means that, using the seven iron, you must plan for the ball to travel a quarter of the distance to the hole in the air and roll the remaining three-quarters of the way. Once you accept that, you apply this ratio and pick out a landing spot. I recommend that you chip to a circle and not an exact spot.

Jim's Tips

On long chip shots, it's paramount that you keep the body perfectly still. Swaying could throw off your rhythm and timing and solid contact. To prevent the sway, set your back foot perpendicular to the target line, and place weight in the inside portion of the foot.

Almost all the basic chipping setup elements described in Chapter 2, "How to Get Started," still apply here. The only differences are that you play the ball up in your stance more, keep slightly less weight on your left foot, and keep your hands just slightly ahead of the ball. Why? You want to make more of a shallow hit than a descending blow. Also, grip more firmly than you would normally because you want to hit a fairly low running chip shot with a lot of resistance after impact. And, of course, visualize a good shot before you start your backswing.

The Extra-Long Chip Backswing

As you sweep the club back only slightly inside the target line, keep your leg and hip actions stable. Feel as though you're swinging the club back mostly with the triangle formed by your arms and shoulders. However, I definitely want you to cock your wrists in the backswing. This action promotes feel, touch, and easy power.

The Extra-Long Chip Downswing

As Ken Venturi taught me, the proper feeling on the downswing is dragging the ball to the hole as you swing the club through in a pendulum fashion. If the hands lead the club head in the hitting area, the ball will land on the lower tier and run all the way up to the hole just like a perfectly struck putt.

The Long Bunker Shot

The long bunker shot frightens amateurs, and it's a scary shot even for the tour pros. It is not only sand that has to be dealt with, but also the 60 to 90 feet of green between the ball and the hole. Especially high handicappers wonder how in the heck they are going to reach the hole. Frankly, this shot takes practice, but if you realize that the important technical keys to success are focusing on a spot about an inch behind the ball and hitting that spot using a flatter swing than normal, you'll realize that it can be mastered.

The Long Bunker-Shot Setup

Play the ball closer to your left foot than your right foot. Set your feet parallel to the target line, or drop your right foot back farther from the target line, so that you're in a closed stance position. Spread your feet about shoulder width apart to promote a shallower plane of swing.

One secret to playing a long chip well is swinging the club through in a pendulum fashion, using the triangle formed by the arms and shoulders to control the action.

The Long Bunker-Shot Backswing

Make a complete turn of the hips and shoulders, but don't elevate the club on the backswing as much as you would normally. You ultimately want to take a shallower cut of sand. This swing is much like the one you would use to play a full wood shot. Just be sure that you take sand first. You must never hit the ball first.

The Long Bunker-Shot Downswing

Because of the length of the shot, you have to cut closer to the ball—about an inch behind it. So, when you reach the end of your backswing, concentrate on unwinding your body and accelerating the club with your hands and arms all the way through to the finish.

Bet You Didn't Know

In teaching the long bunker shot and playing it himself, Ken Venturi imagines he's picking the ball off carpet. This mental image encourages him to make a shallow cut through the sand in the hitting area.

A vital swing key, on bunker shots, is accelerating the club into the finish with your hands and arms.

The Long Putt

Newly built courses tend to feature expansive greens on short par-three and short par-four holes. Many course designers believe that if they make it easy for you to reach a hole in regulation figures, you have to earn par by two, putting from a long distance. And, trust me, getting down from more than 50 feet in two putts is a hard task (let alone a *snake* or a *roller coaster*), unless you know how to plan out the putt and execute it.

The Long-Putt Setup

Look over the putt carefully, and take time to visualize the ball rolling along a particular line to the hole. Translate this speed into feel and determine how long a stroke you must make to propel the ball to the hole. Unless the green is severely sloped, speed should be your ultimate priority on long putts. Your chief goal should be to drop the ball into an imaginary 3-foot circle anywhere around the hole.

When you've figured the speed and translated the distance to stroke tempo and length, stand more erect, because that enhances your perspective of the line and your feel for distance. Take a wider stance than normal to promote a slightly longer stroke. Allow your arms to extend downward in a relaxed fashion, à la Justin Leonard style, to encourage a tension-free action. As far as the other basics, including ball position, follow those that were discussed in Chapter 2. Also, you may want to try setting your eyes just inside the target line, as this helps promote a slight inside square and inside path, which is actually just a miniature golf swing.

The Long-Putt Backswing

Make a pendulum-type arms and shoulders stroke, but allow the right wrist to hinge slightly for better feel. Don't fight the putter head moving inside the target line slightly. On long putts, the putter will naturally move slightly inside, which is perfectly okay. Make your backstroke as rhythmic as possible and keep the putter head moving back relatively low to the ground.

The Long-Putt Downswing

While keeping your head and body still let the putter head flow all the way through to your finish. Let the movement of the putter unhinge your right wrist naturally, so that you swing the putter face squarely into the back of the ball.

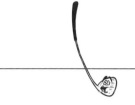

Swing Lingo

A putt of over 50 feet in length is called a **snake**. A long putt over a hill is called a roller coaster.

Jim's Tips

On long putts, follow the example of 1992 Masters Champion Fred Couples. Couples stays carefree to prevent feeling pressured to hole out. His "if it goes in, fine, if it doesn't, that's fine too" mind-set is the attitude to adopt if the putts aren't dropping. You may find this helps you to make a more relaxed stroke and to turn a sour putting game sweet. Concentrate solely on rolling the ball with a pure stroke.

When hitting a long putt, the putter's head should move slightly inside the target line on the backswing.

The Least You Need to Know

➤ When there are no hazards blocking the green's entranceway, the pitch-and-run is a good shot-making option.

➤ On long chips, feel like you're dragging the ball to the hole with the club head.

➤ A key to playing the long bunker shot is contacting the sand about one inch behind the ball and making a full finish.

➤ To promote good feel on long putts, let your right wrist hinge slightly.

Chapter 5

Common Trouble Shots

In This Chapter

➤ Secrets to hitting pitch shots off hilly lies

➤ Chipping off hard ground and other spots of bother

➤ Dealing with buried lies in bunkers

➤ Putting up with intimidating putting situations

When you reach the stage where you feel confident about playing a variety of long shots, including drives, fairway woods, and long and medium irons, you will still tray from the straight and narrow and be confronted with a tough lie. Even top pros on the PGA, Senior PGA, and LPGA Tours miss fairways and greens, so they must depend on their imaginations and hard-earned, shot-making talents to recover. Ironically, even when pro golfers do hit the middle of a fairway or green, they sometimes still miss the green and leave themselves in very difficult places.

Playing pitch shots off a downhill lie, hitting a chip off hard ground, playing a bunker shot out of wet sand, and hitting a putt across a severely sloped green, are all common course situations that you have to learn to deal with in order to shoot lower scores. Let me now review some of the more common pitching, chipping, bunker play, and putting lies that you will need to handle.

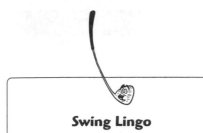

Pitch Outs

Part of the challenge of golf is the challenge of pitching the ball out of a trouble spot and hitting it on the green. There's nothing better than scoring *par* or *birdie* when it seemed you were going to score *bogie* or *double bogie*.

When playing pitch shots from awkward lies in the fairway and rough, you often need to make slight alterations in your setup and swing. For example, when the ball is in a *divot,* you must set more of your weight on your left foot, swing on a steeper plane, and hit down more sharply. Club selection is affected, too. If you normally hit an eight iron from a particular distance, you will need a nine iron. The reason is that you are de-lofting the club at impact; therefore, you change the effective loft of the club. In other words, the nine iron becomes an eight iron. This strategy is part of the planning process that makes golf such a challenging game. You not only have to know what to do, you have to know how to get the job done.

Going Downhill

Pretend that you are out in the fairway at a distance from the green where you would normally hit a pitching wedge. The ball is sitting on a downhill lie. By applying some simple principles of cause and effect, you can approach this shot confidently and hit the ball as solidly as you do when playing off a level lie.

Choose one less club—in this case, a sand wedge. The reason is that at impact you hit down sharply on the ball and, in effect, take some of the loft off the club.

Allow the natural tendency to lean left, because that's the very position that encourages you to align your shoulders parallel to the slope and swing along it through the hitting area. Because the tendency is to hit a *fade* off this lie, allow for this flight pattern by aiming a few yards right.

Once you set up correctly in relation to the ball (which should be played back slightly in your stance to enable you to make the cleanest possible contact while the club is still descending on a steep angle), swing the club back to the three-quarter point. This compact swing enhances your balance—as does keeping your head still.

Trigger the downward motion by rotating your hips and simultaneously swinging the club down with your hands and arms. While maintaining a steady head, try to feel as though you are chasing the ball down the slope with the club head. That's the best insurance you can have for getting the ball in the air.

Going Uphill

You face an uphill pitch shot off a fairway lie. You are sand wedge distance from the hole. What do you do?

The first thing you must do is switch clubs. Because of the uphill slope, the effective loft of the club increases at impact. To compensate, choose a pitching wedge.

Address the ball so that you can swing with the slope of the hill. When you address the ball, you're naturally going to set more weight on your right foot than normal if you are right-handed. But that's okay; leaning hard left prevents you from setting your shoulders parallel to the slope and thus causes you to pound the club into the hill.

In the backswing, protect against swaying your body to your right by keeping your left foot planted on the ground.

Because you set up with most of your weight on your right side, and because you inevitably fight gravity when you start the downswing, it becomes difficult to shift your lower body weight to your left foot and clear your hips normally. Because you tend to hang back, your hands roll over faster than usual. As a result, the clubface turns over through impact, imparting right-to-left spin on the ball. To compensate, align your feet and body a few yards right of the target. Also, tighter grip pressure in the left hand will help to keep the face square through impact.

Swing Lingo

A shot **fades** when it moves to the right in the air. On the downswing, the upper body tends to slide past the ball, preventing the complete release of the hands. This slight hindrance to the releasing action causes the clubface to stay open through impact, and the path of the club to be slightly outside.

Jim's Tips

If you become confused about where to position the ball on hilly lies, remember to play it nearest the higher foot.

Above Ground

When playing a fairway pitch shot from a ball-above-the-feet lie, aim right of target to allow for the slope curving the ball left. Alternatively, set up square to the target, and compensate by opening the clubface. The more severe the slope, the more you should aim right and open the clubface. Take one extra club and use a more compact swing for more control.

Aim right of the target when hitting a pitch off a ball-above-the-feet lie.

Ball Below Feet

In playing a fairway pitch shot from a ball-below-the-feet lie, aim left of target to allow for the slope curving the ball right. The more severe the slope, the more you should aim left.

Down and Dirty

The first priority in facing a shot out of a divot hole is to relax. If you keep your cool, your muscles are able to work freely during the swing.

When setting up, play the ball closer to your back foot, with the clubface slightly hooded—looking downward slightly. Set yourself in position to hit with a sharp descending blow. Remember, however, hooding the clubface reduces its effective loft. Therefore, if the distance calls for a sand wedge, make a slightly shorter golf swing.

In setting up to play a pitch from a divot hole, position the ball closer to your right foot. This address helps promote a sharp descending hit.

Employ a steep, compact backswing by pulling the club almost straight up in the air with your hands and arms. However, be sure to turn your shoulders. If you simply lift the club up, you will not generate sufficient power.

On the downswing, drive your knees toward the target while swinging the club through with both hands. This sharp angle of descent enables you to hit down forcefully, extract the ball from the divot hole, and propel it toward the green.

Knock, Knock

You are 75 yards from the hole. There is a strong wind in your face, and you are hitting to a pin positioned in the front portion of the green, some 20 feet behind a deep bunker. What do you do? You play a knockdown—a low shot that produces a whole lot of backspin, takes one bounce, and then settles near the hole. A high shot will often balloon too high and bury in that front bunker.

Bet You Didn't Know

Many high handicap golfers are under the impression that pros play a knockdown shot only with a strong wind in the face. Wrong! When facing a relatively short downwind shot to a green fronted by bunkers, professionals, such as Tiger Woods, punch the ball under the wind.

When playing the knockdown, set up square to the target with the ball played a few inches back from your normal position for a pitching wedge. Playing the ball there places you in position to hit with your hands leading the club head, thereby setting up the sharp angle needed for producing backspin.

In the takeaway, elevate your hands and the club head to help set up a steep downward blow.

Your downswing keys are moving the club low to the ground, toward the target through impact, and keeping the left hand/left wrist unit firm as you punch the ball.

Don't Get Needled

Whether or not you ever visit one of golf's greatest destinations, the Pinehurst Resort and Country Club in North Carolina, you will probably still play a course with fairways lined with pine trees. When you do, you better know how to play a pitch shot off pine needles.

When you face such a lie, know right away that you must hit the ball on the descent in order to produce a solid shot. If you try to sweep the ball off the needles, you will not make solid contact.

At address, prevent slippage, loss of balance, and ultimately a mishit by taking a narrow stance. Set the club just behind the ball, but off the ground slightly. Be very careful not to touch the pine needles with the club head, which can easily cause the ball to move. Keep your hands a couple of inches ahead of the ball to encourage an upright plane. Hold the club just above the needles.

Make an upright backswing, allowing your wrists to hinge freely. Coming down, pull the club down squarely into the back of the ball with your hands and arms leading the club.

Grass Roots

When the ball lies in grass that is growing toward the target, the good news is that this lie offers less resistance to the club head. The bad news is that this lie helps produce a flyer, which is a shot that flies farther than normal. The reason is that when grass intervenes between the ball and clubface at impact, the grooves on the club are unable to grab the ball. In such circumstances, it's difficult to determine exactly how fast the ball will come off the clubface, and thus how far it will fly and roll.

Therefore, to play this shot, compensate by taking a smaller swing, depending on how thick the grass is—the heavier the grass, the firmer the stroke. For example, in playing a shot out of thick grass, allow for the resistance by swinging more firmly. Take several practice swings near the ball to get the proper feel.

Death Moves

When getting ready to play a shot off pine needles, be careful about picking up any nearby twigs or stones because you could shake up the loosely knitted needles, cause the ball to move, and incur a penalty. That's also why I recommend that you not set the club down on the needles when taking your address.

Jim's Tips

When pros are faced with iron shots from a slight flyer lie they often play their normal club for the distance at hand. However, they swing on an out-to-in path rather than an inside-square inside path. This type of swing produces a soft-landing fade, which flies slightly from left to right. So when setting up, aim slightly left of target, and open the clubface slightly.

Way Out

When grass grows away from the target and back at you, the way to hit the ball out is to select a stronger club because this type of lie reduces club head speed upon impact and the distance the ball will carry.

In playing the shot, make an upright backswing. This upright arc allows you to drive the clubface down into the ball so that it catches less grass and encounters less resistance.

Lob It

When the ball is sitting in light rough next to the green, and you have to hit over a bunker to a tight pin, a superlofted shot with a lob wedge is the perfect play.

When taking your address, set the clubface back more than normal to increase its natural loft even more. Grip more firmly with your left hand, and maintain that secure hold in the hitting area to discourage your right hand from turning over and closing at impact.

Bet You Didn't Know

Phil Mickelson is one of the greatest lob-wedge players in the game. However, he does a couple of things I wouldn't recommend you do, unless you just want to have a little fun. He swings the club well past the parallel point in the backswing with an open clubface and hits under the ball at practically maximum speed. The ball goes almost straight up and drops onto the green like a butterfly. Believe me—this takes talent, a ton of practice, and the nerves of a safecracker.

Make a long and controlled backswing, letting the wrists hinge freely. Unhinge your wrists coming down, so that you bring the clubface down toward the ball and then under it with the open clubface.

Chip Outs

If there is one guarantee in golf, it's that during a round you face a host of chipping situations. This is true because of different lies you inevitably confront in the fringe, including high grass and trodden-down dirt called hardpan. Additionally, the greens differ from course to course. There are slow greens, fast greens, flat greens, and sloping greens. And then there is the element of distance. Sometimes the holes themselves are placed in the front of the green, the middle of the green, or the back of the green. Mix all these elements together and you have quite a challenge on your hands. What follows are some of the common chip shots that you will need to play sooner or later.

Hard to Believe

To play a short chip off hardpan with a pitching wedge, play the ball back in your stance (closer to your right foot) and set your hands a couple of inches ahead of the ball. This address position promotes a downward hit, which is perfect for popping the ball onto the green.

Swing back, allowing your wrists to hinge, promoting a more upright plane and a sharp solid hit.

Swing the club down into the ball, using a hit-and-hold action. This means that you will resist the follow through by firming up the grip and left wrist. Because the wedge contains more mass in the club head than other short clubs, such as an eight iron, you can use a shorter stroke for the required distance, reducing the odds of a mishit.

Chip off the Old Block

Pretend that your ball is to the side of the green, behind a bunker with a low lip. The lie is tight and the pin is situated very close to the fringe.

When blocked by a shallow bunker, you do not have to choose a sand wedge and try to lift the ball into the air because you stand a good chance of mishitting the shot. Instead, play a creative running chip shot through the bunker by using a 7, 8, or 9 iron. You want the ball to skip through the bunker with just enough speed to roll to within a few feet of the hole.

To execute this shot, play the ball back in a narrow stance with your hands ahead. Make a short stiff-wristed backswing. Let your hands lead the club head on the downswing. If played correctly, this technique produces a low shot that runs through the trap and fringe and trickles to the hole.

Death Moves

Don't ever try to lift the ball off hardpan, otherwise you'll probably top the ball (hit the top half of it) and send it flying over the green. Either pick the ball clean or strike down, but never lift.

Bank on It

You have just hit your approach ten yards over the green. You are below a grassy bank and an elevated green. The grass on the bank is pretty short and the ground underneath fairly firm. The pin is cut on the top level of the green. This is one of golf's toughest shots if you play it with a wedge, because there is very little margin for error. The percentage shot is a chip played with a short iron. (You could use a 7, 8, or 9 iron, whichever makes you feel more comfortable. Just be sure to set your hands farther ahead of the ball to reduce the effective loft of the club even more.)

The strategy is to carry the ball into the bank so that it skips before popping up onto the green and trickles to the hole. To accomplish this goal, be sure to play the ball back slightly in your stance; make a short, firm-wristed backswing, keeping the club fairly low to the ground; and come into the ball with the club's handle leading the way.

Skull It

Every few rounds, you'll hit a shot over the green and it will finish against the first cut of rough. Let's say you did just that and the ball is only a few yards from the hole. What do you do?

In such a situation, it's difficult to control the chip. Chances are that the longer grass will get between your club and ball, making it very hard to stop the shot quickly enough. The smartest and simplest shot is to skull it with a sand wedge.

Raise the club off the ground, rather than resting it down in the grass so that its protruding leading edge lines up with the ball's equator. Use your normal putting grip and address position. Next, swing the club back with your arms and shoulders. The wrists must stay quiet for you to make a level and steady stroke. It's also crucial that you keep your head still, so as not to sway off the ball and disrupt your balance. Using your putting motion, stoke through smoothly, and the ball will roll like a putt. It might have extra topspin, and you will be surprised at how easy this shot is once you get the hang of it. The reason that it works well in these situations is because the club head is raised above the high grass behind you.

On the forward swing, remember to stroke the ball just as you would a putt, except let the leading edge of the sand wedge bump or nudge the top half of the ball. When the ball is struck, it will skid for a slight distance before picking up true overspin just as a putt would.

Bet You Didn't Know

When Tiger Woods is confronted with a ball resting against the first cut of rough, he uses a three wood to chip. Tiger plays the ball off his right instep, in a very narrow stance. He places 70 percent of his weight on his left foot. Going back, he hinges his right wrist to elevate the club. Coming down, he unhinges the wrist until impact, and hits against a firm left wrist. This shot works well with a fairway metal wood because the rounded head easily glides through the rough. An iron will catch in the rough, and the clubface is often affected negatively.

When setting up to play a bump-shot, line the sand wedge's leading edge up with the ball's equator.

Bunker Bail-Outs

In Chapter 3, "Building Blocks," I discussed the club and body movements necessary for hitting the basic bunker shot. I am now going to take your bunker game into a new dimension by teaching you how to deal with more difficult lies. I'm not talking about the real crazy shots just yet. You are not yet at that level. What I'm about to give you here are simple, easy-to-follow instructions on how to bail out of awkward bunker situations you are destined to confront during a round.

Plug It Up

Here's what to do when you find your ball plugged: The ball is buried halfway or more in the sand, with little or no crater of sand around it. To be prepared, let me tell you right up front that what you will be doing is pretty much the opposite of the basic bunker shot technique.

In this plugged situation, set the face of your sand wedge behind the ball and above the sand slightly, with its face hooded (closed). Set about 75 percent of your weight on your left foot. Play the ball back in your stance. Put your hands ahead of the ball. Grip the club firmly. All of this advice is just the reverse of our normal bunker setup. That's because you don't want the club to dig and go deep into the sand, and the follow through is not important for this shot.

Make an upright swing, but instead of releasing through the shot, contact the sand about an inch behind the ball, burying the club into the sand. The ball will come out quite fast, or hot, so you do not need to swing down all that quickly. (This is often a very pleasant surprise to students.)

To hit a good recovery shot from a buried lie in a bunker, hit down sharply, and then stop.

All Wet

Wet sand is often more compact and firm, so the sand wedge tends to bounce off it rather than slip under it. To avoid this, use a technique I learned from Gary Player, undoubtedly one of the greatest living bunker players.

Player uses either a pitching wedge or a lob wedge instead of a sand wedge. These clubs feature less bounce and the lob wedge has added loft, which makes getting the ball airborne a whole lot easier. Furthermore, the shallow sole of these wedges cut through the wet sand without much resistance. Player's most vital swing keys are gripping the club more firmly in his left hand (because that helps him hold the clubface open through impact) and hitting slightly closer to the ball. Remember that the ball comes out easier and faster in compacted sand.

Up Tight

The ball sits cleanly in dry, fluffy sand, close to a high lip. You are hitting to a tight pin. Take a *strong right-hand grip* and choke down on the club so that your right hand is partially on the shaft. Also be sure to open the clubface. (I learned these keys from watching master short game player Seve Ballesteros.) These two simple setup adjustments should help you swing the club on an upright plane and slip the club under the ball so that it floats softly over the lip and stops quickly. Gripping down enables you to swing faster, which helps to get the ball higher without having the ball go too far.

Putting Problem Solvers

Don't let the billiard-table look of a typical green give you the impression that all greens are level and quick. Some greens are slow. Also, most greens are sloped, which means you have to concentrate harder on figuring the degree of break and the proper speed to hit the ball. Uphill and downhill putts are tricky and require different strategies, as do wet greens.

Let's now take a look at the secrets to putting well in tough situations.

Jim's Tips

To play out of a partially plugged lie (the ball less than half-buried in sand), simply use less force. In playing a fried egg lie (the ball sitting down in the center of a crater of sand), strike the sand on the edge of the crater and use more force to extract more sand. Remember that not all buried lies are equal. You must learn to identify the different types of situations and make slight adjustments.

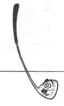

Swing Lingo

Taking a **strong right-hand grip** means turning your hand away from the target, and more under the club, so that the V formed by your thumb and forefinger points up at your right shoulder.

low Going

Based on my experience as both teacher and player, I believe that a heavy putter is better on slow greens because it discourages you from speeding up your stroke. You can make a smoothly paced putting action and reach the hole. Still, if your favorite putter is light, you must adjust by making a longer and firmer stroke. An excellent mental image that works for many students is to simply imagine a second cup several feet behind the hole and putt to that.

Fast Forward

On extremely fast greens, it can sometimes be very difficult to maintain good distance control when using a heavy putter. This is especially true when facing a steep downhill putt. If you like your heavy putter, make your normal stroke, except lighten the hit by contacting the ball more toward the toe of the putter face. This will deaden the hit and help to control the speed. Personally, I just take an extra short and extra slow stroke and visualize stoking my putt just a few inches. To do this, visualize a line in front of your ball. Depending upon the length and speed of your putt, adjust the length of that line. Then putt to the end of your imaginary line.

Death Moves

On longer putts, don't ever make the mistakes of playing a right-to-left breaking putt off your left toe, or a left-to-right breaking putt nearer your right foot. If you do, you stand very little chance of getting the ball started along the proper line and sinking the putt. That's because of the arc of your stroke. Poor positioning will make your long putting much more difficult.

All Wet

The most critical technical point to remember, when putting on wet, dewy surfaces, is to allow for about half as much break as under dry conditions. Often you will face wet conditions with early morning tee times. Because we have to stroke the putt harder, the initial break is almost entirely eliminated. As the sun dries out the greens, you will notice that your putts break more.

Curling Cues

Here's what two-time Masters Champion José Maria Olazabal does on sharp-breaking putts. In assessing the break, he looks for the high side of the hole—the point where the ball will start breaking—just as the great South African Bobby Locke did. (Locke has been voted one of the top 10 putters of the twentieth century.) When José sees that the slope of the green breaks from right to left, he plays the ball closer to his right foot. This unique address key—that I recommend you consider adopting—virtually forces you to swing out at the putt in the precise direction the ball should start rolling. If the putt breaks in the opposite direction, he plays the ball closer to his left foot. These deft position changes can work wonders for some golfers. Give it a try. It might be the magic you need.

When to Putt

New golfers think that because the ball is on the fringe they have to use a chipping club. Let me tell you, even the pros sometimes putt the ball if the circumstances dictate. Let's say, for example, your ball sits in manicured fringe, 15 feet from the hole on a level green. In such a situation, go through your normal putting routine. Next, simply employ the normal basic putting stroke taught to you in Chapter 3. The oldest rule in golf might be "whenever you can putt, putt." Often your worst putt is better than your best chip!

Jim's Tips

Chip, rather than putt, if the grain of the fringe grass is too heavy, the grass is too high, or there is mud on the ball.

The Least You Need to Know

➤ When pitching out of a divot or another bad lie, play the ball back in your stance to promote a descending hit.

➤ Don't be afraid to hit chips with a three or four wood, as Tiger Woods sometimes does.

➤ Swing easier when playing a shot from a plugged lie in sand.

➤ On breaking putts, aim at the point where the ball will start curving.

Chapter 6

Wild Shots

Over the course of the previous chapters, we have covered in detail the basic elements involved in setting up for pitch shots, chip shots, bunker shots, and putts. Together, we have also covered the proper backswing and downswing actions for playing short shots, as well as longer versions of those same shots and trouble shots, too.

Golf is a game of the sublime, the not so sublime, and the ridiculous. What follows are secrets to playing wild shots from ridiculous lies from which you have to recover because of a bad drive, a poor approach into the green, or simply bad luck. You've got the right equipment now. You know the importance of mental imagery. You have been given drills to groove good short-game techniques. Therefore, I think you now are ready to handle these shots.

Wild Pitch Shots

I have been to courses all over the globe watching pros and amateurs, so you would have thought I'd seen everything. That's not so. Almost every time I get in a golf cart at Doral, visit another course to play, or take a student out for a playing lesson, I see at least one lie or course situation I have never seen before.

As good as the pros are, they also have to play wild pitch shots from wild lies. I have seen professional golfers get in crazy on-course predicaments a lot of times in which they have to use their imagination and good technical know-how to recover. You must do the same.

Let me show you how to hit four wild shots I have seen pros play with a wedge. I would not call these common situations. By the same token, I would not call them uncommon either. I've witnessed pros in these situations numerous times. My point is that if these talented golfers have had to play these types of pitch shots, you can bet your best golf ball that you will too.

Border-Control Pitch

You have just hit a highly controlled right-to-left tee shot, on a very short par-four hole of an executive course. You are so proud and happy about your drive that you can't wait to walk down the fairway and hit your approach shot to a green with the hole located on the right side.

Skipping ahead, you arrive at your ball. You are only sand-wedge distance from the hole, but the lie is one you have never seen before. The ball is sitting on the border where the fairway ends and the rough begins.

Death Moves

When the ball lies on the border of the fairway and rough, avoid taking the club back along an exaggerated inside path. The club will tend to snag in the grass, throwing off your swing tempo, timing, rhythm, and plane.

I admit this wild lie can be very distracting, but there is no reason to fear it. The secret is to avoid the rough in the backswing by swinging the club along an outside-inside path, rather than on an inside-square-inside path. Let me explain what I mean. Normally, the club swings back slightly inside the target line, returns to a square position at impact (clubface perpendicular to target), and then swings back to the inside when you hit through the ball. On this swing, you direct the club away from the target line on the backswing and then across it slightly at impact, with the clubface slightly open to impart soft left-to-right cut spin on the ball. The soft cut is the perfect shot in this situation, because if played correctly the ball drifts over the left side of the green and then moves toward the hole. It is also a good percentage shot, because if you fail to hit the ball exactly as planned, it will still finish on the left side of the green where you can two-putt for par.

Select a pitching wedge instead of a sand wedge, because hitting a soft cut causes you to lose a little distance. Set up open with your feet, knees, hips, and shoulders pointing slightly left of target. Hold the club head above the grass to further prevent the club snagging. Aim the clubface at the hole, to allow for the outside-in swing. Also, hold on more firmly than normal with the last three fingers of your left hand at address, and maintain that hold throughout the swing because this helps keep the clubface slightly open at impact.

Swing the club back outside the target line, then down into the ball, trying to hold back the follow-through. This firm hit-and-hold action, combined with a slightly open clubface position at impact, causes the ball to float softly from left to right, all the while moving toward the hole.

Stick-It Pitch

This time you hit a tee shot down the right side of the fairway, seemingly in the perfect place to attack the hole cut on the left side of the green. The problem is that when you walk to your ball you notice it resting against a small branch, which probably fell off a nearby tree and was blown onto the fairway. According to the rules, you are allowed to deem the lie unplayable, penalize yourself one stroke, and drop the ball. But, I don't advise you do this, particularly since this branch is quite thin.

Even though a thin branch or twig is behind your ball, you can still hit a solid shot. Start by playing the ball nearer your back foot, as this will encourage an upright backswing and sharp angle of descent. It's this sharp angle of attack that allows you to make the cleanest possible contact with the ball.

On the backswing, allow your wrists to hinge freely as you make a fluid shoulder and hip turn. For maximum control, swing the club to the three-quarter point.

On the downswing, use active hand action as you direct the club more powerfully than normal into impact. This is one of those few times in golf that you should have the sense that you are pulling the club down with your hands and arms. The added speed you generate will be transmitted to the club head, allowing you to plow though the branch and hit the ball onto the green.

Death Moves

If you move a twig that's resting against the ball, and the ball moves out of its original position, you incur a one stroke penalty and have to place the ball back in its original position.

The Desert Pitch

During your golfing life, you are bound to make a trip to the desert. If you travel out to Arizona or to our schools at PGA West in La Quinta, California, to play golf, I guarantee you will find yourself playing a shot off the desert sand. Because the afternoon wind blows the sand around, miniature sand piles often are formed. If your ball lands on one of these tiny piles of sand, don't play the same shot you would if the sand were firm. Whenever you get in one of these spots, the trick is to pick the ball cleanly off the top of the pile using a sweeping action instead of a digging action.

When setting up, be certain to set your feet in a closed position, as this helps promote a slightly flatter plane. Balance your weight evenly on both feet and play the ball from where you feel you can make clean, solid contact. Set your hands in line with the ball. If you let your hands get out well ahead of the ball, you position yourself to steepen the plane of swing. Again, when dealing with soft sand, you want to sweep, not dig.

On the backswing, encourage a more rounded swing by rotating your shoulders on a flatter axis and allow the clubface to fan open slightly.

Coming down, rotate your shoulders in the opposite direction, and swing the club through fluidly with your hands and arms. If the pin is *tucked left* and you want to impart some draw spin on the ball, exaggerate the rotation of your right hand and forearm. This action allows the toe of the club (the side of the club head farthest from you) to lead its heel, which helps produce a draw spin—similar to the top spin action in tennis or ping pong.

Death Moves

If playing a pitch off a soft area of desert sand, avoid hitting down sharply so that you don't stick the club down deeply into the sand and hit a fat shot. Instead, pick the ball cleanly off the top of the pile.

Swing Lingo

If a pin is **tucked left,** it is located on the left side of the green, often at the back, and often behind a bunker.

Tree-Climber Pitch

The ball is in light rough, yet there is some cushion of grass underneath it. You have a fairly tall tree in front of you, seemingly blocking you from hitting the green that's approximately 55 yards behind it.

A novice golfer would automatically play a recovery shot out sideways, to the fairway. While in some cases this is the correct play, you can also easily loft the ball extra high by using a technique I learned from watching tour professionals in action.

The shot is played different from the way a standard pitch is played. You contact the ball at the very bottom of your swing arc or even slightly on the upswing, leaving your weight back on your right foot, as Sergio Garcia and other pros do when playing this shot. Because the club's effective loft is increased slightly at impact, you need to use a stronger club; in this case probably a gap wedge instead of a sand wedge.

The idea is to hit this shot as softly as possible so that it sits down quickly on the green. Therefore, set up open with the ball played opposite the instep of your left foot. Aiming left of target encourages an upright swing, while the forward ball position helps you stay back and under the shot. Lean most of your weight right and keep it there. The paramount key to playing this shot successfully is setting and keeping your weight on your right side during the entire swing, which puts your hands behind the ball at impact for even more loft. Grip lighter than normal, because this enables your hands and wrists to work freely and promotes the long, slow, loose swing that you need for this situation. The last technical point of the setup involves clubface position; lay the club head back slightly so that its face is angled up more toward the sky.

Jim's Tips

When the ball sits atop soft and pliable rough grass, it is far easier to hit the shot high. In fact, sometimes you have to swing much harder than you would expect because the effective loft of the club increases so much at impact. Practice will tell you which club works best.

When swinging back, hinge your wrists early in the takeaway, and keep your arms relaxed. These keys promote that long, loose swing you need for playing this shot well.

Control the downswing with your hands and arms, and make sure you release the club freely and finish high.

Wild Chip Shots

Chipping has such an innocent ring to it you probably think it just isn't possible to face a wild chip shot situation. Forget about it! You will not believe the trouble you can get into near a green, especially if you become one of those golfers who travels from course to course.

Let me show you how to play three chips, starting with one requiring you to play left-handed, which if you normally play right-handed, will be a mindblower. Next, I show you how to rebound a chip shot off a tree. Last, I show you how to hit a one-handed chip in a very unique way. In golf, as in life, when there are obstacles that block your way, you gotta do what you gotta do. Brighten up, things could be worse. German pro golfer Bernhard Langer once had to chip a ball that was lodged in a tree.

Employ a slightly longer and looser ("wristy") pitching swing when hitting a shot out of rough over trees.

The Left-Handed Chip

Your shot has landed to the right of a green, even with the hole. The ball is sitting cleanly in light rough, and you are only 20 yards from the hole. There are no hazards between you and the hole. You only have more light rough and manicured fringe grass between you and the green.

Normally, this would be a relatively easy shot. But what makes the situation so wild is that the ball is so close to a tree that there is just no way you can set up to the ball and play it right-handed as you normally do. In this situation, rather than take a drop and incur an unplayable lie penalty, hit the shot left-handed.

At address, reverse your hand positions on the grip end of a lofted club, and turn the club over so that its toe faces down and is in a position to contact the ball. Before you swing, take practice swings to gain a feel for the unorthodox action.

Swing the club back and through with your arms, employing as short and comfortable an action as is humanly possible. Practice this shot from time to time in your backyard or at the range. Sooner or later this situation will arise. When you pull it off in a match, it will impress or perhaps even shock your playing partners. It might even win you a bet.

Jim's Tips

When you play a left-handed shot with a right-handed club, the ball tends to fly left slightly off the angled clubface. So, allow for that when you aim.

The Rebound Chip

You probably realize that golf is a highly unpredictable game. That being said, you will be less shocked to hear that there will come a time when the ball is so close to a tree you can't make a normal right-handed backswing or an unorthodox left-handed backswing.

If you find yourself confronting this lie, you are to the side of a nearby unguarded green, and the tree trunk blocking you is wide enough, try playing a rebound shot. Don't be concerned about safety. First of all, this shot requires very little power. Because you are so close to the green, it won't require tremendous force. Second, to play it, face the tree, but set your entire body to the left of the tree's trunk. In other words, you are out of the direct line of fire. Third, aim to hit an area of the trunk, just above the tree's base. That way, the ball is not likely to ricochet off line. Rather, the ball will rebound relatively straight back off the tree, fly low, and scurry through the intervening grass between you and the hole, then onto the green toward the pin. Oh, how sweet this is when you successfully hit this shot. It's absolutely devastating to your opponents.

Play this shot with one of your wedges and choke down slightly for control. Take a narrow stance and place 70 percent of your weight on your left foot. Set your hands well ahead of the ball, which should be played closer to your right foot. Your exaggerated hands-ahead position will reduce the effective loft of the wedge, which is perfect for your desired shot-making goals.

Employ a slow, short backswing action. Swing down on quite a sharp angle so that the ball pops up a bit and hits the target you picked out on the tree's trunk.

When playing a rebound chip, swing down on a sharp angle to pop the ball into the tree.

The Right-Handed Pitch

Here's another wild shot to play, when your ball is next to the base of a tree and you are stymied. Imagine that your ball is sitting only 10 yards to the right side of a green. As in the previous situation, there are no hazards between the tree and the hole. Realistically, you could hit the green, if you could just get the ball rolling. But you see problems. First, the ball is so close to the tree that, even though you can face the hole, there is not enough room to swing the club back. As soon as you take the club away, it will hit the tree. Second, a left-hand only swing won't cut it. The ball is directly in front of the tree. Third, the tree is so thin that you would not even think about rebounding the ball off its trunk. What do you do? The answer: Play a right-handed shot—backwards!

Stand to the left side of the tree with your feet together, your back facing the target, and the ball played off your right foot. The club you should have in your right hand is a pitching wedge because of its loft and sharp leading edge. Grip down about three inches for maximum control. In completing your unorthodox address, extend your right arm fully and lean the handle of club a few inches toward the hole. This sharp angle will help you hit down sharply and pop the ball out.

Make a short, steep backswing and simply chop down on the ball.

Death Moves

When you face a situation in which you think you can realistically rebound the ball off a tree and onto a nearby green, don't go for too much distance. If you do, the risk is not worth the reward. You are better off deeming the ball unplayable and penalizing yourself one shot.

Wild Bunker Shots

In preparing you further for the wild, I must teach you how to recover from some crazy bunker lies. So, by the time you finish reading this section, you will have these important scoring shots in your shot-making arsenal.

Before I begin though, I have a surprise for you. As an added bonus I teach you how to hit a shot out of water by using a bunker-play technique. This seems like the wildest shot of all, but it is really not that difficult to play. But don't let your regular playing partners know that. When you blast the ball out of water, let them think your expert recovery was a stroke of genius.

Jim's Tips

When hitting the backwards right-handed chip, let your right wrist hinge so that you promote a steep backswing plane, a solid downward strike, and added club-head feel.

The Long Downhill Bunker Shot

The first thing you must do is set your shoulders parallel to the sandy slope. To reach the hole, you need to take a thinner cut of sand. So spread your feet a few inches wider than the width of your shoulders, because this stance encourages a steeper plane of swing. Play the ball just behind of the midpoint in your stance, and open the face of your sand wedge.

On the backswing, pick up the club quickly with your hands, and minimize the turning action of your hips. Exaggerating the coiling action of the body leads to a loss of balance and a mishit shot. Don't make this mistake.

It's important to drive your knees and lower body toward the target on the downswing. But the most important key of all is to swing down along the slope.

Death Moves

When setting up to play a long downhill bunker shot, don't ever play the ball forward of the midpoint in your stance. That position will almost always make you hit too far behind the ball. In short, you may never get out of the bunker, let alone hit the ball near the hole.

The Long Buried-Lie Bunker Shot

Approximately 30 yards from the green, your ball is half-buried in a high-lipped bunker, which is unguarded by a hazard. To recover, use a shot I learned from John Andrisani, former senior editor of instruction at *Golf Magazine*, who learned it from Seve Ballesteros, who learned it from Neil Coles, the renowned former European Tour player. Believe it or not, this shot is best played with a nine iron, because this club features fewer degrees of loft and a thinner flange than the sand wedge. You would have to be Hercules to reach the green by using a sand wedge and splashing the ball out.

In setting up, play the ball just to the right of the midpoint of your stance. Make a compact backswing. Swing the club down into a spot in the sand, a half-inch behind the ball. The ball will pop up, carry the lip, then run fast toward the hole.

Jim's Tips

Set your hands back to the centerline of your body for the downhill bunker shot, sometimes even farther back. This keeps the loft on your sand wedge and enables you to get the height that you need.

The Water Blast

There are courses that feature green-side water hazards that run right up to the edge of the bunker. To the right of the second green at the Lake Nona Golf Club in Orlando, Florida, there is such a dual hazard. When playing there, or on any other course that shares this feature, you could find your ball lying on the sand, but half-submerged in water. This situation can also occur in the shallow part of a creek or water hazard.

To recover, use a sand wedge and lay the clubface wide open. Align your body open to the target line, with the ball played opposite your left instep. This forward ball position further promotes a high, soft-landing shot.

Swing the club up on a very steep angle, allowing your wrists to hinge freely.

The closer you are to the pin, the farther behind the ball you should make contact with the water. Play it just like you would a bunker shot. To give you a general gauge, if you face a shot of around 15 yards, hit two inches behind the ball.

Death Moves

It is against the rules to ground your club in a hazard—let its sole touch the water. So, in playing a water blast shot, hold the club slightly above the water's surface, at least 2 inches behind the ball. The penalty for touching the water prior to swinging is severe—two strokes in medal play and loss of the hole in match play.

Open the face of a sand wedge in preparing to hit the water blast shot.

Wild Putts

By now, you realize that the putter is maybe the most important club in your bag. Well, you haven't seen anything yet. In this section, I show you how to use your putter when you are not on the green. You are going to learn how to play one wild shot from sand and one wild shot from rough, using the putter.

Jim's Tips

I've found that using extra wrist action is very helpful in playing the putter shot out of sand because it provides easy power.

Swing Lingo

A **pop** is a short shot played with a variety of clubs, including the putter. When you hit this shot, you make a very short wristy backswing, and then hit down sharply on the ball (or a spot just behind it), stopping at impact. You sort of give it a stab or pop with the club. The ball pops out of the lie. (I suppose this word has a double meaning.)

The Sand-Cheater Putt

To a novice golfer, putting from the sand sounds absurd. Trust me, when your ball is sitting reasonably close to the hole in a low-lipped, green-side bunker, the putt is the perfect play.

The rules prevent you from resting the club on the sand, so to be safe and to promote a purely rolled putt, line up the putter face with the equator of ball.

Use your normal long putting stroke, but contact the top half of the ball. The shot you hit will carry overspin, which is good because it will propel the ball through the sand and fringe grass and then to the hole.

The Putter Pop Shot

Here's a creative shot I learned from many years of teaching ladies clinics at the clubs I worked at in New York. It's called a putter *pop*. You use it when the ball is half-submerged in rough grass around the green and you've got plenty of green to work with.

Set up with the ball back. By back, I mean way back. Play this shot from behind your back foot. Use a narrow stance with your hands well ahead of the putter head, and 70 percent of your weight on your left foot. Grip well down on the shaft.

Employ a very short and upright backswing, making sure to hinge your right wrist. The putter head goes almost straight up.

Bring the club down into the top portion of the ball on an extremely sharp angle, and stop. The ball will pop up into the air, bounce a couple of times in the fringe, land on the green, and roll quite fast with overspin to the hole. I've found this to be the most effective shot for most amateurs to play. Once you get it, the shot is idiot proof. By that I mean that you get it on the green every time. With a wedge, the odds are that most amateurs will miss the green half the time.

These unorthodox hand and ball positions are necessary for playing a putter pop shot from Bermuda grass rough.

The Least You Need to Know

➤ When playing a cut shot with a pitching wedge, hold on to the club more firmly with your left hand, through impact.

➤ When playing a right-handed chip shot, hinge your right wrist to encourage a steep backswing and sharp downward hit.

➤ When the ball lies half-submerged in a water hazard by the green, pretend you are playing a bunker shot.

➤ When you use the putter to recover from Bermuda rough near the green, hit down on the ball.

The Power-Wedge Formula

> **In This Chapter**
>
> ➤ Understanding the power lie
>
> ➤ Thinking power
>
> ➤ Taking a different stance on the setup
>
> ➤ Knowing the value of restricting hip turn on the backswing
>
> ➤ Understanding the value of an extended through-swing

Hitting the ball powerfully is one of the most alluring factors among golfers. If you want proof of this, retire to the 19th hole (bar/restaurant) of your local course. This is the place where players congregate after a round with their playing partners, often to relive their round over a lemonade, coffee, cold beer, or club sandwich. The stories told in this somewhat sacred gathering place are always amusing because players tell each other about what they did or should have done on the course.

One thing you can always be certain about in any 19th hole is hearing anecdotes about powerful shots. One player will brag about hitting a drive and a wedge to a particular par four, while another will tell his tale about hitting a wedge to a par-three hole with an ocean breeze coming right into his face.

There is no doubt that hitting powerful shots makes the game more fun. And ever since big hitters John Daly and Tiger Woods arrived on the tour scene, its made this aspect of the game an obsession among golfers. I have no problem with power, provided it's understood that there is a time and place to use it.

In this chapter, I enlighten you on the subject of power, and tell you how to hit your wedge shots a little farther while still maintaining control. There are definitely advantages to being a strong wedge player, provided you can control your distances. As Tiger Woods discovered, there is no reason to hit wedges powerfully if the ball carries the green and lands in trouble. Let's get started with today's lesson.

Defining Power

Jim's Tips

Swinging at a slightly faster tempo is not the only link to powerful shots. The clubface must also meet the ball squarely at impact. Furthermore, in upping the pace of your swing, you must still rhythmically coordinate the movement of the body with that of the club.

Some golfers just want to hit the ball powerfully because it gives them a sense of satisfaction. It does good things for their ego. Frankly, I have no problem with this, provided that you understand that whenever you bring power into the shot-making equation, you run the risk of swinging too fast and throwing off the tempo, timing, and rhythm of your swing. When this happens, you are likely to lose your balance and not hit the shot you envisioned. Therefore, it is important to know precisely what power is so that you can generate it while swinging within yourself.

I want to make it clear that when discussing power in this chapter, I am talking about hitting powerfully controlled wedge shots from good lies on the fairway. I am not talking about trouble shots. I already discussed those in Chapter 5, "Common Trouble Shots," and taught you how a steeper swing and sharp descending hit work best when the rough grass grows toward you or when you need to extract the ball out of a fairly deep divot hole. But I'm getting ahead of myself. Defining power and pinpointing the specific elements involved in a powerful swing is so vitally important that I want to tackle this subject at a snail's pace.

Green-Light/Red-Light Situations

In understanding the art of using power to your benefit, it's critical that you understand when to go and when to fold. Your decision to do either should be directly related to the course situation, the lie of the ball, and your personality type.

Let's say that the lie is good, but the yardage to the hole and the wind direction make you question what club to hit—a smooth nine or a hard pitching wedge. Well, if you are an aggressive player, who feels more comfortable and gets better results hitting the ball hard rather than finessing the shot, this is a green-light situation. The pitching wedge is the best choice of club. Just remember that the harder you swing, the more spin you impart on the ball. Therefore, it is possible to fly your wedge shot all the way to the hole only to see it spin back 15 or 20 feet.

Let's take another example. Pretend that you are out on the fairway, assessing your approach shot into an extremely short par four, or your third shot on a par-five. You tell yourself that a normal swing with a sand wedge will not propel the ball all the way to the hole. What's more, you realize that a pitching wedge is too much club. This shot-making dilemma is called being in-between clubs, or a *tweener.* I don't have any trouble with you hitting a sand wedge a little harder here to ensure that you reach the hole. But before reaching for your club, look at the lie. You could be in a red light situation. If the fairway grass is longer and lush, rather than tight, the ball will automatically fly a little farther. That's because grass will intervene between the ball and the club-face at impact and cause the ball to fly at least 10 yards farther than normal. So a normal swing with a sand wedge will do the job. And if it's wet, you better think about gearing back to a lob wedge. When moisture enters the equation, the ball flies even farther. My point is don't be so quick to hit your sand wedge more powerfully. Sometimes, a normal swing works nicely.

Swing Lingo

The term used among golfers to describe a situation when a player is between clubs is **tweener.** For example, you face a tweener when you can't decide whether to hit a smooth pitching wedge or a hard sand wedge.

The Power Mind-Set

When you make up your mind that, for whatever reason, a powerful wedge shot is what you want to play, you must prepare yourself mentally.

In getting ready to play a long wedge shot, it's critical that you put yourself into what's commonly referred to as the zone: a cocoon of intense concentration. It doesn't really matter how you click on the switch so long as when you do, you immediately start focusing more intently on the ball and your target. It's also helpful to make practice swings that match perfectly the swing you intend to put on the ball.

Just before stepping into the ball, it's critical that you see yourself swinging rhythmically and hitting the ball along a specific path to a specific target. This preswing rehearsal also helps you maintain your focus and high level of confidence.

Death Moves

Don't simply make lazy practice swings that barely resemble the swing you intend to employ. The whole idea of making a serious practice swing is to rehearse the intended swinging action. That way, when it comes time to hit the real shot, you feel extremely confident and relaxed. This is especially true in your short game.

Swing Lingo

Takeaway refers to the movement away from the ball. As you draw the club head away from the ball, the initial move is called the takeaway. The **flat spot** is the area at the bottom of the swing arc. A strong weight shift increases the length of the flat spot. All long hitters have an extended flat spot in the hitting zone.

Jim's Tips

The type of stance you take for your power-wedge setup is a personal thing—a matter of what works best. My advice, however, is to stand with your feet and body parallel, or pretty much parallel, to the target line. This stance gives you the best chance of ensuring square contact, especially when you are swinging faster.

The Power-Wedge Setup

When you step into the ball, position it a touch farther forward than normal and take a stance that's wider by a couple of inches. Moving the ball up further in your stance promotes a wider *takeaway* and allows the club to move low to the ground through impact for a longer period of time. You need this longer *flat spot* in your swing to hit the ball more powerfully. If you play the ball back in your stance, as you do when hitting out of a divot hole, the swing you make has more of an up and down look to it than a down and through look. The wider stance gives you a stronger foundation and enables you to retain good balance while swinging more powerfully. Balancing your weight evenly on the ball of each foot also ensures good balance during the power-wedge swing.

Set your hands slightly ahead of the ball because this prevents a quick pick-up action of the club in the takeaway, a steep swing, and a sharp angle of descent. Remember, you want your downswing to be more streamlined, so that the club travels lower to the ground coming into impact. It's this action that produces a shot that flies slightly lower than normal and travels farther.

In gripping the club, hold the club a little more lightly than normally, as this allows you to generate faster club-head speed.

Something else you can experiment with is dropping your hands down a tad lower and standing only an inch or two farther away from the ball. Both these keys essentially flatten the natural lie of the club and allow you to swing on a slightly flatter plane. In setting up to hit a powerful wedge shot, you should do everything possible to guard against swinging on too steep a plane. However, you don't want to encourage an overly flat plane either. So, hit balls in practice to see what address yields the best results.

Take a slightly wider stance than normal when setting up to hit a power-wedge shot.

The Power-Wedge Backswing

When looking to generate more power on the backswing, it's advantageous to swing the club on a wider arc. You create a wider arc by taking the club back relatively low to the ground in the takeaway and feeling your weight shift to the inside of your right foot and leg. Incidentally, never let your weight shift to the outside of your right foot, otherwise you run into balance and shot-making problems. When power is your goal, you must delay the full hinging action of the wrists by letting the swinging weight of the club head take care of this naturally.

Swinging your hands well past your body, with the left arm extended fully and the right arm bent only slightly, is vital to creating a wide and powerful swing arc.

Another critical link to power is the nature of the turn. Many golfers are wrongly under the impression that the more you turn your shoulders and hips, the more powerful the shot. I proved this wrong in 1993 when conducting a study of PGA Tour professionals with golf teacher Mike McTeigue. Using a special device called a SportSense Swing Motion Trainer, we discovered that the most powerful hitters had a bigger differential or gap between their powerful shoulder turn and restricted hip turn. Yes, restricted hip turn. To widen the gap, I recommend that most golfers minimize the action of the lower body on the backswing. If you happen to be one of those golfers who has the flexibility to make a strong coiling action of the shoulders, make certain to restrict your hip turn. Two ways to restrict hip turn are setting the right foot perpendicular to the target line at address and keeping the right knee flexed during the backswing.

When swinging the club back to the top, one more thing is important. You never want to swing the club back so far that the wrists collapse or over hinge because this fault causes power to leak out of the swing. Put yourself in the best position by making a strong compact action.

Death Moves

When hitting the power-wedge shot, don't consciously hinge the wrists or let them hinge automatically by keeping your right elbow tight to your body. If you do, you narrow the swing arc and promote a steep downswing action.

Bet You Didn't Know

Tiger Woods is one of the most powerful wedge players in the game, yet he employs a compact backswing. He used to swing the club back to parallel—club shaft parallel to the ground—but he's learned that he can generate as much, or more, power using a shorter swing. Moreover, the shorter swing has enhanced his control.

The Power-Wedge Downswing

One key to employing a powerful yet controlled downswing is to make a solid shift-and-rotate action of the lower body. As Ben Hogan proved, the more fluidly you shift your hips laterally before rotating your left hip in a counterclockwise direction, the faster the arms and hands move, the faster the club comes into impact, and the farther you hit the ball. However, you never want to make such a fast shift that the left hip spins out to the left of target, or else you cause your right shoulder to jut outward. When this happens to a player, he or she tends to swing the club across the ball. You want the club to swing down the target line at impact, with its face precisely perpendicular to the ball and target. So, what you should be thinking about is making a power-generating, fluid, shift-and-rotate action. Yes, fluid is the correct buzzword for you and every other golfer who is trying to hit the ball powerfully.

Shifting the hips toward the target at the start of the downswing will help you generate added arm-hand-club speed.

As the lower body leads and weight shifts to your left foot, it's equally critical that you maintain your width of swing by letting your arms drop down naturally and your wrists unhinge all by themselves. Consciously concentrating on flailing the arms and bringing the club faster into the ball by snapping the wrists are disastrous. Let the shift-and-rotate action of the hips and the powerful unwinding action of big muscles in your shoulders gets the job done for you.

As to recreating the flat spot through impact, and swinging into the proper finish, here's how you make those things happen. Imagine that there is another ball a couple of inches in front of the one you will actually hit. If you strive to hit the imaginary ball, you swing low and powerfully through the ball and arrive in a good finish position before you know it.

Developing a powerful swing takes practice. I'm saying that to prepare you for the next chapter, which teaches you drills designed to help you physically ingrain the correct power-swing movements into your technique.

Jim's Tips

Late in the evening, test your maximum wedge distance on the golf course. I suggest you hit five balls with each of your wedges and carefully pace off how far they go. Furthermore, it's a good idea to hit each club in two opposite directions. Also test uphill and downhill situations. You can tape the results on the shaft of each wedge until you are certain of each club's potential.

Bet You Didn't Know

During the early and mid 1970s, when Lee Trevino was winning major championships, he played powerful pitching wedge shots better than anyone else. The chief reason was that he had a long flat spot in his swing.

The Least You Need to Know

➤ Square contact with the ball, not just fast club-head speed, is necessary for hitting powerfully accurate wedge shots.

➤ Certain lies enable you to hit the ball farther by using your normal pitching-wedge swing.

➤ Concentrating intently on the ball and target help you produce more powerful wedge shots.

➤ When playing a power-wedge shot, create a wider arc of swing by delaying the hinging action of your wrists.

➤ Don't underestimate the power of the shift-and-rotate action.

Chapter 8

Power-Swing Drills

In This Chapter

➤ Creating a wider swing arc

➤ The importance of fluid lower-body action on the downswing

➤ Employing a balanced swing

➤ Ways to ensure a well-timed swing

After reading the last chapter, and following each step for building a power-wedge game technique, you should have a basic understanding of the mechanics involved. What's left now is to learn the individual elements of the backswing and downswing by rehearsing them over and over individually until you can then blend them together into one fluid, uninterrupted motion. The best way to reach this ambitious but realistic goal is to work on drills.

The drills I give you involve the backswing and downswing only. I'm staying away from the address because I think the best way to practice it is in front of a mirror so that you can see what you are doing wrong, if anything, and then make the necessary adjustments. Another good idea is to have a professional check your body and club-face alignments—ball and hand positions.

You should not proceed with the following backswing and downswing drills until you have your wedge setup down. So, you may want to practice it over and over and then check it for accuracy and confirm that it is technically correct.

Because I want your technique to be rhythmic, I also provide you with some helpful drills for promoting good balance and timing during the swing.

Backswing Drills

The entire backswing motion takes less than a second from the time you start the club back to the time you reach the top. The following drills are designed to help you ingrain the proper motions into what is referred to as muscle memory. All this means is that, through drill work, the golf muscles in your body, namely those in the hips, shoulders, and arms, learn their proper "job description" in the swing.

Death Moves

When working on the take-two drill, don't try to consciously pull the club back with your hands in an extra low motion. Instead, swing the club away with the hands, arms, and shoulders. The second ball will simply get in the way of the club head as you employ a smooth takeaway action. It is critical to get the club up and in balance on the backswing. It must not go low and around the body.

The Take-Two Drill

One of the best ways I know to learn a better take-away action is to practice brushing over a ball placed along the target line six inches behind the one you are addressing.

In swinging back, concentrate on directing the movement of the pitching wedge just over the second ball with the big muscles in your arms and shoulders.

The Catch-It Drill

To get used to the feeling of swinging a pitching wedge with good extension in the arms, have a friend squat directly behind your line of flight, about six feet behind the ball, with his or her hand extended. Next, make your takeaway action while trying to put the club head into his or her hand. This is a great way to feel the arm-club extension and get the wrists set properly early on in the swing. Remember, if the wrists overhinge, the arc narrows, ultimately causing you to lose power.

The Rope Drill

Mike Dunaway, the Arkansas-based power hitter who John Daly admits is longer than he is, invented a drill that I think will work wonders for you. It will teach you to feel the vital pivot and turning motions of the backswing so that you are more apt to repeat them easily when playing a power-wedge shot on the fairway. For this drill, you need two props that can be purchased at your local hardware store: a 6-foot piece of rope and a large eyebolt with a hole big enough to slip the rope through, leaving some room for it to move freely.

Place the eyebolt in the grass on your local practice tee or in your backyard. Next, thread the rope through it.

Hold an end of the rope in each hand. Take your swing address, making believe the eyebolt is the ball. Next, pull gently on the rope using your right arm. Immediately, you will sense how the body should rotate, particularly the hips.

The Dowel Drill

This drill encourages a full shoulder turn. Place a long wooden dowel on the ground, extending it straight back from the front of the ball toward the area between your feet. Address the ball as you would to hit a power-wedge shot. Make your backswing, trying to turn your left shoulder past the dowel. Keep practicing this drill until you feel your left shoulder turn nicely under your chin and behind the ball.

Wall Drill

To check that you are swinging correctly, stand next to a wall so that the heels of your shoes are about two feet from it. Next, swing back. If the club hits the wall, you know that you are probably overusing your hands, instead of letting the club be directed back and up more with your arms and shoulders. The swinging weight of the club head should hinge your right wrist automatically once you reach the halfway point in the backswing. If you don't feel this happening, consciously hinge the right wrist at that point of your swing, and continue doing so until you get used to swinging the pitching wedge on the proper plane. You should not hit the wall.

Jim's Tips

When practicing the rope drill, freeze the backswing position for a few seconds so that you can ingrain the feeling of coiling the hips clockwise. If you feel that the hips are turning too much, repeat the drill, placing your right foot perpendicular to the target line. This address key stops you from overturning.

Swing Lingo

If you hear a golfer use the term **flat swing,** it simply means that the club is being directed well inside the target line, often behind the body, on a flat or rounded angle or plane.

Downswing Drills

On average, it takes a player approximately one-fifth of a second to swing the club from the top of the backswing into the ball. The downward motion is over in a snap and virtually operates on automatic pilot. Although this is true, you still should learn the vital positions that, together, make up the downswing movement. That way, when you are out on the course, the positions flow together smoothly. Once you set the downswing in motion by using a shifting and rotating action of the hips and lower body, the other movements of the swing fall into place, much as touching a single domino causes the others in a row to fall.

Working on drills enables you to learn each movement of the downswing so that the movement of the body coordinates in sync with the movement of the club.

The Shaft Drill

Here's a drill I learned from Ken Venturi, designed to help you learn to rotate your left hip at the start of the downswing. It's this rotation that clears the way for the club to be swung freely into the ball. You don't need a ball for this drill, but you do need an old club shaft.

Stick a club shaft in the ground. Make sure that the shaft in the ground is straight up from the outside of your left foot, and then take your wedge address position. Next, make your power-wedge backswing. Start down, concentrating on the shift-and-rotate action of the hips. The idea is to make a slight lateral shift, then rotate or clear your left hip out of the way so that it doesn't contact the shaft.

If it does hit the shaft, you know you have committed a major downswing fault: You have not closed the gap. Instead, you have spun out. If you knock the shaft over, you've slid too much.

Bet You Didn't Know

In 1992, I worked with Tom Kite, who was fighting his tendency to slide his hips laterally on the downswing. Tom's tendency was to get his lower body so far out ahead of the swinging club that, at impact, he left the face of the club open. The result was a weak short-iron shot. I helped Tom ingrain the shift-and-rotate action of the left hip. By moving the ball back in his stance and turning better through impact, Tom regained his laser-like accuracy and much more distance. I'm happy to say that he went on to win the '92 U.S. Open.

The Split-Grip Drill

To learn what it feels like to release the club properly on the downswing and to release the club freely through impact with your hands and arms, hit pitching wedge shots with your hands spread about six inches apart.

Hitting pitch shots with your hands spread apart teaches you how to release the club freely.

Swing the club back and through and I guarantee that you'll immediately feel better body action and your right hand turning over your left. Now grip normally, and hit some pitching wedge shots. You will notice straightaway how much farther you hit the ball.

The Downhill Drill

To learn the feeling of swinging down and through the ball, practice hitting pitching wedge shots off downhill lies. After hitting about 20 shots, hit power-pitch shots off a flat lie. You should notice that your divots are long and shallow and that your shots are flying farther than normal.

To learn how to swing through the ball with the left wrist flat, practice hitting shots off downhill lies.

The Hinge-Retention Drill

Take your full-wedge setup while pretending you have a club in your hand. Swing to the top. Pause. Swing down, concentrating on bringing your right elbow into your right side and in front of your right hip as soon as your left hip clears in a counter-clockwise direction. Feel how this synchronized left hip and right elbow movement helps the right wrist to stay hinged. To generate power, you must retain this right-wrist position late into the forward swing.

Good-Balance Drills

All the top players on the World Ranking List—Tiger Woods, David Duval, Davis Love, Ernie Els, Colin Montgomerie, Mark O'Meara, Sergio Garcia—exhibit superb balance during the swing.

Woods and Garcia are the classic examples of players who do not hold back, not just when hitting a tee shot. No matter how much they go after the ball, they stay balanced and square the clubface to the target practically every time.

One-Legged Drills

Standing on your right leg only, use your left leg as a prop. Set your left leg back off the target line. Swing back to the top and stop. Do this drill 10 times to make sure you get the feeling of pivoting around your right leg on the backswing. Your weight should be directly on top of the right leg and never to the outside of the right foot.

From the top of the backswing position, balanced on the foot, stop and hold the position. Now bring your left leg back to its proper location. Swing down from the top. Feel your weight smoothly shift onto a solid left leg. Repeat this drill 10 times to make sure you get the feeling of pivoting on your left leg through the impact zone.

Death Moves

When working on the hinge-retention drill, don't ever let your right arm extend away from your body. If you do, you un-hinge your right wrist prematurely and lose power as a result.

Jim's Tips

The pivoting actions you learn via one-legged drills help you maintain balance during the swing. Good balance is a significant link to hitting powerful shots. Practice your balance as often as possible. You cannot overdo this aspect of golf.

Timing Drills

The tempo (speed) of your swing is often related to your personality. Take Sergio Garcia. He is a very energetic young man on the course. Even when he's not playing, he exemplifies the typical A-type personality. It's no wonder his tempo is fast. The opposite is true about PGA Tour player Bruce Lietzke. Bruce is laid back, which may explain why he swings a lot slower than Garcia.

Whether you swing like Garcia or Lietzke doesn't really matter. What does matter is that you time the swing correctly, because good timing is what allows you to synchronize club and body movement and to swing rhythmically.

What follows are two excellent drills that help you develop good timing.

Pump Drill

You do not need a ball for this drill.

Swing back to the top (following the instructions in the previous chapter regarding the power-wedge backswing) and down to the halfway point of the downswing. Pause. At this point in the swing, your weight distribution should be equal—50 percent of your weight on your left foot and 50 percent of your weight on your right. Your knees have pretty much returned to a position parallel to the target line. Your left arm is practically parallel to the target line and your right elbow is close to your side, under the left elbow. Hold this position for several seconds. Practice this pump and pause action repeatedly.

Next, make a fluid shift-and-rotate action of the lower body. If you are timing the movements of the downswing correctly, you will feel the speed of the club head being generated by body motion, not the hands.

Bet You Didn't Know

One of my students, Len Mattice, improved his wedge play and sense of timing by doing the stop-pause-rotate drill. This is one reason he is making more birdies on par-five holes. He hits wedge shots close to the hole. The other reason is that Len is one of the best putters on the PGA Tour.

The Inhale-Exhale Drill

Take your normal power-wedge setup position. Swing back, inhaling slowly and quietly at first and faster as the club approaches the top. Swing down, exhaling harder and harder as you bring the club into the ball at a faster speed.

This drill teaches you to how to build speed gradually and time the backswing and downswing actions.

The Least You Need to Know

➤ The catch-it drill helps you make a solid takeaway.

➤ The shaft drill encourages you to clear you left hip.

➤ The left- and right-leg drills teach you how to pivot correctly and to make a balanced power-wedge swing.

➤ The swing-pause-rotate drill teaches you how to make a well-timed power-wedge swing.

Part 3

Taking Your Short Game to the Next Level

Now it is time to rise to the occasion and start taking responsibility for your own short game. I want you to learn how to do such things as fix faults, which are bound to sneak into your swing from time to time. Also, I want you to manage your game on a full-length, 18-hole course, check your health and fitness levels, and study the pros playing short-game shots during a televised golf tournament. I will give you guidance in all these areas.

To further help you take your short game to the next level, and more clearly understand the instructional message, I sort out any myths about technique that may have been hindering your progress in the areas of pitching, chipping, bunker play, and putting. Additionally, I teach you how to control distance, which is of course a vital part of playing well on and around the green.

Fixing Faults

Often, at the end of a day of golf, the player who makes the fewest mistakes is the winner. Still, even the winner of a competition usually makes some mistakes during a round, because golf is a game that can never be perfected. The more you play golf, the quicker you understand this truism. Sure, you will have great days and shoot a super score over 18 holes. But one thing is certain: Upon reviewing a superb round you will discover that there were at least a couple of shots that were not hit correctly. And they cost you.

Short-game faults are the most frustrating because, as I said before, they are the scoring shots. Playing short-game shots well, if not expertly, is what enables you to save bad ball-striking rounds with the long clubs. Furthermore, a sound short game enables you to break your own personal scoring record on a day when your driving, fairway wood play, and long and medium iron shot-making skills are on the mark.

Another feature of this game that makes it fun is correcting your faults so that they are less likely to happen as often. The typical tour pro works hard to pinpoint swing faults and correct a problem, usually after the round in his or her post-round practice session. This lesson deals with the most common short-game errors made by golfers and how to fix them.

The Shank

This is a shot that flies off the *hosel* at practically a 90-degree angle. The shank (or *socket*) is most commonly hit with the wedge. Golfers who have hit the shank in the past freak out just hearing the word. They don't care what they've heard about the shank being the next closest thing to a perfect shot. All they remember is how ugly and scary the shot looked. What's more, if they hit shanks in practice, they remember themselves hitting one after the other. Yes, shanks are known to come in bunches. When you get a case of the shanks, you should break the chain by returning home, playing a game of cards, having a cup of coffee in the clubhouse, or taking a short drive with your favorite radio station on before returning to the practice tee to fix your problem.

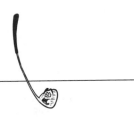

Swing Lingo

Another word used to describe the shank, usually used by European players, is **socket.** That's because they refer to the **hosel,** the neck of the club head, as the socket. Hence the phrase "socket job" refers to a shank.

The worst thing is for you to hit a shank on the course, which I have done more than once during a round of golf. Top pros have too, if that makes you feel better. Let me warn you that when you step up to the next shot, you will not be able to forget about what just happened, and you will probably hit another shank unless you know why this shot occurred and you fix the problem immediately.

The Cause and the Cure

There are many theories on what causes the shank and how to cure it. However, the major cause is swinging the club on the wrong path. The player who hits a shank usually swings the club back on an exaggerated inside path, and then on the downswing, the club swings out over the swing plane with the club's hosel leading a very open clubface. The reason the club starts back inside is that many golfers use their hands to trigger the swinging action, either consciously or subconsciously. This opens the clubface and puts the shaft in a layoff position.

To cure a faulty backswing path, you first must get the club shaft more vertical and up more as you take the club back. This more balanced position of the shaft is crucial to curing the shank. You must trust this technical fact, so to prove I'm right, try the following little experiment.

Face a wall in your home, setting the toe end of your pitching wedge flush to the baseboard molding. Next, rotate your forearms and shoulders in a clockwise direction, all the time looking down at the club head. See how it moves away from the wall along a path closer to you, or on the inside. The turning action of the forearms and shoulders directs the club both open and inside the target line. This puts you in a death position for golf.

Instead of this faulty move, bring the club up so that it's more vertical and not nearly so much inside. The more up and down the club travels, the better. Remember that the more inside the club goes on the backswing, the more it will tend to go inside on the downswing.

The Two-Ball Drill

Almost every top teaching pro I know recommends the two-ball drill to students suffering from a shank problem. It is great way to get the club head swinging more down the line through impact, instead of moving dramatically on an inside-out path. Place a second ball about two or three inches outside the ball you are addressing. Seeing that second ball there will discourage you from swinging out and across your object ball and, instead, virtually force you to swing down the line. Keep inching the outside ball closer to the ball you will hit, until one side of the outer ball is just about even with the toe-end of the club head and until you feel comfortable that you've grooved the proper path. When you first try this drill you will probably be shocked if you hit both balls. However, it dramatically demonstrates the problem and, of course, the cure.

The "Chili Dip"

Next to the shank, one of the most embarrassing and frustrating faults is to hit the ground before striking the ball. This is a fat or heavy chip, commonly referred to as a "chili dip." You may have heard this referred to as chunking, laying the sod over it, or sticking your pick. Three common causes of the chili dip are swaying, dipping, or starting the club head first from the top (or decelerating on the forward swing).

Jim's Tips

Feel free, on chip shots, to hinge your right wrist slightly on the backswing. This action can help you feel the club head. In turn, this feel helps you hit a better shot. Also, I advocate a little more wrist hinge when the lie is bad because you need to swing the club upward slightly to promote a descending hit.

Pushing the club away with your left hand, arm, and shoulder, as I do here, will allow you to keep the club low to the ground at the start of the swing and make a more streamlined downswing action.

The Skull

The third fault type—out of a quartet of ugly shots—is called a *skull*. The player hits the top half of the ball with the leading edge of the club, known to golfers as the belly. Golfers who hit this shot are usually terrified. Instead of hitting down on the ball, they try to lift it. This can happen anywhere on the golf course—the fairway, the bunker, or near the green.

The causes of the skull shot are stroking too flat on the backswing, swaying, staying back too long on your back foot, lifting up through impact, or bending your elbows in the impact zone.

To remedy the skull, trust the sand wedge to enter the sand and lift the ball into the air. If you swing down correctly, according to the basics laid down in Chapter 3, "Building Blocks," and trust the club to work for you, you will be cured of your problem. Don't worry, the sand wedge's flange, through its bounce effect, allows the club to slide through the sand just beneath the ball and lift it into the air.

Swing Lingo

The word used by golfers to describe hitting the top of the ball with bottom of the club, such that it flies low and un-controllably forward, is **skull.**

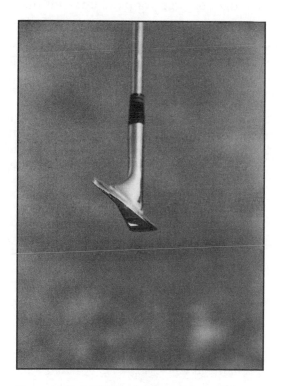

Trust the sand wedge's bounce (left) to help you dig out an area of sand (right), and you are unlikely to hit a skull.

121

Just in case you need some recoaching on the proper requirements for hitting a standard bunker shot, remember to concentrate on entering a general area of sand a few inches behind the ball with the bottom of the club. You must also release the club fully with your right arm so that it passes underneath the ball before exiting on the other side.

It would also help to practice the footprint drill and the tee-time drill presented in Chapter 3.

If you need further help, draw a line in the sand about four to six inches behind the ball and swing down through being sure not to hit the ball.

The Mishit Putt

When watching novices putt, I see them hit the top half of the ball, hit behind the ball and scuff the grass, push the ball to the right of target, or pull putts—hit them left of the target line.

The majority of novice and high-handicap golfers pull putts because they do not keep their left wrist firm in the impact area with the back of the left hand staying square to the putter face. Instead, the left wrist collapses or breaks down, causing the right hand to take control and pull the putter head across the target line.

If you have a tendency to pull putts, try weakening your grip by having the V formed by each thumb and forefinger of your hands pointing pretty much up at your chin. Although the putting grip is a very personalized element of the setup, you can take comfort in knowing that some of the best putters in the game depend on this type of hold.

Bet You Didn't Know

Jack Nicklaus uses a very weak left-hand grip because he feels that this prevents any tendency to rotate the putter head left of target in the forward swing, thereby hitting a pull. He also points both thumbs straight down the shaft in order to feel more security in the hands and wrists. Nicklaus uses a very brisk and solid right arm stroke. His right forearm works like a piston.

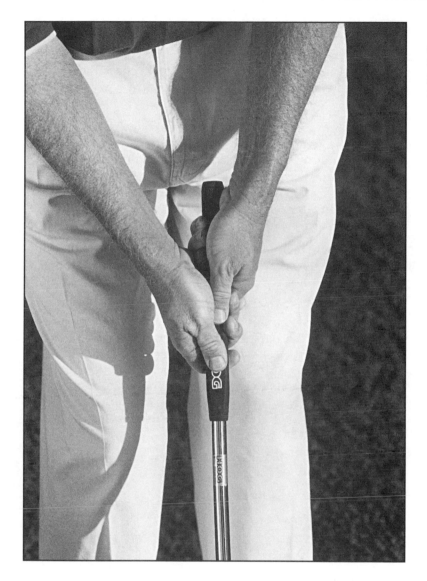

Weakening your left-hand grip, Jack Nicklaus style, can help prevent you from pulling putts left of target.

Jack Nicklaus, like most pro golfers, wants the hands and wrists to stay very quiet during the stroke. The end of the grip should not travel a great distance. To keep the left wrist stable, arch your left wrist up slightly so that there is no indentation between the left forearm and the back of the left hand. This locks the left wrist.

To further ingrain a firm left-wrist position into your existing putting technique—one that will allow you to stroke the putter through to the hole and sink more putts—work on this drill. Use rubber bands to fasten a 6-inch long plastic ruler to the back of your left wrist and hand. Putting while wearing this homemade teaching device discourages you from breaking down your wrist. If you lose the arch in the wrist, the ruler bends.

The Pro Attitude

Before we move on to the next chapter, I want you to realize that you have to keep up with your game the way you care for your car. Just as you must check the oil, break and transmission fluid, and water and gas levels, you must check your setup and swing mechanics.

When finding a fault and working to fix it, the car analogy breaks down. Sometimes, in trying to fix a fault, you actually get worse before you get better. Nobody knows this truism about the game better than the pros. They also experience slump periods, and after going to their personal pros for a private lesson, they sometimes take a couple of weeks to start playing better than they did before. Realize this the next time you start experiencing problems with your pitching, chipping, bunker play, or putting game and start seeking out help. That way, you'll remain patient while persevering.

The tips I have given you should put you on track fairly quickly so that you stop hitting the ugly shots. But, just in case they don't, understand that anytime you implement a change into your existing technique, other parts of your swing change too. It takes time for things to come together.

How fast you improve depends on the work you devote to golf. Obviously, by buying this book you showed the desire to learn to develop a sharp short game or to improve your existing one. So, you made the first step. Maintain that same hunger to improve and, more important, find time to devote at least one solid hour a week to working on the basic shot-making movements and drills I have taught you so far. It's far better to tackle the short game one step at a time than to try to play catch up. Setting high goals for yourself and doing everything that is realistically possible to hit better shots is the pro attitude I want you to adopt.

Bet You Didn't Know

Seve Ballesteros, who many think is still the greatest short game player alive, used to practice from sunup to sunset near his home in Pedrena, Spain. He literally practiced pitches, chips, bunker shots, and putts until the cows came home near his family's farm. Seve also practiced with a only a 3 iron, just to learn the ins and outs of working the club head different ways to hit different shots.

The Least You Need to Know

➤ The inch-closer drill helps you cure a shank.

➤ You'll hit better chip shots if you avoid exaggerated wrist action.

➤ Trust the sand wedge to do the work in sand, and you'll cure a skull problem.

➤ To stop pulling putts, keep your left wrist firm throughout the stroke.

➤ How fast you improve at golf is directly related to how much you practice.

Chapter 10

Management Skills

> ### In This Chapter
>
> ➤ The art of planning out short-game shots
>
> ➤ Having the patience to wait for a golden scoring opportunity
>
> ➤ The value of playing confidently
>
> ➤ Persevering on the golf course
>
> ➤ Playing your own game

Surely in your lifetime, after meeting someone in a high management job, you wondered how he or she ever got to that level. It doesn't matter one bit whether a company man or woman is an Ivy League graduate or not, if the person can't manage people, he or she will not be successful as a manager. You suffer, the company suffers, and all is lost. All the credentials in the world cannot save someone who fails to understand the art of dealing with aggressive and passive employees, in-house personality conflicts, strengths and weaknesses of workers, and much more.

Well, a parallel can be drawn with golf. You can have the best looking swing in the world, but if you don't know how to manage your game by planning shots, playing with patience and confidence, persevering when things are not going your way, and playing your own game, you will never make it as a golfer.

Proper Planning

At a young age, I was told that proper planning prevents poor performance. That advice not only helped me get to where I am in life, but it has helped me play better golf.

There have been many talented power hitters throughout history who never made it because they failed to plan out shots sensibly, particularly pitch shots, chip shots, bunker shots, and putts. The short shots you hit to the green, from around the green, and on the green are tremendously important because this is where the art of scoring comes in. On a par-three hole, you can hit the ball in a buried lie in the bunker and save par by virtue of a great bunker shot and putt. You can hit a bad drive into deep rough on a par-four hole and still save par by pitching out sideways, hitting your next shot on the green, and sinking a putt. You can hit three lousy shots on a par-five hole, face a tough pitch on your fourth shot, and get the ball *up and in* for par. Heck, you might even hole it for a birdie. Few things in golf can positively affect your attitude and your golf score more than a spectacular save or an unexpected hole out. It is also devastating to your opponents.

The art of hitting short-game shots close to the hole is not related to sound technical skills only. A good pitching swing does you little good if you have not allowed for such things as a headwind or a flyer lie. You cannot hit chips close to the hole on sloping greens if you don't allow for such variables as the speed and break in the green. The best bunker swing in the world does not save you when hitting a ball out of a partially plugged lie if you do not know that you must swing easier to allow for the ball coming out hot. And you do not sink breaking putts if you do not take the time to read a green. You must be an expert green reader to be a great putter. (You can take that last line to the bank.)

During a round of golf, you run into various short game situations, all requiring you to plan ahead. The best players in the world never hit a short-game shot before they have considered all the factors that come into play. Like students who take good notes, they know practically every nook and cranny of the course. In fact, all but a few professionals on the PGA, LPGA, and Senior PGA Tournament Series carry notepads with diagrams of each hole and reminder notes about each one.

It's a good idea for you to know your own course like the back of your hand. Therefore, carry a miniature notepad with you on the course. In it, you should write notes reminding yourself, for example, that the first green slopes from left to right more than is noticeable; the bunker by the eighth green is filled with soupy-type sand; the fringe on the right front of the 15th green has sparse grass; and the 18th green is the

Swing Lingo

Up and in is an expression that is used to describe the art of hitting a chip or bunker shot up onto the green and then putting the ball into the hole.

fastest on the course. Reminder notes help you manage your game like a pro. You give yourself the best chance to avoid a hazardous area or to recover when you do find your ball in a tricky lie.

Proper planning means taking the time to analyze the break in a green.

When playing a course that you have not seen before, don't be afraid to ask the head professionals questions about important factors such as the speed of the greens, prevailing wind directions, and the texture of the sand. Ben Hogan used to do this, knowing that the local professional would definitely add a good insight or two that he might miss.

As good a course planner as Hogan was, some experts believe that no golfer was a better strategist than Jack Nicklaus during his winning years on tour. Nicklaus never hit any short-game shot before he had assessed every blade of grass and grain of sand. The one personality trait that made him better than everybody else may have been his attention to detail.

Bet You Didn't Know

Deane Beman, a British Amateur champion, two-time winner of the United States Amateur, and former PGA Tour winner, is recognized as the first golfer to keep a notepad in his back pocket. Beman, who went on to become the commissioner of the PGA Tour, was always a short hitter. Yet, he still turned in winning scores thanks to proper planning and a supershort game.

Beman had a particularly strong short game and was a fantastic putter. As a result he could take a very conservative long-game approach and still shoot very low scores.

Patience

This is the other quality that sets the low-handicap golfer apart from the high-handicap player. Very often, the high handicapper allows his or her ego to run the show on the course. Because of this head problem, many players hit practically every pitch shot along an attacking line and try to sink chips and putts no matter what the circumstances. In the process, they end up wasting valuable strokes instead of saving them through sensible planning.

Conversely, the low-handicap player knows when to be conservative and when to be aggressive. He or she does this by assessing all factors including, first of all, the lie of the ball. Essentially, he or she knows how the ball is going to react in the air and on the ground, no matter what short game shot he or she is playing. More important, the low-handicap player has the patience to wait for opportunities where the odds are highly in their favor.

For example, in a stroke-play tournament, you rarely see a low-handicap player try to blast a ball that's buried under the lip toward the hole. In this situation, I have even seen good players hit the shot backward, after accepting the fact that the best score they will make on the hole is bogie. In the same situation, the typical high-handicap player often keeps blasting away, watching the ball continue to hit the wall of the bunker and roll back toward its original position. A better player can accept a bogie and will usually be sure, in all situations, to avoid the higher numbers.

By the same token, the typical low-handicap player knows to attack the hole when putting only when the conditions favor them. The moral of the story: You have to know when to pick your spots. Just because you are down in a match or behind by a few strokes in a medal play event, don't ever throw caution to the wind. Have the patience to examine all shot-making variables and play the percentages. Remember that your opponent is not exempt from hitting a poor shot or making a mental mistake. Anything can and will eventually happen in golf.

When facing a lie such as this, a patient player will often hit the ball away from the hole to set him- or herself up to score bogie, rather than risk wasting valuable strokes.

Players who proceed with a high degree of golf competence are players who also choose the right club and play the high percentage shot. The longer you play golf, the more you realize that playing golf is a lot like playing chess. It is a strategic game, and the object is to out-think the course. In your early days playing golf, you should take inventory of your strengths and weaknesses and then manage your game accordingly. Later on, as you develop more shots along the way, you can start taking more chances. By developing a strong short game early on, you set yourself up to be a formidable opponent for anyone.

Playing Confidently

To me, confidence means trust. When this trust factor is applied to golf, it simply means thinking that you will hit a good pitch, chip, bunker shot, or putt, often

131

Swing Lingo

In a **medal play** (or stoke play) event, the player with the lowest score wins. **Match play** is a competition by holes. For example, player A wins hole number one against player B by scoring a par four to player B's score of five. Players A and B tie the remaining holes. Therefore, player A wins the match one up.

Death Moves

When practicing your short game, don't just throw some balls down around the chipping green or on the putting surface, and then walk up to them quickly and hit them. Think about each chip shot, assessing chiefly the lie, the slope and speed of the green, and the distance to the hole. On putts, be sure to go carefully through your regular routine. Be sure your practice is producing results. If not, reassess your approach and your technique. Poor practice can be worse than no practice at all.

results in exactly what you pictured, provided your confidence is based on a sound short-game ability developed through purposeful practice.

Purposeful practice does not simply mean going through the motions when hitting shots. It means practicing the basic movements involved in hitting short-game shots over and over until they become second nature. It also means using a variety of clubs to hit shots out of a variety of lies and noting each time how the ball reacts with regard to airtime and ground time. This kind of experimental practice is valuable because it teaches you how to hit new shots by working your body and club in different ways. Confidence comes from success. Success in the short game comes from good mechanics. Good mechanics come from proper practice.

The more diligently and sensibly you practice, the stronger your level of confidence will become. Moreover, when you feel confident, you experience less pressure standing over the ball and ultimately hit a better shot. Another reason you hit a better shot is because confidence helps you relax. The less tension in your golf muscles, the better feel you have for the club head. It also follows that the more feel you have in your hands, the better your chances of hitting the ball to your target.

Perseverance

When I think of persistent players who possess the will to win, one name stands out: Gary Player, the South African Senior PGA Tour player who throughout his career has never given up. Take the 1978 Masters. Going into the fourth and final round, Player was seven strokes behind fellow tour pro Hubert Green. Nevertheless, to the shock of the spectators and other pros competing in this coveted championship, Player fought back to win. Player scored seven birdies in the last 10 holes on his way to a score of 64 and a four-day total of 277. During the final 18 holes, Player hit superb pitches and bunker shots, and sunk chips and putts from everywhere. He even sunk a critical long downhill birdie putt on the last hole when the pressure was on to win.

Practicing difficult shots such as this one, off a bad lie, allows you to play more confidently, because you know you can recover.

All great players, most notably veterans Jack Nicklaus and Johnny Miller and younger players Justin Leonard and Tiger Woods, possess an uncanny ability to will victory.

Miller is best known for shooting a final round 63 at Oakmont in route to winning the 1973 United States Open. Nicklaus is best known for coming out of nowhere to win the 1986 Masters championship at the age of 46. Leonard stormed back to win the 1997 British Open at Scotland's Royal Troon Golf Club. As for Tiger Woods, he seems to keep storming back every week.

133

Jim's Tips

When you get either well ahead or far behind in a medal or match play event, avoid getting ahead of yourself that you see yourself storming back or holding the trophy. Do not allow yourself to think about results. Instead, play the shot at hand. Persevere one step at a time, trying to hit the best possible shot you can each time you step up to the ball. That way, victory takes care of itself and is a result of your fine play.

The reason golfers such as Leonard and Woods persevere and attack the flag when needing to make a great comeback is that they fear nothing. They have worked so hard practicing the short game that they can attack a flag tucked in a corner of the green and not worry about missing their target and landing in a trouble spot near the green. They know well that, no matter how awkward their stance or how bad the lie, they have a shot in their bag that will allow them to save par or make a miraculous birdie. It doesn't matter if they face a short pitch over a bunker to a tight pin, a chip off hard ground, a buried-lie bunker shot, or a twisting long putt. They see no evil and fear no evil, due to a confident mind-set and a will to persevere and take control of any course situation.

When starting a comeback with a string of good shots and a couple of low-scoring holes, let the momentum and confidence build. One of the worst things you can do is to get overexcited by a few consecutive good shots and let your emotions reach too high a level.

Bet You Didn't Know

There was a time when Tiger Woods was overly aggressive. He took an all out effort to another level and sometimes became overly competitive. There were times when he lost his cool. Now, with everything in perspective, he is a mature player who perseveres intelligently. He has definitely improved his short game, and I'm sure this has helped him to be more patient and save great rounds even with a few less than perfect shots.

The best players in the world don't dwell on either a great score or a poor score on a hole. Oh sure, Tiger may pump his fists when making a birdie, but he never walks to the next tee so overly excited that he wails away at a drive, or to the next green ready and raring to attack a 50-foot downhill putt. Also, even the best players sometimes become frustrated by a bad shot; but instead of letting it bother them, they get over it quickly before moving on they learn to put poor shots or bad breaks behind them. Though this is not easy, and not always possible, we all know that there is nothing we can do about the past. Get over it and focus on the most important shot in golf: the next one!

Playing Your Own Game

The next time you compete in a friendly match or even in a more serious competition and you are pitching-wedge distance to a green on a par-three, par-four, or par-five hole, go with your natural shape of shot: a slight fade, soft draw, high shot, low shot. Unless it's windy or the design and features of the green and its surrounding hazards dictate that you must change your technique slightly, go with the shot you are familiar with or the one you most often hit in practice. The great hall of fame teacher Harvey Penick called this the "plain vanilla" shot. By that he meant the golf shot you know and are comfortable hitting. It may not be fancy, but it gets the job done. Plain vanilla can be very productive in the short game.

Another important point to playing your own game involves laying up on par-five holes. This means playing to a safe area where the fairway is wider or is clear of hazards. It's always a consideration, when hitting your second shot on a par-five hole, to hit where you can play a full third shot into the green with any of your wedges. *Part shots* take more feel and practice. Also, in a pressure situation, the last thing most golfers want to face is a short, 40-yard finesse wedge shot form a tight lie.

Until you have developed a strong sense of confidence in hitting a variety of chips and bunker shots, it's also important that you stick to the basic techniques I taught you in Chapter 3, "Building Blocks." I know if you see your playing partner playing a fancy three-wood chip, it's tempting to try the same shot. That's okay, if you are just out for a casual round. But you will be hurting yourself if you try to hit a strange chip like this in competition without practicing it first. A simple rule is that you don't hit

Death Moves

Many amateurs make the common mistake of experimenting with new shots on the course and end up losing vital strokes to par. Save this kind of experimenting for the practice tee. That's the right place to fool around with your pitching swing and to develop new ways of playing a pitch by making slight changes to your normal setup and technique.

Swing Lingo

A **part shot** is a partial shot or a shot that is less than full. It requires an easier swing and, accordingly, the proper adjustments to swing length and swing speed.

shots you are incapable of playing, and don't hit shots you have never practiced. Even top professionals wait until their round is over to try a new short-game stroke. And only if a new pitching, chipping, bunker play technique works in practice will they try it in play.

The same shot philosophy may not hold true on the greens, however. If you are struggling with your putter early in the round and you want to give the cross-handed, left-hand-low technique a try, you don't necessarily wait until the round is finished. You just never know—maybe this kind of grip and putting stroke will work better for you immediately. Remember that putting is called "the other game."

One of the most incredible stories I've heard about trying something new concerned PGA Tour pro Mike Hulbert. He was putting so badly that he actually started putting on the course with his right hand only. Mike changed right during the middle of the tour event and performed quite well. He finished second the following week, putting with only his right arm. So with putting you never know. It's a constant game of slight adjustments according to how you feel and how you are stroking your putts, and of course, whether or not the ball is going into the hole.

The Least You Need to Know

➤ It's important to examine the lie and the course situation before you play a short-game shot.

➤ You should remain patient enough to sometimes play conservatively.

➤ Steady practice boosts your confidence.

➤ If you keep persevering when your game is not right, you may well surprise yourself and come out a winner.

➤ Playing the shot you know you can hit helps you to shoot a lower score.

➤ Test all shots before you play them on the course.

Healthy Habits

When analyzing golf closely, I've noticed a much improved fitness program for the top players of today, compared to those of just a decade ago. Golfers on the PGA, Senior PGA, and LPGA Tours are much more physically fit and health conscious than are most top players on the amateur circuit. This new and improved health trend continues to have its positive effects. Players of all handicaps are being inspired and realizing the connection between being in good shape and playing good golf. Now it's your turn.

When the golf muscles in your body are strong and flexible, it's easier to employ a swing. This helps everywhere, including the short game. Added strength also helps when hitting wedge shots out of deep rough. Additionally, when you eat the right foods, you are less apt to get tired during a round. Consequently, your level of focus is better. As a result, you make fewer errors in strategy and concentrate harder on hitting accurate and perfectly paced pitches, chips, bunker shots, and putts. There are many lessons to be learned about the value of staying healthy, plus knowing how to relax and have fun on the course.

Strengthening Exercises

I think many newcomers to golf fail to realize what an athletic sport golf is and how well you must concentrate over a long period of time. Make no mistake, golf is a very demanding sport requiring a strong, healthy body to maximize performance. Even if you ride in a powered cart. If you are not in shape you tire down the stretch and tend to fold under pressure, especially if you are competing on a hot and humid day.

So that you are ready and raring to go, I will provide you with some strengthening exercises. Strengthening exercises are necessary for training the muscles most involved in the golf swing, particularly those in the legs, arms, hands, wrists, and shoulders. Stronger muscles enable you to make a more efficient well-timed pitching swing. They also enable you to remain strong for all 18 holes, whether it is you or your opponent that's putting pressure on you.

Bet You Didn't Know

Of the past generation of tour golfers, Gary Player was the first to follow a regular strengthening exercise regimen, starting way back in the 1960s. Nowadays, Tiger Woods, Sergio Garcia, and David Duval carry the torch, encouraging younger golfers around the world to make a serious effort to get fit.

It's no coincidence that the most physically fit golfers usually play the best golf. So be sure to follow this regular body-strengthening program. In determining the number of repetitions for each exercise, consult someone knowledgeable in the conditioning field. What's most vital is to exercise properly. Also, realize that this strengthening regimen helps you to become more disciplined, which, in turn, helps you to become more determined to improve your short-game skills.

Running

Running is one of the best exercises for the thigh and calf muscles. Therefore, I'm not surprised that more and more tour professionals are doing this type of exercise. A few years ago, even Arnold Palmer started getting back in shape by doing some roadwork. In strengthening the legs, you build a stronger base to swing from. This stronger foundation enables you to stay balanced during the swing and thus hit better shots.

Running (like cycling, skipping rope, and jogging) is also excellent for building stamina. Many tour professionals ride a bike. Golf, especially competitive golf, can be very draining on the body, so any type of aerobic exercise is good for you and your game.

Dumbbell Lifts

Working with free weights is an excellent way to strengthen the muscles in your forearms and wrists. You need this strength to hit powerful shots from deep rough bordering the fairway, as well as from trouble spots near the green, such as ice plant, which is common on California courses, and heather, which is common on the links courses of the British Isles. Wrist strength can also be good for chipping and putting, because you do not want the wrists to collapse early on in the backswing causing the hands take control. Here's one exercise that can do great things for your body:

1. Sit upright in a chair with both feet flat on the floor.

2. Rest the back of your forearms on your thighs so that your hands hang over your kneecaps and your palms face the sky.

3. Holding a dumbbell in each hand, bring your wrists toward you, while keeping your forearms flush to your thighs.

4. Return slowly to your starting position and repeat the motion.

Jim's Tips

When doing dumbbell lifts, start with a 3- to 5-pound weight in each hand, and then progress to a 10-pound weight—or even more, if you work with a trainer or someone who can show you the proper technique.

Death Moves

When working with weights, be careful not to lift heavy weights when doing bench presses and, for that matter, any exercises that cause you to overbuild the muscles in your upper body. Too much muscle bulk is not good for your golf, as I told one of my students, Sly Stallone.

The Big Weights

This exercise is a little more serious, because it requires a 50-pound barbell. On the positive side, however, regular workouts help you build up strength in your legs and enhance your posture, too. Good posture is a necessary ingredient to swinging the club on the proper plane. Here's what to do:

1. Drape a bath towel around your neck.

2. Spread your feet shoulder-width apart.

3. Lift the barbell from the floor, and rest the bar on the towel at the base of your neck behind your head.

4. Squat down, keeping your heels flat on the ground.

5. Slowly raise up, and then repeat the squat.

Squeezing a Ball

Forget about any fancy sports equipment for exercising the muscles in your hands. Strong hands do help you hit good recovery shots such as a wedge from very heavy rough. However, one of the most basic and best ways to strengthen the hands is by slowly squeezing a tennis ball. Simply squeeze and let go, squeeze and let go. Try to repeat this exercise between 10 and 20 times a day.

Stretching Exercises

It is not enough for the muscles in your body to be strong; they also have to be supple for you to make a fluid pitching swing or rhythmic chip, bunker shot, or putt. You want your muscles to feel oily, rather than stiff, so they work at maximum efficiency. Stretching is probably far underrated by the average golfer, but it definitely is not by professionals, especially the senior tour players. Stretching is crucial to extending your golf skills and improving your range of motion.

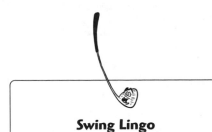

Swing Lingo

A **doughnut** is a heavily weighted circular object that is designed to be attached to a club shaft. When you swing the weighted club, you stretch your golf muscles.

Swinging a Heavy Club

One total-body exercise that stretches every vital golf muscle is swinging a heavy club. You can purchase a weighted club, have your pro remove the grip of an old wedge of yours and fill the club shaft with sand, or purchase a *doughnut* to put around the shaft of your club. (Because most ceilings are at least 8 feet high, the shorter wedge can usually be swung indoors.)

I'm different from most teachers who recommend students swing a very heavily weighted driver to stretch the golf muscles in their hands, wrists, arms, and shoulders. I think this puts too much strain on the body. Besides, when you put an iron, such as a pitching wedge, back in your hand, the tendency is to swing it much too fast. It literally feels like a feather in your hands.

Swinging a club with sand in the shaft (to provide added weight) will help you stretch your golf muscles and swing more freely.

Leg Stretches

To stretch your legs, get down on your hands and knees. Next, raise your right leg, extending it behind you, as far as is comfortably possible. Hold that position for the count of five, before returning to your starting position. Repeat, this time extending your left leg. Proceed slowly, never trying to stretch your legs to the absolute limit.

141

Neck Stretches

A supple neck prevents any possible strain that could occur when hitting a shot that requires you to stay down longer and resist with the upper body—the fried-egg bunker lie being one of them.

To stretch the neck muscles, stand erect and slowly tilt your neck back until your eyes look up toward the sky. Return slowly to the starting position. Try to repeat this exercise 10 times daily.

Diet

The majority of tour professionals eat healthily, setting a good example for amateurs. When you eat the right foods, you feel much more awake on the course and sustain your mental strength for the entire round. You think more clearly too, which is important to making smart shot-making decisions.

Off the course, most top players eat steak, chicken, pasta, potatoes, fruits, and vegetables. They drink water, not alcohol or soda, and they also refrain from eating junk food. On course during a round of golf, most tour pros do little more than eat a piece of fruit or a health bar and drink water or Gatorade. Again, however, I would advise you to consult an expert and design a diet that is right for you.

Bet You Didn't Know

Lee Trevino claims he plays his best golf on an empty stomach. In contrast, fellow Senior PGA Tour player Al Geiberger believes he hits his best shots when he eats a little something during the round. In fact, Geiberger ate peanut-butter-and-jelly sandwiches in route to winning the 1966 PGA championship. Obviously, your best diet will be different from someone else's. Try to determine what helps you to feel strong and alert.

Relaxation

I feel strongly that finding ways to relax during a round is also very healthy and productive for your game. Professional golfers have told me that they let their minds relax in between shots. Some pros think of their family and friends, while others just admire the beautiful scenery or simply remind themselves about how lucky they are to be alive and playing golf. This type of mental escape helps you relax your mind and body so that when you arrive on the next tee or prepare to play an approach shot into a green, you feel clear headed and ready to go.

Knowing they have practiced hard gives professional golfers more confidence. And when you are confident, you tend to be more relaxed. Something else that helps you feel more confident is taking the time to pick a target, staring that target down, making a fluid practice swing, and stepping into what you know is a correct address position. So, be sure to practice your various shot-making routines and the basics for setting up properly.

Playing Games

It's one thing to play golf with your spouse or your kids for the sheer fun of it; it's another thing to play competitively with your friends.

Playing competitively for money is actually excellent for your game. This kind of training teaches you how to handle pressure situations and forces you to take more time and care when hitting a short-game shot. I'm not a believer in competing for anything more than you can comfortably afford, but betting can improve your focus a lot. Incidentally, many tour pros play gambling games during practice rounds. They also bet during the off weeks when at home playing with friends.

Bingle, Bangle, Bungle

This is an amusing game involving three points that will have positive effects on your golf game, particularly with respect to playing better short-game shots. This game is best played with a group of four golfers. One point is awarded to the player who reaches the green first. One point goes to the player whose ball is closest to the hole when all balls are on the green. The third point goes to the player who first hits the ball into the cup. The winner is the player with the most points at the end of the round.

Death Moves

Golf is only a game. Sure you want to shoot a low score. But avoid putting extra pressure on yourself, avoid promoting tension by ignoring your playing partners, and remember to have fun. Between shots, talk to your fellow players or caddy about nongolf subjects. These brief escapes will help you to relax.

Jim's Tips

The next time you play golf, bet on who makes the most up-and-in conversions on all shots around the green (and extra for hole outs). Also, establish a small money pot for the golfer who takes the lowest number of putts for each nine holes you play. This kind of low stakes gambling keeps you and your playing partners competitive and mentally sharp.

Sandies

In the sandies game, the player who gets the ball up and down from any bunker wins a certain amount of money. I like playing this game because it makes me concentrate more intently on employing the right type of swing for the particular bunker shot I'm faced with. I want that sandies cash.

Competing for "trash" will encourage you to concentrate more intensely when facing such lies as this "fried egg."

The Least You Need to Know

➤ Running or riding a bike is good for building strong legs and, in turn, a strong foundation from which to swing.

➤ Swinging a weighted club helps you stretch the muscles in your body and thus employ a more rhythmic action.

➤ Healthy eating habits help you sustain your physical and mental strength for the entire round of 18 holes.

➤ Low-stake money games make you concentrate more intently and help you retain the will to win.

TV Tips

Every year the television ratings for golf jump higher across the networks. And I can see why. It seems the talent gets better all the time. The fine play of Tiger Woods, Sergio Garcia, and David Duval has sure helped add some more heightened excitement to the PGA Tour. Having names like Justin Leonard, Davis Love, Phil Mickelson, Ernie Els, Fred Couples, Mark O'Meara, Vijay Singh, Hal Sutton, and Steve Pate sure help the ratings too.

The Senior PGA Tour ratings have been set afire by the rivalry between Hale Irwin and Bruce Fleisher, although many onlookers I talk to still like watching Jack Nicklaus, Chi Chi Rodriguez, and Lee Trevino. I must admit, I enjoy watching these three veterans as well, simply because they are such creative shot makers and you can learn so much from them.

On the LPGA Tour, there is an array of women worth watching, simply because their setup and swing positions are fundamentally sound. Se Ri Pak sets up to the ball perfectly, and Karrie Webb swings the club as well as anyone I've seen. But if you want to see what I mean by sticking to the basics, watch them. If you want to see power, don't leave your seat when Laura Davies is hitting a driver shot, but she can and does hit some awesome shots around the green.

You can learn a heck of a lot about playing pitch shots, bunker shots, chips, and putts from watching particular players on tour. Let me tell you what some of these players are known for so that the next time you are on your couch, you can sit back and enjoy the show while looking and learning.

Viewing Pitching Experts

What I like so much about watching the pros play on television is that I get a refresher course on the basics. Just watching players like Jeff Maggert, Hale Irwin, and Anika Sorenstam play pitch shots by the book is healthy for your game. These three players are not as exciting to watch as their PGA Tour, Senior PGA Tour, and LPGA Tour counterparts: Tiger Woods, Chi Chi Rodriguez, and Laura Davies respectively. But, as I said, by watching them all you can get a good picture of what it means to set up to the ball according to the basic fundamentals and swing in a technically sound, easy-to-repeat manner.

When watching Maggert, Irwin, and Webb set up to a pitch, note the rhythm and practice moves before they hit the shot. Watch also the way they allow the right wrist to hinge on the backswing—that helps them set the club on an upright plane and enhances their feel. If the network shows the downswing in slow motion, notice their flat left wrist position at impact. The back of the left wrist lines up perfectly with the back of the left forearm. There is no indentation between the left wrist and forearm on a standard pitch. More important, the back of the left hand is square to the clubface, which is point-ing straight at the target. These three players know the ins and outs of preparing for and playing the standard pitch.

Jim's Tips

ESPN's golf commentator Andy North, who is also a two-time U.S. Open Champion, does something very interesting when following the last group in a Senior PGA Tour event. If one of the players hits a super short-game shot, North waits until they leave the green and then shows viewers how to play that particular pitch, chip, bunker shot, or putt. Look and learn.

Draw-Spin Pitch

One of the super shots that Chi Chi Rodriguez has hit more than once in a Senior PGA Tour event is the draw-spin pitch. Chi Chi uses this shot to draw a low pitch around a deep bunker or water hazard on the left front side of the green to a pin tucked behind it. The ball has hook spin, draws slightly in the air, lands, and then spins left to the hole. This is a shot you will have fun hitting in practice and then trying out on the course once you perfect it.

When watching Jeff Maggert, Hale Irwin, and Karrie Webb hit pitch shots on television, look closely at their flat left wrist position at impact, demonstrated by me here.

When setting up to play this creative pitching-wedge shot as Chi Chi does, position the ball just behind the midpoint of your stance, with your hands ahead of it slightly. The more draw spin you want to impart on the ball, the more you should aim your feet and body right of target, and the more you should close the clubface. Most people I teach this shot to do not close the clubface enough, so don't make this error yourself.

When watching a pro play this shot on television, notice the way he swings back and perhaps just slightly to the inside. It's on the downswing, however, that he gets a little more creative. He rotates his right forearm, right wrist, and right hand in a top-spin action. This right-sided rotation helps him impact with the toe end of the club leading its heel. It's this same clubface position that will allow you to hit a low, drawing pitch that turns around the trouble, lands on the green, spins left, and rolls toward the hole.

147

Superhigh Sand-Wedge Shot

No golfer plays the superhigh sand-wedge shot better than Fred Couples. Sooner or later when watching Freddie play a PGA Tour event, you'll see him hit this superhigh shot with a sand wedge. Often the shot will be out of rough to a very tight pin. He sometimes uses this shot to hit the ball over a fairly tall tree to have it land on the green next to the hole and stop virtually dead. Incidentally, we teach this shot at my short game schools. Here are your instruc-tions for playing it like Freddie does.

Take your highest lofted sand wedge and play the ball well forward in your stance. Freddie plays the ball op-posite his left instep to give added height to the shot. Open your stance and set your hands behind the ball slightly, because both these keys further promote a higher shot. Hold the club lightly, being sure to grip the end of the club. Sometimes Freddie hits this shot with the pinkie of his left hand off the butt end of the club. This helps you to make a tension-free swinging action and to release the club more freely on the downswing.

Employ a very long and relaxed backswing, allowing your wrists and hands to work freely. Feel yourself swinging slower than normally. Phil Mickelson and Tiger Woods also hit this shot often and with a lot of success.

The three most important downswing keys are releas-ing the club as soon as possible by unhinging the wrists, hitting on average about two inches behind the ball, and making a full followthrough. Freddie is so great at playing this shot. What's amazing is watching him hit as far as five inches behind the ball if he is playing this shot out of coarse Bermuda grass rough.

Viewing Chipping Experts

To get a good visual picture of what ideal standard chipping techniques look like, watch Davis Love III, Gil Morgan, and Se Ri Pak. All these players open their stances slightly, hinge their wrists a little on the backswing, and make contact with the ball slightly on the descent. So they are worth studying the next time you see them chipping on television. Having said that, you can learn about a different style of chipping invented by Paul Runyan, who won the 1934 PGA championship, and another by Hubert Green.

Here, I demonstrate the superhigh sand wedge shot from Bermuda rough. The grass flying into the air indicates that I contacted an area of turf behind the ball, just like Fred Couples does.

Runyan-Style Chipping

Runyan, who still plays golf at 91, influenced the chipping style of Jack Nicklaus and a large number of other players and teachers. When watching Nicklaus chip during a televised tournament, notice the unique qualities of his setup. He sticks both elbows outward, so if an imaginary line were drawn through the forearms, it would run

Swing Lingo

A **square-to-square stroke** refers to keeping the clubface square to the arc of the swing. It does not refer to keeping the clubface square to the target line.

Jim's Tips

When trying out Hubert Green's chipping method, remember to choke well down on the club as he does, because this helps you to swing the club back on a steeper plane. Hubert will often grip all the way down to the steel below the grip. With this style, Hubert can get down very close to his work and be very aggressive.

parallel to the target line. He bends over quite dramatically from the waist, just as he does when putting, because this gives him a stronger sense of control. Like Runyan, he also sets his feet squarely to the target line to promote a *square-to-square stroke*.

To propel the club back and through, he rocks his shoulders back and forth, using a motion similar to one a parent uses to rock a baby. The wrists stay locked throughout the stroke, which helps the club to swing low to the ground going back and through.

Try this shot after watching television, ideally either on the practice chipping green or course. You will see how this technique produces a very soft-landing shot that rolls the split second it hits the green. It is a terrific shot to hit to a superslick putting surface when there is limited green between your ball and the hole.

Green's Lift-and-Stab Method

Throughout his career on the PGA Tour, Hubert Green was rated one of the finest chippers in the game. If you didn't get a chance to watch Hubert play during the 1970s when he won a bunch of tournaments, or in the '80s, highlighted by his well known 1985 PGA championship win over Lee Trevino, you should watch him these days on the Senior PGA Tour. Green is older, but his chip stroke hasn't changed one bit. You might want to try it, especially if you have trouble hitting finesse chips.

When you use Hubert's method, you can be very aggressive. That's because when you employ Hubert's technique, you hit down on the ball, causing the effective loft of the club to be reduced. This can be a better stroke for nervous types who feel more comfortable hitting down quite firmly on the ball.

Watch Hubert and you will see that he sets up very open, with the ball positioned near his right heel and his hands way out ahead of it. On the backswing, he cocks his wrists dramatically so that he can more easily lift the sand wedge upward with his hands and arms. On the downswing, he simply unhinges his wrists and hits down into the ball abruptly—kind of stabbing it in the back. With this method you will almost never mishit a chip.

Hinging the wrists dramatically on the backswing is critical to playing a lift-and-stab chip like Senior PGA Tour professional Hubert Green.

Bunker Play Experts

Some of the better bunker players on tour—namely Jeff Sluman, Tim Herron, and Stewart Cink—are not superstars. However, because their setups and swing techniques are fundamentally sound (similar to those I taught you in Chapter 2, "How to Get Started," and Chapter 3, "Building Blocks"), they hit the ball up close to the cup time after time.

All tour players are worth watching carefully, and I hope that you practice your bunker play techniques using them as models. Let me now share with you two special shots that I've learned from two of the greatest bunker artists.

151

The "Dairy Queen" Bunker Shot

The unique special short bunker shot technique called the *"Dairy Queen,"* taught to me by Claude Harmon, is designed to lift the ball over a very high bunker lip and stop it quickly on a fast green. Harmon used to play this shot frequently at New York's Winged Foot Golf Club, a course known for its very steep bunkers and exceptionally fast greens. He also taught it to me and, of course, to thousands of his other students. In case you haven't noticed, Tiger Woods has dramatically improved his short bunker shots. He learned his technique from my good friend Butch Harmon, Claude's eldest son.

One player who employs Harmon's short bunker shot method is Tom Watson, who just so happens to be one of the all-time greatest sand players. The next time you're sitting on your couch watching a Senior PGA Tour event, look for Watson and study his method. It is specially designed to help you loft the ball over a very high lip and stop it quickly on a fast putting surface.

When Watson sets up, note his weak grip and how he sets the clubface open by not leaning the shaft forward. Often he leans the club shaft back away from the target, as did Claude. Watch how quickly Watson lifts the club into the air on the backswing, hinging his wrists dramatically to promote the necessary steep plane. As soon as Watson starts his downswing, he releases it with his arms, hands, and wrists, concentrating on thumping the sand about three to four inches behind the ball and making the knuckles of his left hand face upward at impact. Through impact the club stays wide open and scoops a long furrow of sand out from under the ball. The shorter he follows through the shorter the ball travels. When it hits the green it goes nowhere.

Swing Lingo

Harmon called this shot the **"Dairy Queen"** because the golf ball landed so dead on the green that Claude compared it to turning an ice cream cone upside down and dropping the ice cream on the ground.

When I showed this technique to Brad Faxon, he incorporated a slightly higher and extremely narrow finish, mirroring the backswing. Brad renamed this shot the "fondue shot" because he visualized how you would scoop out cheese from a fondue pot. You might find this useful, and I can tell you from first hand experience that it works.

Slip-and-Hold Method

This is another ideal shot when you have very little green to work with. Just in case you don't see me demonstrating it on *The Golf Channel*, here's how to play it using a wide-flanged sand wedge with moderate bounce.

At address, take an extra-wide stance and lower your hands. Also, set your hands behind the ball so you can set the clubface even more open.

When Tom Watson and other pros hit the "Dairy Queen" shot, they scoop sand out of the bunker as this divot indicates.

On the backswing, create a wide arc by extending your hands low and away from the body and keeping the wrists quiet.

On the downswing, simply slide the club into the sand behind the ball. To prevent the ball from flying too far, restrict the follow-through. Again, this method produces a long thin furrow of sand. You won't dig the sand ever. This shot can be fantastic, but it won't go as high as the "Dairy Queen" shot.

Viewing Putting Experts

I have been pleased to be around two great PGA Tour players, Brad Faxon and Len Mattiace, students of mine who are recognized as fantastic putters. On short putts, they swing the putter with their arms and shoulders. On longer putts, they incorporate some wrist action into the stroke, while

Jim's Tips

When playing the slip-and-hold bunker shot that I learned from Ken Venturi—winner of the 1964 United States Open and one of the world's best bunker players (even now!)—be sure to hold the club at the very end of the handle. If you choke down on the club, you probably won't get enough speed.

the putter swings on an inside-square-inside path. Karrie Webb, who putts cross-handed and Dottie Pepper are two of the best putters on the LPGA Tour. George Archer has one of the finest strokes on the Senior PGA Tour. You should make a point of watching all these players on television because they use simple rhythmic strokes. But don't look at only the type of stroke they make. Look, too, at how they prepare to putt and at the pace of the stroke.

Bet You Didn't Know

George Archer won the 1969 Masters and many other tournaments on the PGA Tour using a smooth pendulum-type putting stroke. He is considered one of the best ever by his peers. George developed his stroke by huge amounts of practice. He told me that he tried to get at least one 5-hour putting session in every week of the year.

Archer's stroke is classically conventional compared to the one employed by his fellow Senior PGA Tour player Gary Player, whom you should also watch putt on television. Player, who is one of only four men to win all four major championships, has built a career around his unorthodox stroke.

Player's Jab Stroke

A disciple of the great South African putter Bobby Locke, Player sets up closed, with his elbows touching his body. Player hinges the right wrist on the backswing, then unhinges it on the forward swing, stopping at impact. At impact, the blade putter he has used for so many years stops dead. In short, Player hits the ball with sort of a quick jab action. This stroke works especially well on short-length putts. Because the ball rolls faster off the putter face, Player never accelerates—a major problem for poor putters.

Many other great putters have used this type stroke, including the great Isao Aoki. It sure throws a huge boulder in the no hands all shoulders method taught exclusively by some teachers and some schools. Anyone watching golf will see all types of strokes and styles that work wonderfully.

The next time you watch Gary Player putt, note two technical points of his Jab Stroke, demonstrated here by me: 1. A closed stance and 2. An abrupt right wrist hinge on the backswing.

The Least You Need to Know

➤ The draw–spin pitch shot can help you avoid trouble.

➤ The superhigh sand–wedge shot helps you hit over trees to a tight pin.

➤ Chipping like Jack Nicklaus promotes a square-to-square stroke and accurate shots.

➤ If you like to employ a more aggressive chipping action, try copying Hubert Green's method.

➤ Play the "Dairy Queen" shot when hitting out of sand over a very high lip.

➤ Gary Player's jab stroke can help you sink more short putts.

Short-Game Swing Myths

If you are a newcomer to golf, or someone who's played for just a short while, I must tell you what tips to ignore regarding pitching, bunker play, chipping, and putting.

Over the last 20 years, particularly, studies have been done with video and computers involving the very best players in the game. Additionally, prominent instructors who work with tour pros are using videotape. I also use this vehicle, because it is a good way to pinpoint a fault in a player's swing and to disprove myths about technique.

Through studying the techniques of the game's best players, our short-game teachers and other top teachers around the country have discovered that many long-held beliefs about short-game technique are fictitious. So, let me review each short-game department, reveal the relevant myth, and tell you where you have some leeway regarding a particular element of the setup and swing.

Pitching Myths

Almost every student I teach for the first time has to be told that what he or she has heard or read about pitching is not true. Often, this gives students an immediate sense of relief and helps them improve right away because what they were trying to do was difficult or totally incorrect.

Myth One: Square Up

Some teachers still instruct their students to set their feet parallel to the target line, believing that this is the only way to make good swings and good shots. There is, however, no cast-in-bronze rule for setting up to play a pitch. Personally, I prefer my students to set up slightly open when hitting the standard pitch, because I think this gives them a better view of the line and helps them clear their left hip a little more easily on the downswing. Most importantly, this setup restricts the hip turn and greatly discourages an inside takeaway. The majority of pros I've studied set up this way.

Myth Two: Square Clubface Position

It is the general consensus among the golf populace that you must set the clubface down square to the target, with its sweet spot lined up with the back center of the ball. This is also what we generally teach at our schools. However, many pitch shots require an open clubface that must be set at address. The slightly open clubface increases the bounce of the club and helps the wedge slide under the ball. I often see tour players set the clubface in this fashion.

Bet You Didn't Know

Several years ago, *Golf Magazine* showed many top pros lining the ball up close to the heel of the clubface. The editors of that publication explained that because the arms extend to the maximum at impact, the club moves outward slightly. So if you start near the heel, you end up hitting the ball with the sweet spot of the clubface.

This unique position can actually encourage you to swing the club up on the backswing, rather than on a flat plane. Some golfers who set the clubface down squarely swing on a fairly flat plane and on an exaggerated flat plane when the toe portion of the club is close to the ball. The point I'm making is that certain players must do what they must do in order to arrive at impact with the clubface dead square to the ball.

Myth Three: Keep Your Left Arm Straight

This is one of the old adages that doesn't seem to die. I can't tell you how many golfers come to me struggling with tension in their swings and complaining of off-center hits because they try so hard to keep the left arm stiff on the backswing.

Having given thousands of lessons, you must trust me when I tell you that virtually all tour pros have some bend in their left arms. It is okay to allow your left arm to bend slightly on the backswing. Seve Ballesteros is still one of the best pitching-wedge players in the game, and he allows his left arm to bend on the backswing. Seve simply uses a gentle pulling action of the hands to straighten the arm at impact.

Like Seve Ballesteros, I often allow my left arm to bend slightly on the backswing when pitching the ball.

Jim's Tips

For those of you who have too much bend in your left arm, try letting the right wrist hinge on the backswing. This is a good thing to do on wedge shots anyway. When you try to make an extended takeaway too long and with the wrists locked, you tend to overbend or collapse your arm when swinging the club up.

Myth Four: Keep Your Head Still

Keeping your head still goes against natural human motion and hurts your ball-striking ability.

Studying the pros has helped me come to one conclusion about head movement: Your head will move laterally or rotate away from the target during the backswing of a full swing. However, when hitting standard wedge shots, don't let your head rotate or move much at all because, if you will remember, you want to keep most of your weight on your left foot.

Allow your head to rotate and release after you hit the ball. David Duval and Annika Sorenstam go so far as to allow their heads to look at the target before impact. I'm not suggesting you copy these two gifted pros, but I am telling you *not* to fight natural head movement. If you try to keep your head locked, you tend to make a tense, overly mechanical swing and jam the club into the ground at impact.

Chipping Myths

Chipping is not a science, it is an art form requiring steady practice to determine how best to work the clubface to deal with a particular lie. Tempo can change too, depending on what type of shot you are playing. Chipping requires good intuition on the part of the player so that he or she can predict what the ball is going to do in the air and on the ground. This is one reason why I become frustrated when students tell me that they were taught certain chip-swing keys that I know only too well are simply myths.

Myth One: Chip with Your Favorite Club

Many professional golfers on the PGA Tour hit many chip shots with a sand wedge. They simply play the ball back more with their hands well ahead of it to hit a low chip. To hit higher chips that sit down more quickly on the green, they play the ball farther forward in their stance than they normally do and exaggerate their wrist action on the backswing and downswing.

For most golfers, we strongly suggest using at least two or three clubs. As I told you in Chapter 1, "What Is the Short Game?" it's more sensible for you to work hard with three clubs—a seven iron, nine iron, and pitching wedge—so that you develop a variety of good chips shots. Use the sandwedge for short-pitch shots or specialty shots in the rough around the green.

Myth Two: Chip the Way You Putt

This so-called set-in-stone philosophy has hurt millions of golfers, because it has them swinging the club back and forth like robots. The majority of recreational golfers who chip the way they putt lose feel, particularly on long chips, because they grip very firmly and keep their wrists locked. Instead, their chipping stroke should simply be a miniature version of their bigger swings.

Warning: Copy this stiff-wristed chipping stroke and you will lose feel for distance.

On most chips, except the very short ones, you need to hinge the wrists slightly, so that you set the club on a slightly upright plane, which is necessary for hitting the ball slightly on the descent and propelling it into the air so that it carries the fringe and lands on the green.

Bunker Play Myths

Gary Player and Chi Chi Rodriguez are both great bunker players. They made both the open stance setup and the method of hitting an area of sand close behind the ball famous. The success of these players led to the creation of the following myths.

Myth One: Set Up Open

You do not need to set up open to play good bunker shots. Many great bunker players, including five-time British Open Champion Peter Thomson and former PGA and British Open Champion John Daly set up with their right foot dropped back a few inches further from the target line. This closed setup position allows them to swing the club on a shallower swing plane, and take less sand. The square setup is far superior.

Some of the best bunker players in the world, such as John Daly, play from a closed stance like the one shown here.

Most women and many weekend players simply cannot set up open, open the club-face, swing outside in, and get the ball onto the green. They simply do not have the swing speed to do it. They come up short every time unless they skull the ball over the green.

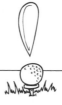

Bet You Didn't Know

Julius Boros, PGA Champion and two-time United States Open Champion, played the majority of bunker shots from a square stance position. He took a very conventional type of swing—very similar to his regular golf swing. The only difference was that it was extra smooth and extra fluid—syrupy.

Take my advice: Trust your sand wedge, which is built to get you out of the bunker. Keep the clubface square and make a normal golf swing. That is, do not swing outside in across the ball. Also, do not block or hold on going through impact. Instead, use a normal release. That means that you must allow your right hand to brush over your left hand. This way you hit quality bunker shots, and you get the ball all the way up to the hole. No other advice in this book is more important to the general golf population!

Myth Two: Take a Weak Grip

You do not need to hold the club with a weak grip to play bunker shots well. In fact, Paul Azinger, John Daly, and many other top players on the PGA and European tours take a strong grip, letting the Vs formed by their thumbs and forefingers point at their right shoulder. This swing key also allows them to swing on a flatter swing plane and take a shallow cut of sand.

Putting Myths

New golfers don't realize that putting is the most personalized part of the game. This unawareness makes them fall victim to certain myths regarding the way they should set up and *stroke* the putt.

Swing Lingo

When discussing putting technique, the word **stroke** is often used instead of swing. The putting stroke is the same as the putting swing, except that you have a backstroke and a forward stroke, instead of a backswing and a downswing.

Myth One: Take a Narrow Stance

Although many pros, such as Tiger Woods and David Duval, spread their feet narrowly apart when setting up for a putt, some of the world's greatest putters take a wide stance. Probably the best of all is the successful Senior PGA Tour player Dave Stockton, who is most famous for his 1970 PGA championship win. Stockton still uses a mallet-type putter and employs a fairly long flowing stroke.

You don't have to putt from a narrow stance, like this one used by Tiger Woods and David Duval. Feel free to putt from a wide base by spreading your feet shoulder-width apart.

If you presently play from a narrow stance and feel you make a short up-and-down choppy stroke, try spreading your feet a few inches farther apart. You may discover that the ball rolls more purely across the green.

Myth Two: Set Your Eyes Over the Ball

Many great putters, most notably Jack Nicklaus, set up with their eyes over the target line and their head behind the ball. This position enables them to see the line more clearly and to make a straight back-and-through stroke. However, both Ben Crenshaw and Brad Faxon, who I consider the two best putters in the world over the past 20 years, set their eyes inside the target line. Justin Leonard, the 1997 British Open Champion, sets his eyes far inside the line with the putter head far away from his body. Scott Hoch, an all time top money winner, sets his eyes outside the line.

So what is the answer? You must set up so that you see the proper line in your mind's eye. Putting is not a science.

Jim's Tips

If you decide to try putting from a wide stance to promote a level back and through stroke, balance your weight evenly on the central portion of both feet. Also, crouch over on short putts and stand more erect on long putts, as Jack Burke taught me.

Bet You Didn't Know

Students tell me all the time that they have been taught to set their eyes over the ball. Maybe you have been too. If it's working for you, by all means stay with it. If not, experiment by positioning the ball farther away from your foot line and body. You might be shocked that you see the line much better and make a better stroke.

Myth Three: Employ a Shoulder Stroke

I'll concede that the majority of pros control the stroke with their arms and shoulders for putts of within 20 feet of the hole. They incorporate wrist action into their stroke only when the putt is longer, and they depend on the added feel this slight wrist-action stroke provides. However, there are still many tour professionals using both hands and arms. Putting with your shoulders dominating takes a ton of practice.

If you are having problems putting with a pendulum-type shoulder stroke, don't believe that you must stick with this stroke. It is a myth that this kind of stroke is the only way. Three legends of golf, Bobby Jones, Arnold Palmer, and Billy Casper all used their wrists to control the movement of the putter on the backstroke and forward stroke. Let's also not forget Crenshaw, Faxon, Player, Burke, Hogan, Snead, Nicklaus, Ballesteros, Stewart, Els, Kite, and Montgomerie to name a few who are not shoulder-dominated putters. So please don't tell me there is only one way.

Myth Four: Follow the 17-Inch Rule

I have a tremendous respect for short-game expert Dave Pelz. However, I don't agree with his philosophy of hitting a putt at a speed that allows the ball to roll 17 inches past the hole if it fails to drop into it. The first reason I consider this mythical is that green speeds vary from slow to medium paced, to fast, to superfast. Second, it's ludicrous to assume that this speed will be the same for any length putt, which is what Pelz teaches. Third, accepting this myth turns you into such a bold putter that, on superfast sloping greens, you will have problems with distance control and will probably three putt a bunch of them.

Death Moves

On a steep downhill putt on a superfast green, don't think of rolling the ball 17 inches past the hole because you'll probably roll the ball off the green. On a steep uphill putt, on a superslow green, don't think of rolling the ball 17 inches past the hole because the ball probably will not reach the hole. You may need to think of rolling the ball up to 36 inches past the hole.

I disagree with much of the putting philosophy and general short game philosophy taught at several well-known schools. At the McLean Schools, our short-game team is dedicated to dispelling myths and teaching what has been proven to work on the toughest testing ground in golf: the PGA Tour.

I accept that Tom Watson is a bold putter who was one of the best ever during his heyday of the early 1980s. However, most great putters of the past and present die the ball into the hole. This simply means that they stroke the ball at a pace that allows it to either fall gently into the hole or stop very close to it. A short list of great die putters includes Bobby Jones, Jack Nicklaus, Brad Faxon, Ben Crenshaw, Gary Player, Loren Roberts, Colin Montgomerie, and Jim Furyk. Even Tiger Woods has switched from being a bold putter to a die putter. He made that switch after rolling a ball from one side of one green into the water on the other side of the green during the 1997 Ryder Cup matches.

Let me sum it up this way: There are offensive putts and defensive putts, those you go after aggressively and those you even try to leave short. All of golf is a game of risks. Golf shots are all somewhat of a gamble where you must judge the odds. Smart players take risks when the odds are in their favor. Putts over 20 feet have high odds. It's not worth it to aggressively slam putts at the hole. Take the advice given to me by Jackie Burke: Don't use up too much energy by trying to be perfect on 30- and 40-foot putts. Instead, focus on speed and making a good roll. Perfect speed will leave you an easy tap in anywhere around the hole. Do that, and some days those putts all go in. As Burke has said, "Give luck a chance."

The Least You Need to Know

➤ When hitting pitch shots, feel free to let your left arm bend slightly on the backswing.

➤ You should not chip exactly the way you putt.

➤ Bunker shots don't have to be played from an open stance.

➤ Many die putters are great putters.

Chapter 14

Distance Control

Plunk!

In This Chapter

➤ Hitting pinpoint pitch shots

➤ Judging airtime and roll time on chip shots

➤ How to hit bunker shots close to the hole

➤ Keys to hitting perfectly paced putts

No matter what caliber of golfer you are, novice or expert, if you have not seen the pros play live at a championship site, you are missing an experience of a lifetime. Not only do you get to see all your favorite players in action, you get to see them show off their short-game talents.

What's so amazing about athletes who make their living playing golf is their ability to control the distance of the golf ball with pinpoint accuracy. Whether they are hitting a pitch shot, bunker shot, chip, or a putt, they are rarely off by much.

Some of you think the typical tour professional's prowess is largely innate, and moreover, that you yourself can never develop a pro-type short game. Frankly, no matter how hard you practice, it would be very difficult to match a Tiger Woods short game. Tiger is, after all, a true magician, especially around the greens. Nevertheless, by absorbing the secrets from the pros that I pass on to you about how to hit short-game shots close to the hole, you will be ready to take your game to a higher level.

Pinpoint Pitching

You know by now that the typical PGA Tour pro does not hit pitch shots, for example, from 60 yards out from the green, the same way every time. One time the ball lands short of the hole and bounces a couple of times before rolling up next to the hole. Another time, the same player hits a pitch shot that lands about 10 feet past the hole and then spins back toward it. Other times, the player hits a shot that flies very low, lands next to the hole, and *checks*. Another time, the player hits a soft floater that drops down next to the hole as softly as a feather pillow.

When I watch great golfers hit a variety of pitch shots, I am reminded of great pianists. When I listen to a world-class concert pianist, it sometimes sounds as if the piano features hundreds and hundreds of different keys, rather than just 52 white keys and 36 black keys. I appreciate the pianist's gift for altering the speed, pressure, and angle at which he or she touches the keys to create different sounds. In the same way, we admire the pro golfer's talent for swinging in a different way to hit different types of shots different distances. That's talent, yes indeed. However, I promise you that you too can develop this ability by learning what the typical pro has done to nurture this talent.

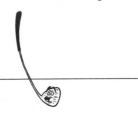

Swing Lingo

A ball that **checks** is a ball that simply stops or grabs the green quickly, after one or more bounces. That is why you often hear a player yell, "Check! Check!" if they believe the shot is flying too far.

Measure by Measure

The first order of business is to follow the examples set by such golfing greats as Bobby Jones, Ben Hogan, Jack Nicklaus, Johnny Miller, Seve Ballesteros, Lee Trevino, and Tiger Woods. You must measure the average distance you hit your pitching wedge, gap wedge, sand wedge, and lob wedge, assuming you carry all four of these clubs in your bag. If not, at least go to a practice range and measure how far you hit the ball, on average, with your pitching wedge and sand wedge. Make sure that you hit shots off real grass, not artificial grass, because the latter may not give you the same reading. Hit a minimum of 25 balls with each club and then go pace off the distance. When figuring your average, throw out any shots hit fat or skulled so that you get a proper average.

Vary the Conditions

In taking this exercise to an even more sophisticated stage, hit the same number of balls into a wind, with the wind at your back, into crosswinds, out of light rough, heavy rough, wet rough, and dry rough. Once again, record your averages. I do not recommend that you hit all these shots and make all these calculations in one day. Give yourself a week or even two weeks to figure out your distances.

If you carry four wedges in your golf bag, know the average distance you hit with each club.

I know this sounds like a heck of a lot of work. It *is* a heck of a lot of work. However, once you start playing golf and reaping the rewards, you will be glad you put so much effort into your short game.

Change Your Swing

When practicing out of different lies with different clubs, record your average distances for short, long, smooth, syrupy, and brisk swings—with square, laid-open, and hooded clubfaces. This is how good players become great. They practice smart and hard and know their wedge games so well that they can handle any course situation and hit shots with pinpoint accuracy and superb distance control.

Bet You Didn't Know

Ben Hogan was so fanatical about distance control that he purposely practiced hitting wedge shots when he felt fatigued and overexcited. Doing his math, he calculated the average distance that he hit shots when experiencing each bodily and emotional condition. My point is that he was more of a hard worker than he was a magician. The great ones do a lot more than most people know.

Precision Chipping

All great chip-shot players assess a number of variables before they pick out a club. These include the lie of the ball; the yardage between the ball and the spot on the green where they plan to land the ball; the slope and speed of the green they are hitting to; and, without question, the distance to the hole.

The following are some of the questions about the pros that I suspect you want answered:

➤ How do the pros know what club to select?

➤ How do they know where to position the ball in their stance?

➤ How do they know whether to open the clubface or set it down square to the ball and target?

➤ How do they know where to position the ball in their stance?

➤ How do they know how far to swing the club back and through?

➤ How do they know how hard to swing?

➤ How do they know where to land the ball?

➤ How do they know how far the ball will roll?

In a nutshell, the answer to all your questions is the same: hard, honest, experimental practice.

For you to be able to hit chips close to the hole (or in it!), you must be willing to practice creatively and purposefully. Bad lies, good lies, level greens, sloping greens, fast greens, slow greens, long distances, short distances—each combination of variables dictates a specific club and shot-making choice. Therefore, I suggest you practice hitting chips out of various lies with various clubs. Keep practicing until you learn by experience which combinations involving club, clubface position, length of swing, and speed of swing work best for you in terms of producing the precise amount of airtime and roll time that you seek for a particular shot.

Bull's Eye Bunker Shots

Before you can evolve into a first-class bunker player, you must recognize all the cause and effect permutations that revolve around technique. For example, a ball flies faster out of a partially plugged lie. Furthermore, a sand wedge featuring less than 10 degrees of bounce works best out of firm sand, while a sand wedge featuring at least 14 degrees of bounce works best in soft sand. If you swing from out to in, you impart soft left-to-right cut-spin on the ball, while if you swing on a flatter plane, you take a thinner slice of sand and hit the ball lower. Also, if you choke down on your club with your right hand on the steel and your grip stronger, you find it easy to hit the ball up quickly over a high lip and land it softly. The list of things you must know goes on.

Jim's Tips

If at all possible, when honing your distance-control skills with various chipping clubs, practice hitting shots at different courses. The more data you can record on paper and in your brain about how the ball reacts in different conditions, say on firm greens versus soft greens, the better.

Bet You Didn't Know

Some tour players own at least three different sand wedges with different type bounces. During a practice round on the course they will be competing on in a tournament, they hit shots out of bunkers with each sand wedge to see which works best. As tour conditions become more standardized and conditions in bunkers more similar, the need for different wedges is lessened. This is not true, however, for the amateur who travels from course to course.

Because I have shown you how to play the standard bunker shot, the long bunker shot, common trouble bunker shots, and more wild bunker shots, you have a head start on other golfers who have not had such an education. Still, in order to learn how to hit the ball consistently within a six-foot circle around the hole—or the bull's eye, the hole itself—you have to experiment in practice.

Through trial and error during practice is how pros such as Seve Ballesteros, José Maria Olazabal, and Sergio Garcia developed into superb bunker players, able to judge a shot practically right down to the inch. The reason they have such a handle on distance control is that they have practiced hitting shots out of every conceivable bunker lie with a sand wedge, lob wedge, gap wedge, and pitching wedge. This is why this trio of great professionals and other superb bunker players can visualize shots so accurately. They are not merely imagining a certain shot; they are replaying one they have hit and studied over and over during practice.

When facing a shot like this in a bunker, a pitching wedge and a square clubface position at address can work wonders, provided you swing on an upright plane. José Maria Olazabal, Seve Ballesteros, and Sergio Garcia all learned this through hard practice.

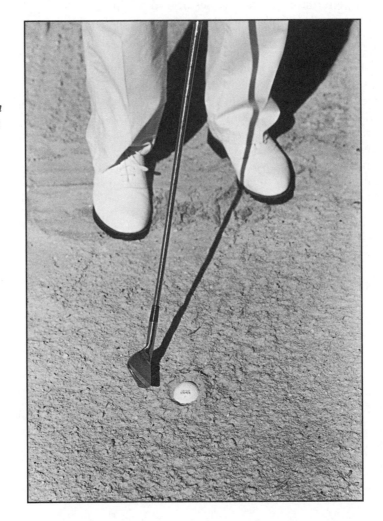

Take the time to vary your technique and tempo of your swing in practice, and you will be surprised how many new shots you learn. The more shots you have in your bag, the more equipped you will be to pick the right one to play for the distance at hand, and the more fun you will have at the *beach*.

Putting Perfection

Harry Vardon and Ben Hogan knew it. Sam Snead and Tiger Woods know it. And Tom Watson definitely knows it. Putting can drive you crazy. In Watson's case, he's gone from being the world's greatest putter to being one of the worst from inside three feet to being at least adequate again.

Putting can make you feel frazzled, especially when some putts fall short of the hole while others zip by it.

Regardless of how good a putter you are, you are going to have bad days. The secret is to limit those bad days by improving your distance-control days. You can really improve your technique by aiming at no hole for long periods of time. Just hit putts across the green so that you concentrate intently on speed, as Jack Burke taught me. Or, you can work on the following distance-control improvement drills.

25 x 25 Drill

Take your normal putting address, facing a hole about 25 feet away. Next, turn your head and stare at the hole. Maintain that position while hitting about 25 putts.

Just doing this drill once enhances your ability to judge the pace of a putt and improves your eye-hand coordination. When you return to your normal setup position, you tend to make the proper length and speed of stroke necessary for rolling the ball the perfect distance. It really gets you away from overcontrolling your putter.

Swing Lingo

When a player says he hit a shot in the **beach**, he is talking about the sand bunker.

Death Moves

On days when your distance control is off, don't immediately change your stroke or buy a new putter. You could just be having a bad day due to changes in metabolism or lack of feel in your hands. You're not alone. Even the world's greatest painters wake up some mornings not able to work their brush the way they want. One day, one week, or even one month does not make you a bad putter. It's your performance over a long period that counts. Don't let short-term poor putting destroy your good attitude.

Here, I'm practicing the 25 × 25 drill.

String Drill

Lay a 3-foot long string horizontally on an area of your local course's putting green. Now, move back 35 feet from the string and lay another 3-foot long piece of string down on the green. Next, putt six balls toward the string 35 feet away, trying to lag each one up as close to the string without hitting it, just as pool players do when lagging short of the cushion or as you did as a kid pitching pennies. When you have putted all six balls, hit them in the other direction. Go back and fourth six times, and you should see some big improvement in your distance control.

Plumb-Bob Green Reading

If your eyesight is fine but you still have problems with accuracy and distance control, practice the following plumb-bob drill before putting to several different holes on the putting green.

Stand directly behind the ball, with your shoulders parallel to the horizon. Hold your putter vertically, at arm's length in front of you, with only your right thumb and forefinger holding the very top end of the putter grip. Line up so the club shaft obscures the ball then close your non-dominant eye. If the shaft now appears to be to the left of the hole, the putt will break from left to right. If the shaft aligns to the right of the hole, the putt will break in the opposite direction. If the shaft appears to cover the hole, allow for no break.

Here, I'm practicing the plumb-bob method of assessing the break or curve in a green.

Bet You Didn't Know

The breaks in the greens at Royal Lytham are very subtle and difficult to read, while Augusta National features the fastest, most tricky sloping greens of any major championship course. Plumb bobbing the line can help you determine the break point on putts you are unsure of or have difficulty seeing with your normal sighting procedure.

If you find that this way of assessing the break helps you to read the line better and hit putts the correct distance, by all means use it. Two of the best putters of all time, left-hander Bob Charles and right-hander Ben Crenshaw, both use this system of determining the break in a green. And it pays off; their distance control on breaking putts is superb, as evidenced by Charles's British Open win at England's Royal Lytham Golf Club and Crenshaw's two victories in the Masters at Georgia's Augusta National Golf Club.

Charles and Crenshaw are not the only two tour professionals who plumb bob. In fact, many pros use this method to determine the correct break. They know to use every option available. The next time you begin to experience problems reading the greens, consider following their example.

The Least You Need to Know

➤ To become good at golf, you must know the average distance you hit pitch shots in varying conditions.

➤ If you expect to chip well consistently, you must be prepared to make subtle changes in your setup and swing.

➤ To hit sand shots on the money, you must know how the ball will react from different lies.

➤ The 25 × 25 putting drill will help your distance control.

Part 4

Dealing with Different Types of Trouble

The old expression, "When the going gets tough the tough get going," certainly applies to the essence of this part of the book.

When you finish reading the next three chapters on dealing with rough, rainy-day weather and grass bunkers, you will be a much more educated player. You will realize how seemingly unimportant elements of the setup, such as grip pressure, play a very critical role in shot making. You will also learn how to make allowances when hitting shots off a wet fairway or to a wet green. And, too, you will learn how to predict how the ball will fly and roll out of a particular grass bunker lie. Only then will you be able to pick the right club and play the right shot.

Rough and Ready

Hitting good touch shots out of rough with a lob wedge when the ball is sitting down slightly, moderately, or deeply is something every better golfer must learn to do. The problem is most club-level weekend players rarely practice these shots.

Because I first introduced you to the lob wedge back in Chapter 2, "How to Get Started," let me remind you that it usually features 60 degrees of loft. If you are a more advanced player and have not yet purchased one, you should because of its advantages over the sand wedge in certain course situations.

The added loft of the lob wedge can help you greatly, if and only if you practice with it. The lob wedge features less bounce than the sand wedge, so at the right time, it has major advantages. Its sharper flange cuts through thick rough more easily than the sand wedge does.

In making a case for the lob wedge, I don't want you to get the impression that it is your saving grace in all situations. Because of varying lies, different length carries over hazards guarding the green, and ever-changing hole positions, the lob wedge requires you to make some subtle technical adjustments when playing out of light or deep rough. I'll go over these, but before I do, I want to discuss a couple of other points involving grip pressure and swing tempo, relative to all the shots I will be discussing.

Grip Pressure

The pressure you grip the club with is one of the least talked about elements of the swing, yet it is one of the most important. Let me say right up front that it's absolutely wrong to think you can play all shots with medium grip pressure. Like most new golfers, you probably have heard this said by at least one of your playing partners or read about it in some golf magazine or book. No knowledgeable and certainly no top players believe in this theory. We realize that different short-game shots require different degrees of grip pressure.

As you have already learned that during play you have to make different length and different type swings to hit the ball solidly, softly, high, or low. In executing shots, grip pressure can run the range of superlight to superfirm. There are even times when you need to grip more firmly with the left hand but lightly with the right. For example, when playing a burning cut into a green from the rough, you must grip more firmly with the left hand to help hold the clubface open. To hit a *soft-cut*, you reduce grip pressure in both hands tremendously.

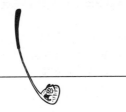

Swing Lingo

A **soft-cut** is a shot that flies gently with left to right spin, lands softly on the green, and spins to the right. This is an ideal shot to play from rough when the ball must fly over a bunker and stop quickly next to a hole that is positioned close behind it.

Obviously, in teaching you various shots, I will give you guidance on this grip element. However, it's up to you to practice on your own too. While hitting out of different type lies with different clubs, change your grip pressure to see how it effects the execution of the shot, plus the flight and roll of the ball. You notice a huge difference in how the golf ball reacts.

The two most important things for you to remember about gripping is: Light pressure allows you to program active hand and wrist action into your lob-wedge swing technique; and firm pressure programs dead hand action into your swing. This is important because when you grip correctly, you do not have to think about using or not using your hands and wrists. Instead, the swing operates essentially on automatic pilot, making it relatively easy for you to repeat good swings over and over.

Bet You Didn't Know

When Fred Couples plays a short lob-wedge shot out of fairly heavy rough, he grips the club so lightly to promote active hand and wrist action that his right hand sometimes comes off the club at impact. Look for this while watching him play this type of shot on television. While you're at it, watch Tiger Woods and Sergio Garcia. I've seen them let go more than once or twice as well. That's light grip pressure!

Swing Tempo

When you get into playing shots such as those discussed here, swing tempo becomes even more critical than, for example, when you play a standard pitch shot to the middle of the green. I like a brisk, firm stroke. Short shots out of rough require much more exactness, particularly when you are hitting over a hazard to a tight pin. When you are playing a standard pitching-wedge approach shot under normal conditions, say into a short par-four hole, you swing at a brisk speed, and the ball flies into the air and lands on the green with a lot of spin and control. Using the same tempo during a round, you can repeat 10 pitch shots off the fairways onto 10 greens and get nearly the same results. However, when playing shots from rough, the conditions involving lie, carry, and spin vary so much that, very often, you need to vary your swing tempo. Of course, feel is everything. You can swing superslow, fairly slow, at medium pace, moderately fast, or use a very high degree of acceleration. There are really no shortcuts to swinging at the right speed. All these speeds and degrees of feel are developed through practice. Still, there are general rules that can help.

Short Light-Rough Lob

Imagine that your ball is lying quite nicely in light rough with a cushion of grass under it, and you are approximately 10 yards from a green unguarded by bunkers. There are about 30 feet of green between the edge of the fringe closest to you and the hole. Just in case you don't know, this is what is considered a classic no-brainer short-game situation.

In setting up to play this shot, play the ball in the middle of a square with slightly open alignments, your hands level with the ball. The cushion underneath the ball

Death Moves

Even when you need to hack your ball out of very deep rough onto the fairway, you swing the lob wedge superfast. For best results, think balance, control, and maximizing acceleration. Trust me, you need a lot of speed to hit the lob wedge any distance out of the deep stuff.

will provide you with more effective loft at impact, so there really is no need to lay the clubface open. In other words, height is already available to you naturally. Because you do not need to play the ball well up in your stance, set your hands even with or perhaps just slightly ahead of the ball and hold the club with a moderate grip pressure. You have plenty of green to work with, so you can hit a shot that will land about 20 feet short of the hole and roll toward it. Put only slightly more weight on your left foot, as this will help stabilize your body.

The shot you are hitting is short, so there is no reason to make a very long swing with a lot of wrist action. The best players play this shot using a three-quarter-length action. In this case I would follow the example set by such short-game wizards as Sergio Garcia, who employ the short-swing action. You can afford to keep your hands out of the swing because of the close proximity of the hole. A fluid arm swing aided by some lower body action through the shot provides you with the acceleration to propel the ball to the hole.

If your ball lies quite cleanly in light rough, like this, with a cushion of grass under it, and there are no hazards in front of the green, there really is no need to lay the club face open.

When swinging down, push your right knee gently toward the target. Because the ball is in light rough, there is no need for you to pull the club down hard with your hands to dig the ball out. All you need to do is accelerate your arms into a short follow-through. There is no need to concentrate on making a long followthrough action here; although, for a higher, softer shot, this is recommended. The power generated by the swinging action of the arms is made slightly stronger by the right knee action. Also, the 60 degrees of loft and the cushioned lie will automatically help you hit the ball into the air. As for the degree of roll, this depends on all the factors that I've asked you to check. Those include the hardness of the green, wind direction, and speed of the green. And one more important factor that I have not mentioned is the type of ball you use. A hard cover, two-piece ball will fly higher and with less spin than a soft cover, multi-layered or wound ball.

Jim's Tips

When playing the short pitch from light rough, use your right knee as a focal point. Ken Venturi has taught players such as Tom Watson, Tom Weiskopf, and John Cook to use the right knee as an accelerator. You time your hands and your right knee to develop a consistent feel for any short shot pitch.

There is some flexibility in playing this shot. So, if you feel more comfortable adding a little wrist action into your action and making a slightly longer backswing, go right ahead.

Long High-Rough Lob

The ball is sitting down in heavy rough, 20 yards from the green, and you have to hit over a bunker to a tight pin position. What do you do?

As you can probably imagine, when just thinking logically about the lie and situation, it is necessary for you to change your swing technique dramatically in order to hit a good recovery shot. If you have guessed that you will need to accelerate the club much faster in the impact zone, you are right. Added speed is necessary for the club to plow through the grass behind the ball, slide underneath it, and keep the club head moving to your finish.

When setting up to play this shot, open your body and stance. This will enable you to swing the club freely, back slightly outside the target line, and then slightly across *the line* slightly in the impact zone with high acceleration. To program added height into the shot, play the ball off your left heel, set your hands behind the ball, and lay the clubface of your sand wedge open. If you own a lob wedge, keep the face square. Grip the club lightly enough to promote live hand and wrist action but firmly enough to allow the clubface to withstand the powerful forces acting on it at impact and guard against it being twisted into a closed position by the blades of tall grass.

185

If you confront this lie in a rough, and you must carry a bunker, lay the club face open.

Swing Lingo

In describing the backswing outside the target line and down across it through impact, golfers loosely refer to the target line as **the line;** thus, the phrases outside the line, across the line.

The chief shot-making goals on the downswing are to cut across the ball slightly and hit down and through it so that you can hit a very high shot that lands slightly to the left of the hole and spins toward it. Understand that when trying to swing the club across the target line and ball, you must not pull the club violently with your hands. Simply set up left.

When swinging down, use your lower body to shift. I would suggest a shuttle of the knees toward the target because this action has positive side effects. First, it enables you to swing the club with added speed while still maintaining a smooth rhythm. Second, it allows the upper body to rock back away from the target. In turn, this slight rocking action enables you to stay well behind the ball through impact, with your right shoulder dipping downward slightly. As a result, the club swings down into the grass behind the ball and then nicely under it. And because you stay back, you can throw the ball high into the air. In the hitting area, it's critical to use active hand action.

In hitting the long high-rough lob, notice how my knees work toward the target while my upper body leans back.

Gravitate to a High Position

There's one more thing to mention about playing the long, high-rough lob that is very critical. It's something that the top professionals do. They see themselves swinging into a high finish position before even setting up and then try to match that ideal position when it comes time to hit the ball. The image of a high finish position,

Death Moves

When playing a lob out of heavy rough to a tight pin, do not try to hit down into the grass on a sharp angle, because the club will dig and lose speed. Instead, think of slipping the club just under the ball and finishing all the way through with your eyes and belt buckle facing the target.

Jim's Tips

If your ball sits down deeply in coarse, dense Bermuda rough, swing the club twice as fast as you think you should. This is a lie that requires maximum acceleration of the arms, wrists, hands, and club to extract the ball. Remember that the ball will go shorter than you expect.

which is what you ultimately want to arrive at, helps you to accelerate the club through the high rough behind the ball and then down under it.

When All Else Fails

If the ball is sitting down so deeply in heavy rough that it's a struggle just to see it, that's your signal to just hit it back somewhere onto the manicured fairway, even if that means hitting the shot toward the tee. Get the ball strategically to a place that will best allow for a simple chip and putt.

Setup to make a steep backswing and to hit the ball sharply on the descent using an abrupt chopping action, play the ball just behind the midpoint in a narrow open stance, take a powerful grip, set your hands a couple of inches ahead of the ball, and put 70 percent of your weight on your left foot. This is one of those instances when you should hold the club very firmly with both hands so that you can better resist the forces of impact.

Swing the club back on a very steep angle. Leave the your weight on your left foot as you swing up to the top. Going down and through, feel your left arm and hand pull the club into the impact zone. This will help to prevent any violent twisting of the club.

You can also drive your legs toward the target on the downswing without getting out too far ahead of the ball. And if you find you have difficulty timing the downswing, follow the example set by PGA Tour player Steve Pate. He swings the club to the top, pauses, and then pulls it down hard into the grass behind the ball.

It's difficult to predict exactly how the ball will come out. If you do everything right and accelerate the club through impact, the ball will come out a little hot. Allow for this when picking a landing spot, or else you could finish up in deep rough on the other side of the fairway.

The Least You Need to Know

➤ Certain lob-wedge shots require you to grip more firmly.

➤ In some course situations, a slower swing tempo works best.

➤ If the ball sits on a cushion of grass, you will usually increase the effective loft of the clubface at impact and hit a higher shot automatically.

➤ In heavy rough, grip the club lightly enough to promote active hand action, but firmly enough to allow the clubface to withstand the force of impact.

➤ When facing an extremely bad lie in heavy rough, cut your losses and hit a shot safely back to the fairway.

Chapter 16

Rainy Day Golf

In This Chapter

➤ Packing a rain suit

➤ Two towels

➤ Staying smooth

➤ Making allowances for wet ground

➤ Keeping your cool in the rain

Don't believe what you hear about it never raining on a golf course. No matter where you live, you are going to play golf in bad weather. Even if you live in sunny Florida or California, you are going to wake up to rain or occasionally encounter it after you begin your round.

If you're dealt a rainy day, the most you can do is to be prepared, but that doesn't simply mean protecting your body with an umbrella and keeping your clubs dry. It means carrying other accessories. It also means making adjustments to your swing, shot-making game, and mindset that enable you to handle this frustrating course condition.

Rain Gear

To give yourself the best chance of beating the course in a stroke-play competition, or an opponent in a match-play event, such as a company tournament or club championship final, you must carry in your golf bag all the essential gear for helping you handle the rain.

A light drizzle is one thing, heavy rain is another. You can handle drizzle easily. However, if the rain is pelting down and your opponent is prepared but you are not, I think you know who is probably going to win the match. Every pro on the PGA, LPGA, and Senior PGA Tours realizes that being fully prepared in rainy weather is one of the secrets to playing winning golf. What's so great about being prepared is that it allows you to replace anxiety with confidence. When the rain is falling and you possess the "right stuff" mentally and physically, you're likely to still return a good score.

Suit Up

The rain jacket and pants suit is something you should never leave home without. Although you can find cold weather suits, rain suits are usually made of very thin and pliable material, called Gore-Tex, so they can be easily folded and stored in your bag. The typical rain suit is light, so it will not present a heart-strain problem if you prefer to carry your own bag rather than ride in a powered cart.

What's really special about the newer, top-of-the-line rain suits is that the material breathes. So if you're playing in rain, you can play in comfort. It wasn't so long ago when playing in a rain suit was torture. In fact, a player could sweat off as much as five pounds playing in one of the old hot suits.

Bet You Didn't Know

About 10 years ago, the typical rain suit was so noisy that, when a player wearing one moved just a little bit, it was easy for a fellow player to be distracted. The old suits used to make sort of a "swish–swish" sound. Today's rain gear is quiet and made of less cumbersome material. So if you're hitting a shot, say a pitching wedge from 75 yards out from the green, you feel free, not restricted.

Bring Your Umbrella

It's surprising how many golfers I see with no umbrella in the special slipcase of their golf bag. If there is a chance for rain, you never see a top professional without an umbrella, because they realize the importance of keeping the body and clubs dry. Golf umbrellas are much bigger than those umbrellas that we all usually carry when protecting ourselves from the rain. In fact, they are so big that they can protect you, your caddy if you have one, and your bag of clubs. Visit your local pro shop and speak to the head professional or to one of his or her assistants about buying a good golf umbrella. Umbrellas are available in many price ranges, with the most expensive ones featuring the logo of the particular manufacturer.

Extra Gloves

There are water-resistant golf gloves on the market that really give you a good grip on the club. Still, you should carry at least one extra glove with you, because even these gloves get somewhat slippery after a couple hours play.

If you're a new golfer who prefers to play with a thin calfskin leather glove, I suggest you bring at least three extra ones with you to carry you through a rainy day round. These gloves normally provide you with added feel for the club. However, this feel goes out the window real fast on a rainy day because the grip becomes slippery very quickly. To delay this negative effect, ask your pro to show you one of the new products that you can rub or spray on your glove to give it a supersticky feel.

Two Towels

When you play golf on a rainy day, you need two towels. You need one towel to clean the dirt and water off the clubface of each club, to prevent hitting flyer shots. Remember—a flyer is a shot that flies longer than normal because of grass, sand, dirt, or moisture between the ball and the clubface at impact. You need to carry a second towel as a backup for seriously rainy days. There are some new grips now available that resist water, so you may want to ask your local golf professional to show you selections of these. If you like, the pro or one of his or her assistants can change your grips for you at a minimal cost—something you really should do once or twice a year.

Jim's Tips

If you start the round in light rain, but the forecast is for heavier weather, tuck an additional dry towel in the side pocket of your bag. It's better to be safe than sorry, especially if you are playing in an important match.

Stay Smooth

Golfers press in the rain—meaning that they swing faster. I can't exactly explain this phenomenon. Maybe it's because they want to get the shot over with fast and get back under their umbrella or under the protection of their cart with a covered top. However, I do not want you to rush your pitches, chips, sand shots, or putts. If you are well equipped with a rain suit, you do not have to worry about catching pneumonia. Additionally, if you're wearing your all-weather glove and your rain suit, you can swing comfortably; maybe not as freely as you would on a sunny spring day, but you can still get the job done. Take your time, focus in, and play a smart golf shot.

Bet You Didn't Know

The typical PGA, LPGA, and Senior PGA Tour pro might be more meticulous about preparing to hit a shot when it's raining than when it's sunny. The pro goes through his or her normal pre-swing routine but usually makes at least one extra practice swing to get used to swinging in a rain suit and to swinging at a slightly slower tempo. The pro also makes sure to remove any loose blades of grass and drops of moisture from the clubface, in order to avoid hitting a flyer.

Shot-Making Allowances

A wet course presents you with new challenges pertaining to the lie and condition of the fairways, rough, greens, fringe grass, and sand. Let's talk about wet conditions that result from light rain falling before or during play. Let's imagine that rain has just fallen on the course that you are about to play, and you are confronted with some difficult situations you are not accustomed to dealing with.

Rainy Day Pitching

One of the biggest concerns on a rainy day is playing a pitch shot off wet turf. In these conditions, avoid playing the ball well back in your stance, swinging on a steep plane, and hitting down sharply. This is not the kind of lie that lends itself to going down after the ball. Instead, move the ball forward in your stance and pick it cleanly off the grass. This will produce a softer shot with less spin, but it is much safer in wet conditions.

Rainy Day Chipping

Believe it or not, chipping in wet conditions is almost always easier. The speed of the greens is slower, and there is less break to factor in. You can be more aggressive knowing that your ball will roll less near the hole. Realize, however, that when playing a running chip with a 6 or 7 iron, your normal airtime-to-roll-time ratios will change. You must land the ball farther into the green, simply because it will not roll as much.

On rainy days, avoid this open stance and very steep swing.

When chipping off wet ground, make a level stroke, making sure to keep the club low to the ground through impact.

Rainy Day Bunker Play

New golfers tend to get confused in wet sand, not knowing whether to hit closer behind the ball or further behind it. To have a clear understanding of this lie, you need to know that the club does not make as deep a cut in wet sand as it does in dry sand. However, this can be a good thing. Powdery sand is actually more difficult to play out of than wet sand. Because powdery sand offers less resistance, the sand wedge digs deeper into the sand. Consequently, the depth of your cut must be judged perfectly to hit a good recovery shot.

Reading what I just said, don't think that playing out of wet sand is free of any dangers. If you hit too close behind the ball, you could send it flying over the green. Also, if the sand is compact, the flange of the sand wedge could bounce off the sand into the top half of the ball. As a result, you will probably hit a low shot that hits the lip and falls back into the sand bunker or rockets far over the green, usually into a very bad place.

So, when playing a shot out of wet sand consider using the gap wedge or pitching wedge and aim about 2 inches behind the ball. Because these clubs have little bounce (flange), they will cut under the firm, compacted sand. You might also play it with a lob wedge as I described in Chapter 5, "Common Trouble Shots," for short shots.

If the sand is wet and compact, plan on hitting farther behind the ball.

197

Rainy Day Putting

When hitting long putts on relatively level greens that are wet, you should hit the ball more firmly. When putting on wet sloping greens, don't forget to allow for about half as much break as you would under dry conditions.

Employ a longer or firmer stroke when the greens are wet. Here, I rehearse that type of stroke.

Bet You Didn't Know

When putting long putts on wet greens, PGA Tour professional Greg Norman contacts higher up on the ball to impart overspin. This unique technique allows him to use the same stroke as he normally would for the distance at hand.

Think Like a Pro

To play golf well in rain, you must apply the old adage "walk, don't run." The pros follow this philosophy, taking more time to select the club, set up to the ball, and visualize the shot. They do something else too: They roll with the punches.

When playing in rain, there will be holes on which you hit a ball fat with a pitching wedge, chunk a chip, skull a sand shot, or leave a ball short on the putting green. This is to be expected, not because you are new at the game, but because playing in the rain is not easy even for the best players in the world.

I have noticed that professionals from other countries are particularly good on rainy days and perhaps a little better than professionals from the United States. The reason for this is that pros on the European PGA Tour visit many different countries and constantly play in worse conditions. They have gotten so accustomed to fickle weather that they just accept rain and patiently deal with it as best they can. On the other hand, pros in the U.S. generally play on courses built in ideal climates. You will have to play a few times in rain to learn just how to deal with these adverse conditions. But once you do, stick to it, no matter how hard it rains. One more thing: A good rain hat never hurt either.

Jim's Tips

If you hit a bad shot on a rainy day, because you swung too hard and lost your balance or because you lost your hold on the club's handle, move on and accept the challenge that the weather presents you. On your next shot, take the time necessary to prepare yourself. Once you get going the wrong way and give up in bad weather, it's definitely all over. There is almost no limit to how high your score can go.

The Least You Need to Know

➤ A rain suit and a golf umbrella can do wonders for your score on a rainy day.

➤ Bring more than one glove along with you, just in case it rains on the golf course.

➤ Practice every now and then in rainy conditions.

➤ Swing more smoothly in rain.

➤ Don't allow for as much break when putting on wet greens.

➤ If the club's handle slips in your hand because it's wet, and you hit a bad shot, accept this as part of the challenge of playing in rainy weather and confidently move on.

Chapter 17

Grass Bunkers

In This Chapter

➤ Reacting to grass bunker lies

➤ Deciding what club to play

➤ Setting up correctly

➤ Hitting on-target shots

➤ Having faith in your swing technique

Many of the courses being built today feature grass bunkers located as far away from a green as 90 yards or right up next to the putting surface, as is usually the case. This trend certainly became much more noticeable in 1982, when course architect Pete Dye designed the Tournament Players Club course in Ponte Vedra, Florida, which is the home of the PGA Tour and the annual site for the Tournament Players Championship (TPC).

Since the first TPC course opened, others have been built around the country by Dye and other architects in cities such as Hartford, Connecticut, and Scottsdale, Arizona. Regardless of who the architect is, this exciting feature has survived and offers a special challenge to golfers.

Grass bunkers are essentially bunkers with grass instead of sand. However, they are usually featured in clusters, with the terrain rolling up and up and down from one grass bunker to the next. Consequently, you can find yourself hitting a very short or fairly long shot, depending whether you are in a grass bunker located near the green or in one farther away from it. When landing in a grass bunker, you just never know how you are going to find your ball lying. It can be sitting perched up on grass or sitting down in it. You can face a level lie, uphill lie, or downhill lie. The ball can be above or below your feet. All these lies add a new dimension to the game and present you with shot situations that you must know how to handle to shoot a good score.

Bet You Didn't Know

To the right of the 18th green at the original TPC course in Ponte Vedra, Florida, there is a big cluster of grass bunkers. Because the Tour Players Championship is played here every year, all types of shots have been played by the world's greatest on national television. There have been numerous occasions when a top tour player has simply tried to put his ball in the center of the green—sometimes just playing to make a bogie.

Reaction Time

Before deciding what club to hit in a grass bunker, you must carefully study the lie. You must imagine yourself setting up in a manner that best enables you to hit a recovery shot out of the grass toward your target. Sometimes, as I said earlier, the ball will be sitting in a grass bunker farther out from the green, while other times it will be lying very near the putting surface. These two lies require different techniques, and the best way of getting a feel for the specific swing is to visualize it. Visualize yourself hitting the ball with a particular club, and see it fly and roll a certain distance in your mind's eye. If you are looking to stop the ball quickly from a grass bunker that is located near the green, you will often need to swing the club on an out-to-in path, in order to impart soft-landing cut spin on the ball. When looking to advance the ball to the green from a grass bunker farther out in the fairway, you will need to cock your wrists early, swing on a steep plane, and make sharp contact with the ball on the descent.

Here, I'm reacting to the ball sitting down deeply in grass, and thinking about what shot to play.

Club Selection

The club you select is a personal choice, but the better player will always choose the simplest shot. The selection process should be related to the visualization process. In short, the club you visualize yourself playing and hitting a good shot with should be your choice. However, there are other factors to consider when selecting a club for playing a grass bunker:

➤ As a general rule, when hitting off an uphill lie, take *one more club* to allow for the effective loft of the club increasing at impact.

➤ When playing a shot off a downhill lie, take *one less club* to allow for the effective loft of the club decreasing at impact, because you'll be hitting more sharply downward and playing the ball farther back in your stance.

Since the ball is on a sharp downhill slope, I'll probably decide to use the more lofted lob wedge (rather than the gap wedge, pitching wedge, or sand wedge) to hit this relatively short pitch over trouble.

➤ If the ball is above your feet, it will tend to turn from right to left in the air and roll more upon landing. Therefore, consider taking one less club.

➤ If the ball is below your feet in a grass bunker, the ball will tend to turn from left to right in the air, causing you to lose some distance. Therefore, consider taking one more club.

Once you select the club, take at least two practice swings to be sure that it feels right in your hand. Next, make an even stronger effort to visualize a good shot. This will help you employ the right swing for the shot you face.

Setting Up for Success

The most important things to remember about taking your address when preparing to hit any shot from a grass bunker involve aim. The following are the basic rules that apply:

➤ When playing a straight shot off a level lie, aim the clubface directly at the hole or perpendicular to it.

➤ When intending to impart left-to-right cut spin on the ball, aim the clubface to a target right of the target line and aim your body well left.

Swing Lingo

In golfer's language, **one more club** refers to a less lofted or stronger club—for instance, a sand wedge rather than a lob wedge. The term **one less club** refers to a more lofted or weaker club—for instance, a lob wedge instead of a sand wedge. Now you know why golf is sometimes called "a game of opposites."

➤ When playing a shot off a side-hill lie with the ball above your feet, allow for the ball drawing or hooking by aiming the clubface at a target right of the green. The more you think the ball will curve, the farther right you should aim.

➤ When playing a shot off a side-hill lie with the ball below your feet, allow for the ball turning right by aiming the clubface and your body at a target left of the green.

➤ When playing a shot off a steep downhill lie, allow for the ball flying off to the right by aiming slightly left of your final target.

➤ When playing a shot off a steep uphill lie, allow for the ball flying left of target by aiming slightly right of your final target.

Targeting Shots

When hitting a long, blind pitch shot (the green is not visible) from the pit of a grass bunker, a good way to promote accuracy is to aim at an interim target in front of the ball. This preswing alignment aid will give you a strong feeling of security that you are aiming the clubface correctly. The same philosophy holds true if you are playing a short shot to a green that's visible and aiming at a landing spot on its surface.

Here, I aim the club at a light area of grass about 3 feet in front of the ball, since this helps promote an accurate shot.

Bet You Didn't Know

Throughout his illustrious career, Jack Nicklaus has depended on picking an interim target between the ball and the hole. This spot-alignment preswing process has helped him hit accurate clutch shots in major championships. This same disciplined procedure can help you become a more accurate shot maker. I suggest you pick out some object such as a discolored piece of grass somewhere along your intended target line. Nicklaus always picks something about one foot in front of his ball. However, other players are successful using an intermediate target up to 20 yards ahead.

Trusting Your Technique

What's left to do now is to make the transition from the setup to the swing and see how all of the elements come together in playing various key shots from a grass bunker.

After setting up, your chief concern is to trust your technique so that you hit shots confidently. This is precisely why you must always plant a positive thought or image in your mind prior to swinging. Confidence, trust, and commitment will often determine the success of any golf shot. Once you decide on a shot, go with it.

Positive images come from learning about lies and being able to predict pretty much what the outcome of a shot is going to be. What makes the game so darn challenging and sometimes frustrating is that the longer you play it, the more you realize that there are so many combinations of elements involved in hitting a shot that improvisation is necessary. There is a big difference between playing a shot off an uphill lie with the ball sitting down and the pin 10 feet away from you, and playing a shot from a clean uphill lie with plenty of green to work with. The former takes much more finesse.

Death Moves

Do not let a negative thought cross your mind before you hit a shot out of a grass bunker. According to Dr. Fran Pirozzolo, one of the top sports psychologists, good shots result from positive thoughts. If the last thought before you hit any ball out of grass bunker is negative ("Don't hit this downhill chip fat"), odds are that you will mishit the shot. Replace any negative thoughts with a final positive image. Your last thought prior to hitting a shot will be your strongest thought.

Jim's Tips

The most important link to putting the percentages in your favor is playing a shot you know you can play—one you have practiced often. Too many players fall into the trap of gambling out of grass bunkers. Go with your strengths. Play shots that you trust. Do not play shots you have never practiced unless, of course, you do not care about your score.

It is this complexity of varying elements that makes it necessary for you to devote some time to practicing hitting shots from grass bunkers. The only way to be able to react more quickly to a lie during play, to know the right club, and to know what the ball is going to do in the air and on the ground is to learn from experience. That means taking the time to try out different clubs in grass bunkers. It also means varying the lies and the distance of the shots. Preparation through dedicated practice is the only true avenue to becoming a proficient grass bunker player. Only after hitting hundreds of practice shots will you ever understand how to put the percentages in your favor and build the groundwork for creating positive images in your head. It is also a big reason we include some short game work in every school we give and why our short game schools have been so successful.

Your most ambitious goal of becoming a short-game wizard can be accomplished if you use a step-by-step approach, working from the elements of the setup, to the backswing, to the downswing. You will be surprised at how quickly you learn how to just look at a lie and know what club to choose and how to swing, particularly if you remind yourself of one simple formula: Body control plus club control equals ball flight and roll control.

It's essential that you know which setup positions tend to produce which paths and planes of swing. For example, standing very open with your hands well ahead of the ball causes the club to swing on an out-to-in path. To control the clubface while swinging on such a path and to get the ball to spin from left to right (instead of being pulled left of target), it is important to hold more firmly with the left hand. The ball lands softly, and then spins toward the right, ideally to the hole. Once you learn to control your body (by taking the proper setup) and the path of the club, you will control the flight and roll of the ball. All this knowledge takes time to learn, but before you can become a good grass bunker player, it must be stored in your mind.

The road to improvement will not be free of bumps. Finesse shots take time to learn and groove. Even the best grass bunker players had to put their time in. The secret is learning how to play these shots so that they are in your bag for life.

Downhill Grass Bunker Shot

Set your body perpendicular to the slope, play the ball closer to your higher foot, put more weight on your front foot, swing the club on a steeper plane using a free-hinging action of the wrists, and chase the ball down the slope through impact.

Generally, the steeper and more grassy the slope, and the more you need to loft the ball into the air, the more you should open the face of the club. Do not expect to perfect this shot right away, because it is one of the toughest to play.

When looking to advance the ball farther down the fairway or onto the green, open the clubface less and hit closer to the ball.

Uphill Grass Bunker Shot

Set your body perpendicular to the slope, play the ball closer to your higher foot, set more weight on your back foot, and swing the club up and back normally with its arc following the slope. If the ball is sitting down, use active wrist action on the backswing, then hit down more sharply using a hit-and-hold action. When swinging this way, sort of stab the grass behind the ball and stop. This action causes the club to pop the ball high into the air.

Above-the-Feet Grass Bunker Shot

Because the ball sits in the grass well above you, grip down on the club and stand more erect than normal. To help you maintain your balance and stay in control of the club, set yourself into the slope by putting slightly more weight on your toes. Naturally, this lie makes you swing on a slightly flatter plane and will help you clip the ball cleanly off the grass. What you do not want to do is swing the club up and down on a steep plane, because you stand a good chance of jamming the club head into the ground at impact and hitting the ball heavy.

Jim's Tips

When playing a very short uphill shot, use one less-lofted club and swing up the slope through impact. However, it is not necessary to hinge your wrists. An all-arm action will work just fine. The ball will tend to rise quickly and land softly, so allow for this when picking out an aiming spot on the green. Try aiming at the top of the flagstick rather than at the hole.

Swing Lingo

If you are instructed by a teacher to **maintain your level,** or you hear another player use this phrase, it simply means to stay in the posture first established at address and throughout the entire swinging action. Do not rise up or dip down.

Ball-Below-Feet Grass Bunker Shot

Because the ball sits in the grass below you, grip the club at the very top of the handle, and bend slightly more at the ball-and-socket joints of the hips and knees. To help you maintain good balance, and stay in control of the club, set yourself into the slope by putting slightly more weight on your heels. It is imperative that while making a backswing, you keep your head still, because any swaying action will probably lead to a mishit shot. Try to *maintain your level* during the downswing, so that you encourage solid contact. If you stand up as the club enters the hitting area, you will either hit the top half of the ball or miss it completely.

When playing very short shots with the ball below your feet, it is okay to grip down on the club and close the face at address to compensate for the ball turning slightly right in the air. As for the length of the swing, the same rule that applies to other short grass bunker shots applies here. You must practice to figure out what length and speed of stroke works best for each shot you face.

The Least You Need to Know

➤ Before picking a club to play any shot out of a grass bunker, you must see the shot played perfectly in your mind's eye.

➤ One standard setup position will not work for playing all kinds of shots out of grass bunkers.

➤ When playing shots off hilly lies in grass bunkers, sometimes you must aim away from the target.

➤ Once you are comfortable with your setup, trust the technique you have worked so hard to perfect in practice.

Part 5

Rounding Out Your Short Game

This is where I get into the fine points of the short game, namely how to swing with good tempo, timing, and rhythm, and how to spin the ball when hitting a pitch, chip, bunker shot, or putt. Spinning the ball isn't for amusement, as you will quickly learn. You impart spin on the ball for a specific purpose, relative to the shot-making situation.

To round out your game, it is essential that you also learn how to practice before the round, after the round, and at home, working on much more than just perfecting a synchronized, well-timed swing and putting spin on the ball. You must also do such things as read the right magazines and watch the right videos.

Chapter 18

You Got That Swing

In This Chapter

➤ Swinging at a speed that works for you

➤ Good timing tips

➤ The right rhythm

➤ Developing touch with your short-game clubs

In the same way that a car engine can not run without pistons, a battery, spark plugs, and a radiator, a golf swing can not run right without the elements of tempo, timing, and rhythm. Furthermore, in the same way that you have to get a feel for driving your car, you need to get a feel for swinging the club certain ways to hit pitch shots, chips, bunkers shots, and putts. That's where the other important element of touch (also called feel) enters the picture.

Many golfers, particularly high-handicap players, have no idea what these four terms—tempo, timing, rhythm, and touch—mean. Pro golfers, on the other hand, encapsulate these terms, realizing that without these keys they could never propel the ball to a specified target. In this chapter, I teach you how to tie together these four critical keys to swinging efficiently and hitting pitch shots, chip shots, bunker shots, and putts the correct distance.

Tempo

The next time you watch the pros playing golf, either live at a tournament site or on television, note the differences in the speed or *tempo* of their swings. Some players such as David Duval, Tiger Woods, and Sergio Garcia play a lot of small shots with a quick tempo. Other players, such as Ernie Els, Phil Mickelson, and Fred Couples look like they are swinging in slow motion when hitting a shot, especially on high lob shots.

Personality and Tempo

I mentioned in Chapter 8, "Power-Swing Drills," that the speed of the swing often can be related to the player's personality. For example, Ernie Els is a very laid-back type of person, while Sergio Garcia is high-strung. Respectively, each is a perfect match between personality and tempo of the swing.

In citing these examples, I am not suggesting that if your personality matches Els's or Garcia's you should swing like them. That's because I know that this paralleling does not always run true to form. For example, David Duval, a fast and powerful hitter of the ball, is quite a laid-back individual. Still, you need to take the relationship between personality and swing speed into consideration when you enter a slump. You may be making the mistake many amateurs do in copying their favorite PGA Tour player's swing. Just because you are a quiet Ernie Els–type person doesn't necessarily mean that you should swing like he does. Yet there is an excellent chance that he would be the perfect model for you to copy.

In the case of recreational golfers, when their pitching swing tempo goes off, bad things happen. Either they make a very deliberate backswing, which is too slow, and slash at the ball on the downswing, or they swing back very fast. Pros make a smooth takeaway action and gradually build speed as the club gets closer to impact. This steady acceleration is what you want. You must always strive to hit through the ball and avoid a deceleration, or a quitting, at the bottom of the arc.

Swing Lingo

Your **tempo** is the pace at which you swing the golf club.

Jim's Tips

Generally speaking, if your full pitch shots fall off to the right, either in a gentle fade pattern or a more severe slice pattern, your tempo is too slow. If your shots turn to the left, in either a draw or hook pattern, the tempo of your swing is too fast.

Determining Your Tempo

One of the best ways to determine the pitching tempo or speed of swing is to do the following drill:

Hit a full pitch shot using a medium-speed tempo, and then continue hitting more shots, each time swinging faster. As soon as your shots start drifting off course, gear back to the speed that promotes accurate shots and carries the ball a consistent distance.

When practicing full pitch shots, start swinging at medium speed and watch the flight of the ball closely.

Bet You Didn't Know

Bob Tway, a professional known for his smooth tempo, swung at the perfect speed when hitting a ball out of the bunker on the final hole of the 1986 PGA championship. Tway holed the shot to beat the Australian superstar Greg Norman. Facing a very difficult short bunker shot at the famed Inverness Golf Club in Toledo, Ohio, Tway used perfect tempo pace and technique to rob Greg and win his first major championship.

Once you determine you ideal speed for a full pitch, try hitting to a green from 75 yards out from the green, then 60, 50, 40, 30, 20, and finally 10 yards out, until you figure out what speed and length of swing works best for the distance at hand—a tremendous exercise.

With regard to assessing whether you are swinging too fast or slow on chip shots and putts, look where the ball finishes in relationship to the position of the hole. Short and right indicates that your tempo is too slow, long and left usually means you're swinging too fast.

On bunker shots, too deep a cut of sand is the best indication that your are swinging too fast, while simply leaving the ball well short of the hole tells you that you lack acceleration through the ball.

To remedy your tempo problems, follow the basics presented in Chapter 3, "Building Blocks," then practice them until you see consistent results in your distance control.

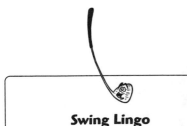

Swing Lingo

Timing is the synchronization of the club, arms, and body to execute the desired shot.

Timing

Have you ever unexpectedly run into an old friend who you needed to see for some reason? It usually goes something like, "Hey, perfect timing, I was just thinking about you and was going to call." Well, if this sounds familiar, you will have an easier time understanding *timing* in the golf swing—that somewhat indescribable element that allows you to tie together the end of the backswing with the start of the downswing, such that one motion flows into the other.

When timing the pitching swing, there is a definite distinction in speed. In the case of a bunker shot, you set the club quite deliberately and then splash the sand. In the case of a chip, you swing back quietly with little or sometimes no wrist hinge, depending on the shot, and then make crisp contact with the ball slightly on the descent. When putting, the stroke works more like a pendulum—tick on the backswing, tock on the downswing.

You hit good pitch shots, chip shots, bunker shots, and putts when various parts of your body come into the swinging action precisely at the right time. You hit bad shots when you disrupt timing by doing such things as twisting your hips briskly on the backswing or making an *over-the-top* move on the downswing. These death moves or faults in your technique play havoc with your timing.

Turning the hips dramatically on the backswing will throw off the timing of your pitching swing.

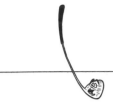

Swing Lingo

Coming **over the top** is a faulty move that is marked by the right shoulder jutting outward at the start of the downswing. This death move causes you to swing over your plane line and deliver the club across the target line through impact. This move is more prevalent on full shots and almost always leads to some kind of bad shot, usually a pull.

Jim's Tips

PGA Tour player Ernie Els is a great model for timing your swing. On chips he leaves maybe just a light scuff in the grass. He merely flows through the ball in a bunker. Even on long putts, his putter flows as quietly as a slow-moving mountain stream, due to perfect timing.

Getting accustomed to timing the swing correctly is much like getting used to working the gas pedal of a car. Just as traffic situations vary and require different degrees of acceleration, so do golf shots. Whether you are hitting a pitch, chip, bunker shot, or putt, you have to know when to swing faster and when to swing slower. Just as you have to time the pressing down and releasing action of the gas pedal, you have to learn to time the golf swing. When hitting golf shots, the secret is moving the parts of your body at the right time and at the right speed, and this, my friends, can only be learned through practice. Practice teaches you what parts of your body come into play for a particular shot and when the parts must start and stop working, such that you time the action perfectly.

Rhythm

If you already play golf, you know that when you hit a good shot the entire action feels tension-free and totally effortless. That's when you've got the feel of a true swing, ladies and gentlemen, and *rhythm* is at work. When the backswing flows fluidly into the downswing and the entire action becomes one uninterrupted motion, you feel like you are floating through the impact area, and everything is working on automatic pilot. The secret is to repeat this seemingly effortless motion so that you can consistently hit good shots.

Believe it or not, the eyes are very involved in your ability to swing rhythmically. If you don't believe this is true, go to a pro tournament and watch the pros hitting pitch shots, chips, bunker shots, and putts and see if their smooth rhythm doesn't rub off on you. It will, I guarantee.

The next best thing to watching the pros play and seeing how they swing smoothly and time both the backswing and downswing action is to visualize a good swing you made and repeat it when you hit a particular short-game shot. This visualization process helps you to feel the swing in your golf muscles and to transmit that feeling to the golf club through your hands and arms.

Bet You Didn't Know

Jack Nicklaus has always said that he never hit the ball until he first visualized the perfect swing and shot play in his head. Nicklaus calls this preswing visualization process "going to the movies." It's highly recommended that you preview all of your shots before you hit them.

Whether you're pitching, chipping, hitting a bunker shot, or a putting, it is not enough to have each individual part of the swing down pat. Unless the action operates at the right tempo, is timed properly, and flows together rhythmically, it is not going to consistently produce good shots. Frankly, the difference between just a swing and a well-timed rhythmic swing is as drastic as the difference between the architectural plans for a house and the finished house. This is why you must spend time on the practice tee, just as Tiger Woods does, and Nicklaus and Hogan did before him, working out any kinks in your technique that prevent the movement of the body and the movement of the club to work in sync.

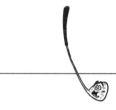

Swing Lingo

You can have a quicker or slower swing tempo and still have great **rhythm.** When your swing flows at a pleasing pace, it repeats for you like the beat of a song.

Most golfers need to learn each vital swing movement involved in pitching, chipping, bunker play, and putting one at a time. Once you have each one down, you hit balls until you feel the isolated movements flowing together.

One of the actions of the swing that can encourage good tempo, timing, and rhythm is the waggle. The waggle is a personalized trigger used by the player to start the swing, and it relaxes the hands, arms, and body. Players depend on waggle actions because they allow for a smooth transition from the static address position to the swing itself. And, thus, spark a nicely flowing chain action that makes the swing run virtually on automatic pilot. Each individual short-game shot may call for its own special waggle because it previews the swing action for the particular shot.

Jim's Tips

A waggle is good way to trigger any short-game shot. On pitches, Gary Player kicks his right knee inward to start the swing. Tom Watson presses his hands just slightly toward the target. I like my students to make rehearsal practice swings and then move directly to the ball and execute the shot. The practice swing and the waggle flow together.

Swing Lingo

Touch is synonymous with feel or the ability of the golfer to hit shots close to the hole. That's what a golf commentator, such as Ken Venturi, means when he or she says that a particular player has good touch on the greens. The sensation of touch or feel involves the eyes that see the target.

Whatever it takes for you to realize the importance of tempo, timing, and rhythm, and the incredibly important role they play in the swing is what really counts. So go to work and start piecing together your pitching, chipping, bunker play, and putting swings.

Touch

Short-game shots make up the most important scoring aspects of the game. You can hit two of your greatest shots to the front of the green of a long par four, but without the ability to chip the ball close to the hole and sink the putt, those two power shots do not complete the mission. What matters most is shooting the lowest possible score on each hole. And in order to do that you have to be able to master pitch shots, chips, bunker shots, and putts.

As important as tempo, timing, and rhythm are to the swing, good *touch* is what enables you to hit the ball close to the hole when pitching, chipping, and hitting bunker shots. It's also what enables you to knock the ball into the cup once you are on the green.

Touch is not necessarily a gift you are born with, but rather can be a learned skill. If you practice the drills I gave you for pitching, chipping, bunker play, and putting, presented in Chapter 3, you may believe what I am saying is true. I say that because I know that these drills probably helped you develop good techniques and, more important, distance control. I am now giving you four additional drills, one for each short-game department.

Cord Drill: For Pitching Touch

Being able to hit the ball on varying trajectories is one of the most critical links to distance control and good touch, particularly on short pitches. The cord drill helps you develop this skill.

Purchase a brightly colored, 20-foot length of thin cord and two 7-foot high metal poles from a hardware store. Stick the poles one foot into the ground, and tie the cord from one pole to the other, at a height of two feet above the ground. Stand 20 feet away and try to hit 10 pitch shots over the cord, being sure not to look up before impact. Move the cord from a height of two feet to a height of four feet, and hit 10 shots. Finally, slide the cord right to the top, at six feet, and hit another 10 shots. Vary the distance you stand from the rope and use all of your wedges. Soon you will begin to develop trajectory control, which is crucial to mastering your shots around the green.

Toss Drill: For Chipping Touch

Empty out a bag or bucket of golf balls onto the fringe of the chipping green at your local course or practice range. Pick out four holes on the green, at varying distances from you. Estimate where you must land the ball for it to trickle to the hole.

Death Moves

Do not freeze your head and eyes to the ground when hitting pitch shots. This invariably causes tension and a robotic swing. Tight hands, arms, shoulders, and neck muscles absolutely kill you in golf.

Next, toss five balls to the closest hole you picked out, concentrating on the strength and arm action you used to propel the ball to your landing spot. Now, try to incorporate the same tempo, timing, and rhythm of your tossing action to your swinging action. You'll be surprised at how good your distance control becomes as you toss the balls to the different holes you aimed for, and then hit real chip shots to them.

Tossing a ball toward a hole can help you determine the right swing speed and thus improve your distance control on chip shots.

Right-Hand Drill: For Bunker-Play Touch

There is no doubt that golf is a two-sided game, some golfers favoring the left side and others the right. Nowhere is this truer than in bunkers, because the right-sided hand action that's necessary for hitting a good recovery shot is essentially a throwing action (assuming you are a right-handed golfer). To familiarize yourself with this action, practice hitting shots with only your right hand.

Draw two lines in the sand approximately 10 inches apart. Swing back and through, releasing the club into the sand about four inches behind the ball. Be sure to splash the sand and continue all the way to the finish. Make numerous practice swings attempting to land your club head in the area between the two lines. When you can consistently swing down into the sand between the two lines, begin to hit with one hand.

To improve your bunker play touch, practice hitting shots with only your right hand.

Bet You Didn't Know

Hitting practice bunker shots with only his right hand on the club was a trademark of the famous Claude Harmon. It's no wonder he won the 1948 Masters tournament at Augusta National, a course where bunkers are aplenty.

Claude became one of the best bunker players of all time and passed this drill on to his many top assistants, his four sons, and luckily me. One of his sons, Butch, is the coach for Tiger Woods. You can see much of Claude's teaching in Tiger's bunker game.

Grip-Pressure Drill: For Putting Touch

Some great putters grip firmly with both hands, while others grip lightly. Other great putters grip more firmly with the left hand to help them guide the putter back and through, and more lightly with the right to help them control distance and give them added touch. As you know, to a certain degree, grip pressure is a personal thing. So, work on the following drill to find the pressure that enables you to enhance your touch.

Pick out three targets on the putting green, one 10 feet away, one 20 feet away, and one 30 feet away. Next, hit 10 putts to each hole, using a two-handed light grip, a two-handed firm grip. Determine which pressure provides you with the best feel, and then try it on the course. You can vary the pressure for different types of putts and continually upgrade the feel you need to putt your best.

The Least You Need to Know

➤ The tempo of your swing should increase through all of your golf shots.

➤ Rhythm synchronizes the movement of the body with the movement of the club.

➤ Working on drills teaches you to develop touch on pitch shots, chips, bunker shots, and putts.

Spin It!

It's now time to get a bit more sophisticated and advanced at hitting pitch shots, chips, bunker shots, and putts. As a complete novice or veteran high-handicap player looking to improve, you probably are somewhat envious of the way professionals hit short-game shots. In fact, on more than one occasion while practicing you have probably wondered why you can't hit at least two or three difficult shots during a round the way they do. You are not alone.

Recreational golfers who have seen the pros play are especially intrigued when they see a pro hit a wedge shot past the hole, then spin it backwards toward the cup. They think it is neat the way they do that. Well, it may look like fun, but to a PGA Tour pro it is only part of his or her job. If the pro spins the ball it is not for amusement. Imparting spin on the ball is part of a calculated plan of attack and, of course, it is a result of proper shot execution. The goal is to hit a particular short-game shot close to the hole, and the professional does whatever it takes to accomplish that goal.

Swing Lingo

When a pin is tucked behind a cavernous bunker or water hazard, it is sometimes referred to as a **sucker pin.** Incidentally, pin placement is synonymous with hole placement, and flagstick is synonymous with pin. A sucker pin often entices golfers to take big risks for big rewards.

Jim's Tips

When playing a backspin pitch, you must swing the club up quickly and then bring it down into the ball at a sharp angle of attack. In order to promote the desired swing plane, take a page out of the lesson book of John Jacobs, the famous golf instructor from England. He advises students to swing the arms on a more upright plane than the shoulders.

What golfers such as you don't realize is that the pros don't depend only on backspin. Depending on the situation and the shot they are playing with a particular club, they depend on imparting other types of spin on the ball, namely hook spin, slice spin, and overspin. Learning how to put spin on the ball is what today's lesson is all about.

Backspin

In some pitching situations, being able to impart backspin on the ball is a huge advantage. The most common situation where this applies is when you face a full pitch shot from the fairway to a green featuring water or a deep bunker in front of it, and the pin is located about close in from the edge of the hazard.

Inexperienced players often try to hit a miracle shot to the *sucker pin* that lands just over water or a bunker guarding the front of the green, while the pro plays the percentages. Often, the pro does not flirt with hazards, but chooses instead to hit the ball beyond the sucker pin and spin it back to the hole. This is why the pro usually scores birdie or par on a hole, while the amateur who attempts shots that he or she cannot play. Learn from this mistake, and follow the example set by the pros on the PGA, LPGA, and Senior PGA Tours.

If you watch the pros play a backspin shot, you will often notice that a thin strip of turf is cut out of the ground and flies into the air. This piece of turf is called a divot. To clear up any confusion about how to take a divot—and believe me many golfers are confused—understand that when a good golfer takes a divot he or she hits the ball first, not the grass. This is an absolute and basic fundamental that cannot be repeated too often: first the ball and then the divot, or as we like to say at our schools, first the little ball (golf) and then the big ball (earth).

I often have seen club-level players trying to impart backspin on the ball by purposely driving the club underneath the ball. They actually believe the club strikes the ground first. When you do this, you may dig up the turf all right, but your divot will be thick rather than thin, and the ball will land well short of the target. This is called "hitting a fat shot."

Three secrets to hitting a pitch with backspin are setting up slightly open, playing the ball back in the stance, and swinging the club up on a steep plane.

The technique for playing a backspin pitch from the fairway is actually quite simple. Set up slightly open with the ball well back in your stance and your hands ahead of it. Put about 60 to 70 percent of your weight on your front foot. Swing the club up on a steep angle, letting the wrists hinge freely. Swing the club down at a steep angle with the hands leading, so that you hit down sharply and stop at impact, using a firm hit-and-hold action, meaning that your lead wrist does not break down. The ball is virtually squeezed or pinched off the turf. The divot starts beyond where the ball was, and the ball sizzles with backspin. You must never try to lift the ball into the air, which causes the leading wrist to unhinge and breakdown.

The shot I just described will fly quite high, so if hitting into the wind, play the burning wedge—a good shot to play if the pin is also situated in the back of the green.

Burning Wedge Shot

This is a shot I learned while playing in Texas during my college days stint at the University of Houston. It is the perfect shot from the 75- to 100-yard range. It is also an exciting shot because the ball flies on a low trajectory, takes two or three small hops, checks, and holds as if it were on a string.

The setup for the burning wedge shot is very similar to that for the backspin shot, except that its purpose is to fly lower and advance prior to checking up. Stand a little closer to the ball, grip more firmly with the left hand, and stand a little more open so that, if anything, you take the club back outside the target line, Lee Trevino style. Some players take the club straight back and then up, and that's okay.

Grip more firmly with the left hand when playing the burning wedge shot.

As with the backspin shot, you have to guard against swinging the club back on a flat plane. When swinging back, keep the takeaway narrow (this is tremendously important), the hands close to the body, and the action compact. Do not swing beyond the three-quarter point.

On the downswing, the club should loop or drop to the inside on a sharp angle of attack. When bringing the club down, keep the image of squeezing the ball clearly in mind and retain firm pressure in your left hand. These keys will encourage you to hit down very sharply with the hands leading and the back of the left wrist flat at impact.

Analyzing Divots

Ideally, your divots should point straight at the target or just slightly to the left when making the proper golf swing. They should also be shallow in nature. These factors tell you that you made a good swing and that your clubs suit you.

Death Moves

When hitting the burning wedge shot, don't try to arrive in a high finish position or you will hit the ball extra high. Striving for a short, low finish will encourage you to squeeze the ball with the clubface at impact and send it flying on a trajectory that allows it to burn or bore through the wind.

Shallow divots that point straight at the target are a sign of a well-played pitch.

229

Deep divots indicate that your swing is too steep. Mere scrapes in the turf or no divot indicate that you either stood up before impact, causing you to lose the flex in your knees, or there was some breakdown of the lead wrist. A divot that points considerably to the left of the target tells you that you came over the shot, or that you are swinging the club on an exaggerated out-to-in path. A divot that points considerably right of the target tells you that the lie of your club is too upright, or that you are swinging the club along an exaggerated in-to-out path.

Hook Spin

When the ball sits in the front fringe and the hole is situated in the very back of the green, say 50 feet away, you should probably play a 6, 7, or 8 iron, because these clubs will roll the ball nicely to the hole. However, this is a shot that is not all that easy to hit if the ball lies in very tightly mowed fringe grass. Therefore, unless you practice this very shot, you are likely to feel uncomfortable playing it on the course. In fact, you can skull the ball if you are not careful.

If you feel uneasy playing a 6 or 7 iron, play a more lofted nine iron and impart some hook spin on the ball. This enables you to make the same speed stroke with a club featuring more loft and still reach the hole. You apply hook spin by closing the face at address and by turning the toe of the club head down through impact. This simply means that you impart hook spin to the ball just as you would in ping-pong or tennis. Your hands roll the face of the implement.

Bet You Didn't Know

Gary Player has played the hook-spin chip throughout his entire career, because he prefers playing a more lofted club from the tight fringe. Gary has won championships all around the world thanks to a fantastic short game. The late Bobby Locke, his fellow South African, preferred to chip in the same way. And he was certainly one of the best ever. The hook-spin chip will roll beautifully and is actually quite easy to learn and execute.

The most important technical keys for playing this shot are ...

➤ Playing the ball in the middle of slightly closed stance.

➤ Lightening your grip pressure for an easier release.

➤ Gently releasing your right forearm and hand over your left forearm and hand through impact so that the toe of the club leads its heel.

The shot you produce will turn slightly from right to left and roll all the way to the hole situated at the back of green.

Slice Spin

There is one bunker method that, although different than the ones I have mentioned thus far in this book, is quite popular when the ball sits in the sand close to the lip and the pin is close behind the lip facing you. It involves slicing the ball out of the sand.

To play the slice-spin bunker shot, set up with your feet, knees, hips, and shoulders aiming well left of the pin. Open the clubface so that it points to the right of your *bodyline* and virtually straight at the hole. The higher the lip and the higher and softer you want to hit the shot, the more you should lay the clubface of your sand wedge open. Your bodyline represents the line on which you swing the club. Play the ball forward in your stance with your hands slightly behind it. The ball will start slightly left of the hole and then spin quite dramatically toward the hole when it hits the green.

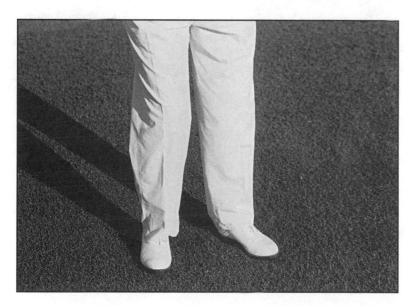

This exaggerated open stance is necessary for playing a slice-spin shot out or a bunker (or off grass). When you take such a stance, an imaginary line running across the toes of both feet points well left of target.

Swing Lingo

A reference to **bodyline** simply means imaginary lines running through your feet, knees, hips, and shoulders. If you are taking an open stance, your bodyline aims left of target. When you set up closed, your bodyline aims right.

Death Moves

I normally encourage a little wrist action on long putts or on slow greens. Using a small amount of wrist action gives you a tremendous amount of feel and touch. Locking your wrists and arms and depending solely on a shoulder stroke is a killer for long distance putting. It is very awkward and unnatural, which usually leads to mishitting the putt.

Take the club up on an upright plane, swinging slightly outside your bodyline and allowing your wrists to hinge and arms to be superrelaxed.

Swing down along your bodyline, retaining pressure in your left hand to discourage yourself from releasing your right hand and forearm over your left. You should feel that the right hand is working under your left through impact, and directing the club head's bounce to hit an area of sand from one to four inches behind the ball, depending on the depth and texture. For less sand, you must stroke nearer to the ball because the flange of your sand wedge will tend to bounce off the firmer base.

The shot you produce will start left of the flag, perhaps turn slightly to the right in the air, land, and side spin hard toward the hole.

The Overspin Pop

One of the greatest shots you can hit from around the green is also one of the easiest. It is played from almost any type of rough just around the green. You will be surprised how many times you have an opportunity to play the overspin putter pop shot.

Many golf courses have substantial rough around and near the green. When your shot just misses to the right or left or rolls over the green, the ball will nestle into these nasty little rough patches. This leaves one of the more difficult shots you find anywhere. Often I see the amateur fail to even get the shot onto the green. It's the type of shot that can easily be chunked. That's because your swing is so short and easy that the rough grabs your club head and kills the speed and, of course, the shot. It is a terrible feeling to stick the club and see your ball move about one foot, yet it happens all the time.

My friend and excellent short-game teacher Bill Davis of Jupiter Hills Club showed this shot to me years ago, and I've taught it successfully ever since. Here's how you hit the shot:

1. Do not use any type of wedge; use your putter instead.

2. Grip far down on your putter—all the way down to the steel—so that your hands are only 30 inches or so from the putter head.

3. Place the ball super far back in your stance. In fact, the ball must be positioned behind your back foot.

4. Now place your hands will forward, which totally delofts your putter face. It also means your putter shaft is leaning tremendously forward and toward the target.

5. Your stroke is nothing more than a simple up and down chop. (If your putter is center shafted or has a large hosel, aim to hit the toe end of the putter face.)

6. The shot will not take much effort or speed. Stay dead steady and contact the back topside of the ball. Your golf ball will pop up and jump over the rough in front. With topspin, it will roll easily to the hole.

Jim's Tips

Once you familiarize yourself with the unique club-to-ball contact involved in imparting overspin on the ball, you will have to put it in practice. You need time to get a feel for how fast the ball comes off the putter face, or the metal wood, and how far the ball rolls when you stroke it.

On the forward stroke, keep your left wrist flat, with the back of it staying square to the putter face. Don't let your hands lag behind the putter head or get well ahead of it. To encourage a smooth and level stroke through the ball, keep your hands level with the putter through impact, or maybe just a tad ahead of it.

As for the most critical secret to success, concentrate on hitting the equator of the ball at impact. This is what enables you to impart the perfect roll.

The Least You Need to Know

➤ When pitching over a bunker or a water hazard to a tight pin, strike down on the ball to impart backspin.

➤ When the pin is cut on the back of the green and a strong wind is in your face, the burning wedge is the perfect play.

➤ The divots you take out of the fairway turf should be shallow.

➤ If you want to hit a long chip with a club that features more loft, impart hook spin on the ball to help you reach the hole.

➤ Hitting a slice spin shot can aid you greatly when you need to loft the ball over a high bunker lip and stop it quickly next to a tight pin.

➤ Use the idiot-proof topspin chip/putt to save stokes from the rough around the green.

Chapter 20

Pre-Round
Practice

In This Chapter

➤ Loosening up your muscles

➤ Getting a feel for clubface-to-ball contact

➤ Practicing your chips

➤ A trip to the beach

➤ Sprucing up your putting touch

Pre-round practice is to golf what sparring is to boxing. Each competitor works in solitude to collect his or her thoughts, gather a sense of confidence and will, warm up the muscles, and get a feel for what he or she is doing.

In the case of golf, I have to look at the top pros and analyze their pre-round habits because it always amazes me how disciplined they are to go through a special routine week after week before a round. Take Jack Nicklaus, for example. He is still recognized as the greatest golfer in the world, yet that doesn't matter to him. As you might suspect of a world class athlete, Nicklaus prepares himself for the round in a calculated way, knowing where to begin and where to end his session.

To become good at golf and give yourself the best possible chance of performing well on the course, you must not rush to the course, grab a bucket of balls from the pro, smash out a few drives, and then run to the tee. Instead, give yourself time to loosen up your muscles, get a feel for hitting the ball different distances with your most vital short-game clubs, and assess how the ball is flying. If, say, you notice that your average pitching wedge flies 10 yards farther than normal, then you must make allowances for this today when playing the course. Let's take a look at what else you should do to prepare for scoring better each time you go out.

Getting Loose

To get loose, begin your pre-round practice session by doing the following:

1. Touch your toes to stretch your hamstring and back muscles.
2. Roll or rotate your head to stretch your neck muscles.
3. Intertwine your fingers and push your hands (palms out) and arms away from your chest to stretch your arm, shoulder, and hand muscles.
4. Slide a pitching wedge through your elbows so that its shaft lies across the middle of your back and stretch by rotating your body away from the target and then toward it.

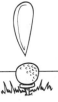

Bet You Didn't Know

The top tour pros usually devote about 30 minutes to working on their pitching, chipping, bunker play, and putting games before playing a competitive round of golf.

Even if you stretched at home, I think you should stretch before the round, particularly if you had to drive a distance to the course. Driving a car can stiffen up your muscles and, if the traffic is bad, you can develop tension too. So it's best to give yourself time to feel good before you play, by going through a steady routine that begins with the simple, quick exercises I have already described or some of your own. I suggest refraining from swinging a heavily weighted driver or three clubs at a time right from the get-go, because these two ways of loosening up can cause you to strain a muscle. I would rather you adopt the Chinese philosophy—every journey starts with one small step—and go easy.

Wedge Work

Assuming that you carry at least a pitching wedge, gap wedge, and a sand wedge in your bag, practice hitting warm-up shots with each club. Start by hitting about

10 shots with the most lofted wedge and then hit the same number of shots with the other two. Begin by aiming at a short target, say at a practice green approximately 20 yards away. Once you go through your first run of 10 balls with each club, hit about the same number of shots to a medium-range target, at about 40 yards out, and then one farther away, say at 60 yards. This wedge work may not seem so exciting, but it is very beneficial to your game. It enables you to further warm up the muscles, makes you start concentrating on a target, provides you with the feel of club to ball, and gives you good feedback on the condition of your swing and ability to control distance.

Start your pre-round practice session by hitting about 10 short shots with your most lofted wedge.

It's too late to revamp your swing just before a round. So if your shots are curving off in one steady direction, take just a little time to see if your ball position or alignment is off. Hopefully, making one or two minor corrections will solve your problems. Hit some longer shots and then come back to the wedge that was giving you a problem.

Jim's Tips

In hitting shots to a target green with various wedges, watch the flight of the ball carefully, and mentally note how far the ball carries. Plugging this data into your head will help you swing at the proper speed and make the right length action out on the course.

Chipping Practice

No matter how great a day you are having, there will be times when you have to hit a chip close to the hole to save par or bogie. To prepare for these times, practice hitting various length chip shots with those clubs you prefer to play from the fringe grass. Try not to practice the basic shot off a clean lie only. Vary the situations. Hit a short chip from a clean lie in the fringe one time, and hit a long chip from a more difficult lie another. If possible, hit downhill chips and uphill chips with a variety of clubs and techniques too. Also, practice hitting shots out of rough if that's what your course features. The whole idea is to simulate the course experience in practice.

When practicing your chip shots, do some experimenting with soft- and hard-covered balls. On fast running greens, the softer ball will perform better. If the course you are going to play has slow greens, you may want to go with a hard-covered ball. Because golf is a game of inches, it pays to experiment and try to find something that serves to your advantage.

Bet You Didn't Know

Pros, such as former U.S. Open winners Ray Floyd and Hale Irwin, try hard to rehearse the short-game playing situation in practice. When practicing a shot, say a chip, they imagine themselves on a particular hole of the course they are about to compete on, facing a particular length chip out of a certain lie. This kind of discipline prepares them for the round, both mentally and physically.

Don't just practice hitting chip shots off good lies. Hit the ball off hardpan like this so you are fully prepared.

Balls of different design perform very differently from each other. On short shots, hard cover balls will jump higher into the air than the softer pro-type balls. However, they will feel much harder, and they will not spin nearly as much. The harder ball will also travel farther on a putt than the same stroke made with a soft-cover ball.

On the Beach

Bunker sand is another part of the game that is neglected by many amateurs because they are often too busy smacking tee shots on the range rather than working on their short game. During a round of 18 holes, you can bet that you will hit a few shots into bunkers guarding the green. The player who can save par from the sand is the one who will probably win a match against an opponent or turn in the lowest score in a head-to-head stroke play game.

One thing that makes sand play so tricky is that the sand in bunkers varies from course to course and sometimes even on the same golf course. Therefore, when you visit a course for the first time, spend some time hitting long and short bunker shots if it has a practice area. That way, you can determine whether or not you will have to hit closer or farther behind the ball on the course, or maybe even use a sand wedge with a different bounce. A sand wedge that features less bounce works better in firm sand, while one with more bounce works best in softer sand.

Recovery techniques also change if the sand is wet from an overnight rain or when you face a plugged lie, partially-plugged lie, or "fried-egg" lie, as described in Chapter 5, "Common Trouble Shots." So be sure you also practice these shots before the round. Hard sand means that your shots will come out faster and farther but usually with more spin.

Before play, smart golfers practice hitting bunker shots out of bad lies.

In starting your practice bunker-play sessions, hit about three shots without aiming at a target. Simply get a feel for the ball thumping the sand and the ball being splashed out over the lip. Then play some shots to different locations. Spend 15 minutes on short bunker shots, 15 minutes on medium-length shots, 15 minutes on long bunker shots, and 15 minutes on buried shots. This will work wonders for organizing your practice time.

Pre-Round Putting Practice

Here we go. Now we are talking about what is arguably the most important club in the bag. I'm a big believer in a structured ritual prior to playing a round of golf. Certainly there will be occasions when you will be pressed for time and will go di-rectly to the first tee. However, it at all possible it is to your advantage to take the time to hit long and short putts before the round, as well as left-to-right and right-to-left breaking putts, so that you get a feel for your stroke and the speed of the greens.

Green speeds vary from course to course and often from day to day at your home track. Usually, the condition and speed of the practice putting green matches that of the greens on the course, so it is a good idea to spend some time putting around it. Rather than hitting three balls to each of the holes set out on a practice putting green, use one ball, because this simulates the course situation and intensifies your concentration. Use one ball for about 10 minutes and focus mainly on getting the proper pace and distance. Then use 10 additional minutes to practice short putts of about three feet. It is a great idea to putt at a tee or pencil stuck in the ground. When you get out onto the golf course, the hole looks the size of a manhole cover.

Bet You Didn't Know

When the pros practice before a competitive round, you often see them rolling putts across both a level part of the putting surface and up and down slopes. They might not even aim at a hole because they know that judging speed is more vital than judging line. They also spend time practicing short putts, usually in the 3- to 5-foot range, because they know they will face these type putts to save par on the course. So will you, so pre-pare like a pro.

When practicing putts, work hard on the basic movements I taught you for setting up and stroking the ball. Also, pay particular attention to the roll of the ball. See if it tends to drift right or left, falls short, or rolls by the cup, and then make minor adjustments to your address or length and speed of stroke to correct any problem.

Be sure to work on the basics of putting before you play a round, particularly those involving the address position—in this case, for long putts.

To groove two vital movements of the stroke, one on the backstroke and one on the forward stroke, work on the following two drills. I encourage students at the Jim McLean golf schools to practice these drills for the simple reason that the drills teach the students to segregate the movements of the left side from the right side. These same drills enable you to feel exactly the role the left hand and wrist play, or if you choose the opposite, the role the right hand and arm play. I believe it is an excellent idea to focus your attention on one side of the body or the other. (Most people do better concentrating on one side and not two.)

Left-Hand-Only Putts

The left hand and wrist are very important to good putting. The left hand must remain quite firm and the left wrist flat for the putter to be guided on the correct path. On short putts, that path is straight back and straight through. On long putts, the putter will swing back inside the ball-hole line, return to a square position at impact with the back of the left wrist lining up with the putter face, and finally back slightly on an inside path in the follow-through.

Holding the putter in just your left hand and stroking long and short putts will give you a good feel for this guiding force in the stroke and help you to develop a sense of security in your left hand and wrist. Practice in 10-minute blocks. After a few sessions, you will develop an excellent feel for how the left wrist remains solid and firm. Then when you put both hands on the club during and actual round of golf, focus solely on that left feel.

Right-Hand-Only Putts

When you putt, the right side can also provide the force with which to propel the ball to the hole. Some great putters, such as Jack Nicklaus, feel like they push the putter through with their right hand, while others feel the right elbow works the putter. Still others feel that the right hand and arm work together as one unit, as I do. The fact is, the right hand and arm can easily be the final point of your putting system.

Hitting putts with only your right hand on the club helps you make a very natural stroke. Practice hitting both long and short putts so that you get a feel for using different degrees of force to hit the ball to the hole.

Jim's Tips

When working on the left-hand-only drill, hit some putts with your glove on and some with your glove off. The majority of right-handed pros take their left-hand glove off when they putt. However, you may feel that leaving it on provides you with more personal feel. Either way is okay.

The Least You Need to Know

➤ It's critical that you loosen up before a round, because flexible muscles allow you to play good-short game shots, particularly long pitches.

➤ Pre-round practice with the wedges you ordinarily carry in your bag prepares you to be target-oriented on the course and helps you to make the right length and speed of swing, relative to the distance of the shot.

➤ Hitting long and short chip shots from different lies with your favorite clubs helps you to prepare for the conditions you will be confronted with on the course.

➤ Practicing various types of bunker shots helps you to get used to the texture of the sand and to judge how far to hit behind the ball from short and long distances.

➤ Hitting just a few putts with only your left hand on the club or a few with just your right hand can be excellent drills to condition your stroke.

Post-Round Practice

During the 1940s and 1950s, Ben Hogan would generally practice hard after every round of tournament golf. No matter how poorly or well he played during competition, you could be sure he would return to the practice area, always looking to improve.

He might spend an hour working out any subtle problems in his technique. Nothing was too small a problem for Hogan. For example, if he felt he was putting the tiniest bit of added pressure on one of his fingers, he would practice taking his grip over and over until he got this right. He was known to stay on the practice tee until sundown.

What many of even the keenest golf fans don't realize is how diligently Hogan practiced the short game, because he knew the value of keeping his pitching, chipping, sand play, and putting games in shape. More importantly, if Hogan believed he had a problem with one of these departments, he didn't want it to hang around. He sat down and tried to figure out what was wrong with his short game technique and then went over to the practice area to work it out. So should you.

Armchair Analysis

The pros know their own games very well. The reason they do is because they have hit thousands and thousands of practice balls and spent thousands of hours thinking about what they do when they pitch, chip, hit bunker shots, and putt. To become a good short-game player and remain one, it is not enough to know the various techniques physically. You must also have a clear intellectual understanding of the ins and outs involved in playing these shots so that when things don't go exactly right on the course, you can fix them during practice after the round.

Bet You Didn't Know

Ben Hogan often sat in a chair on the clubhouse terrace after a round, quietly smoking a cigarette and analyzing his game. When Hogan retired to a quiet spot, you knew he was not happy with something. And frequently that something involved the short game. As angry and frustrated as Hogan was at the time, he was smart enough to know it was best to think about what was wrong with his technique before rushing to hit practice shots and compounding a problem.

I highly recommend Hogan's method of post-round armchair analysis because it enables you to track a problem sensibly and eventually pinpoint it. Of course, I can't tell you what went through Hogan's head when conducting his post-round analysis, but based on what I have learned from other top tour professionals and figured out myself, I'm sure he started his sessions by checking the basics of grip, stance, aim, and alignment.

Setup Checks

One mistake the average golfer makes is to blame his swing or clubs for bad shots. Often, neither is the culprit. Where the player makes his or her mistake is setting up the wrong way to hit a pitch, chip, sand shot, or putt.

The best players in the game constantly check their address positions. In fact, when Jack Nicklaus's teacher Jack Grout was alive, Nicklaus used to try to get together with him once a month to have him check his setup. The reason is that Nicklaus and every other top-notch golfer knows that you can have the most natural and technically sound pitching, chipping, bunker play, and putting swings in the world, but if you fail to do some basic things correctly, such as hold the club with the right degree of pressure or stand the right way, the ball will not hit its intended target. So be sure to take the certain basic fundamentals of the address very seriously.

Feeling the Pressure

At different points in this book, I have stressed the importance of the right grip pressure for you. I have also made it clear that, depending on the shot you are playing and your own personal feel, you should hold the club with a grip pressure somewhere between superlight and superfirm. However, you never want to hold the club so lightly that you lose control of it, and so tightly that you lose feel for the club head. All the same, you must realize that sometimes you need a firm grip to deaden hand action, while other times you need a light grip to liven up hand action.

One of the reasons it is so important for you to practice all the various short-game shots is so that you can determine what grip pressure works the best. It is also essential that, once you find the right pressure, you make a note of this technical point both mentally and physically so that you can refer to it and fix a problem if one crops up.

During your post-round practice session, hit off-beat shots, such as this pitch off a ball-below-feet lie. Determine which grip pressure works best.

Jim's Tips

When practicing, experiment with different degrees of grip pressure. Seve Ballesteros used to do this as a boy and, as a result, taught himself new ways to play pitches, chips, bunker shots, and putts. Once you find the grip pressure and shot that works best, write it down in a little notebook that can fit in your back pocket. Make this your new reference book.

Often, if you really know your game, you can trace a fault in grip pressure just by looking at how the ball is reacting in the air and on the ground. For example, if your pitch shots are flying too low, you can bet you are squeezing the club's handle much too firmly. Frankly though, sometimes no matter how well you know your short game you will be confused. Granted, the notes you made previously will help you get back to form, but not without checking out other areas of your setup and hitting practice shots.

Taking a Stance

The way you stand to the ball is crucial. During a round, the left or right foot can slip into a position that is different from its usual position. However, this minor change to the setup is enough to cause problems in a particular area of your short game. For example, maybe you let your right foot turn outward when playing a standard full pitch shot from the fairway, instead of setting it down perpendicular to the target line. This small change in the position of your right foot is enough to cause your hips to turn too far on the backswing and play havoc with your pitching game.

Although you may feel most comfortable playing short game shots from a slightly open stance because the position gives you a clear picture of the target and provides you with a sense of freedom during the downswing, be cautious not to exaggerate this popular starting position. If you drop your left foot back too far from the target line, you tend to pull your pitch shots, chips, and putts and make too deep a cut in the sand on bunker shots.

Your lesson: Don't take the stance for granted. Make sure you check this element of your setup at the start of your post-round practice session, long before you start ripping your swing apart.

Aim and Alignment Checks

If your distance control is good during play, but your pitches, chips, bunker shots, and putts are failing to head toward the target, your body or clubface alignments are off.

I admit that it is very easy to be off in both of these areas and not notice that something is wrong. So check your alignments carefully during your post-round practice sessions. All the clubface or body has to do is aim a tiny bit too far left or right and you experience directional problems. Remember to lay down clubs to create a small practice station that will easily show poor alignments.

Hitting shots from different positions, such as these putts, will encourage you to concentrate harder on getting your body and clubface alignments correct.

Getting Back in the Swing

It may well be that your setup positions for hitting various short-game shots checks out fine. If that's the case, there is a good chance you are doing something wrong during the actual swing that's causing problems with your shots. You could be jerking the club too far to the inside in the takeaway or letting your right shoulder jut outward during the *change of direction*. Your swing tempo could be too fast, or your swing could be too short or long.

The most important thing for you to do when playing golf is to build up a personal database. In other words, when you see a certain off-target flight pattern or an overly low or high trajectory, you should know your tendencies. Usually the fault can be traced to one or two swing errors. Once you are on to the short game error, you can fix it during your post-round practice, most likely by using the fixes I provided you with in Chapter 9, "Fixing Faults."

Swing Lingo

You may get paired with a low–handicap golfer who is up on technical language, so be prepared. If he or she says you are making an error on the **change of direction,** the reference is to your downswing. Don't worry about the fancy lingo—just keep this observation in mind when trying to solve your shot problem during your post-round practice.

Something else that is vitally important is taking the time to listen to your body, both on the course and during practice. Know the role your shoulders, arms, hands, wrists, hips, knees, and feet play during a particular short-game swing, and know what these movements feel like. Subtle or not so subtle, you must learn the proper sensations in order to swing correctly and fluidly. And when you don't swing correctly and fluidly, know these sensations so that you can regain that good feeling by working out the kinks in your pitching, chipping, bunker play, or putting games during post-round practice. Obviously, when you can't get it together you should seek professional advice. Otherwise, the problem can continue indefinitely or even get worse.

If you don't appreciate what I mean, imagine that you are lost in a major city. Possessing a map helps you find your way, just as knowing the different feel of an individual movement or movements helps you find that lost swinging action.

Jim's Tips

When going to the practice ground to fix a problem, learn to feel the corrective action. If, say, you were making too short a swing on the course when hitting the standard pitch swing, feel your wrists hinge and your arms relax. Keeping tabs on body actions enables you to catch a fault and to fix it immediately once it sneaks into your technique.

I get frustrated when I hear golfers talking so much about the technical aspects of hitting a short-game shot that they forget the importance of feel and the vital role it plays in enabling them to repeat a good pitching swing, chipping stroke, bunker play swing, or putting stroke. I can't stress the importance of learning to feel each body part's job description during the swing. The reason I have encouraged you to groove the most critical actions involved in the various departments of the short game, via drills, is because I believe that by isolating each one, you are more apt to concentrate on feeling it.

When you feel a good swing movement, you then have an easier chance to repeat. Take, for example, writing your name for the first time. If you practice writing each letter individually and are very conscious to feel the movement of the pen, you find it much easier to write your full name using a flowing motion. The same is true about the swings involved in the short game. If, after the round, you practice the individual motions that are faulty, you are able to make them more quickly become part of an integrated uninterrupted flowing motion when you go back out on the course.

Seek Professional Help

Remember that when your short game goes sour and you can't figure out what you are doing wrong no matter hard you try, ask your pro to take a look at the swing you are experiencing problems with and see whether he or she can spot the fault fairly quickly. Allow the teacher time to analyze your faulty short-game swing or stroke more carefully and do some videotaping if necessary.

Even I take lessons. Here, fellow teacher Deborah Donninger is coaching me on where to land a shot with a particular chipping club. Having her point at a spot helps me more clearly visualize the shot.

By watching yourself pitch, chip, hit bunker shots, or putt on videotape, you learn a lot about the technical aspects of your setup and swing. Some of the things you do both good and bad, will surprise you. The idea is to acknowledge those errors and take on the challenge of trying to fix them after the round.

Bet You Didn't Know

Of all the professionals on the PGA Tour, Tom Kite may still be one of the hardest workers. If he senses a problem in his short game and I'm around, he will ask me what I see. After I tell him, he will report faithfully to the practice area and try to fix the problem. The good thing about Tom is that, once he gets the swing right, he hits numerous balls to establish the correct muscle memory.

Most professionals will provide you with drills to fix your problem. Drills are particularly good to work on because they can help you alleviate a chink in your armor before the next round begins. The other advantage is that drills go directly to the source of your problem without you're having to think about the entire swing.

Let's take an example. Say that you are failing to hit good wedge shots because your left wrist is breaking down before impact and your right hand is taking over the downswing. Here's a drill that will help you fix your problem without getting hung up on technique:

1. Stand at a right angle to a wall so that your left shoulder blade is perpendicular to it.

2. Spread your feet apart and position them as you would normally to hit a standard pitching wedge shot.

3. Let your left arm and hand hang down naturally and put your right hand and arm behind your back.

4. Swing back to the top, using no club.

5. Swing down very slowly, trying to press the back of your left hand into the wall, and freeze this position for a few seconds.

6. After working on this drill 10 times in a row and freezing the position for five seconds each time, hit some practice shots. You'll see that your problem of the right hand taking over is fixed and your shots fly on target.

A solid teaching professional can save you a lot of time and aggravation when you're struggling with your game. If you can't book a lesson with the head pro of your local club, ask for his or her recommendation. Many apprentices are very well versed nowadays on the elements of technique, owing largely to the fine job the PGA of America has done conducting seminars and providing instructional information.

The Least You Need to Know

➤ Sitting back in an easy chair at the club and analyzing your short game after a round is a good way to pinpoint faults in your pitching, chipping, bunker play, and putting techniques and to prepare a plan to correct them during your post-round practice.

➤ When trying to track a problem in your short-game technique, start by checking your grip pressure, stance, the alignment of the clubface, and all your body alignments.

➤ When replacing an incorrect swinging motion with a correct motion, it's important that you feel the action. That way, you will be better able to catch a fault in your technique right away and fix it fast.

➤ If a problem in your short-game technique is too subtle to detect, ask the head professional or teaching professional of your country club to give you a lesson—ideally videotaping the shots that are giving you trouble.

At-Home Practice

There are certain types of individuals who, no matter how hard they try, still cannot give a speech in front of an audience. They get so nervous that their hands sweat, they shake, and eventually freeze. The only way to overcome this is to get back in and try again. Often, professional advice helps greatly.

I find that the same human qualities relate to golf. Some players prefer private lessons above group lessons, because they get nervous swinging in front of people. At the McLean Golf Schools, we try to make our students comfortable, but we know schools have many advantages. One huge advantage to working in small groups is that you learn you can hit short-game shots in front of a group. With improved technique in the physical and mental aspects, students gain confidence. The group setting then provides power, and when they face a similar shot during a real round, they do it. But we also offer them instructions on what they can do to improve in and around the privacy of their homes.

Let me be very clear that I have no problem with someone learning at home. In fact, that is one of the reasons I dreamed up the idea to write *Golf School* (Doubleday, 1999), one of my recent books that brings my school curriculum into every golfer's living room.

In this chapter, I am presenting ways for you to work on your game at home. I have my own short game station at my home, as do many other pros, including Greg Norman. Often, tour players would rather pitch, chip, hit bunker shots, and putt than do yard work. Wouldn't you, especially if it this practice helped you shave strokes off your score and enjoy the game more?

Building a Practice Area

At my house, I have a small bunker, various tees set out at different distances, the farthest 75 yards from a practice green that I can pitch and chip to, and hit putts on. The main difference between my practice green and Greg Norman's is that mine is far less expensive and easier to maintain because it is made out of artificial turf rather than real grass. It features padding underneath it, so I can hit pitches and chips to it and have the ball react much like it would on a green you hit to on a golf course. These artificial greens will become more popular. They make practicing at home both fun and very productive.

Bet You Didn't Know

Behind Greg Norman's home in Hobe Sound, Florida, there is an area of fairway that runs between rows of tall royal palms, a green to chip to and putt on, and a practice bunker. This is, of course, the ideal situation. With his hectic schedule, Greg can still find some time during a day to hit at least a few short-game shots and, therefore, remain sharp.

Having a practice station in your own backyard is great because any time you have some spare time, you can practice your short game, alone or with your family and friends. By hitting shots and learning what the ball does in the air and on the ground, you will be able to develop superb eye-hand coordination and distance control, equipping you for play on your local course. Holding contests to see who hits the ball the closest to one of the holes on the putting green, on pitch shots, chips, bunker shots, and putts, can really turn you into a master short-game player. Of course you also can see who shoots the lowest score on the putting green or use any of the many putting drills. All this competition allows you to get used to playing under pressure so that you perform better in a medal play or match play competition at your local course or on another course.

A backyard practice station, inclusive of a bunker, will turn you into a better short-game player.

My suggestion is that you look in the yellow pages or talk to your local golf professional for some guidance, as to what companies build these at-home facilities. The company that built my artificial green with surrounding thicker turf serving as fringe was Synthetic Turf International (561-744-5555). A short game station will add a new dimension to your family life and help you improve your short game while having fun.

Backyard Practice

Those of you that do not have the money or the space available to build such a sophisticated practice area can still work on your short game if you just have a little area of grass in your backyard or even some space in the garage where you can throw down a mat and pitch into a net. Simply hit chips and short pitches with a variety of clubs. This will at least improve your feel, length, and speed of your swing. Also, vary the position of the clubface when hitting these shots. See what happens when you open the clubface more, or shut it down slightly, by playing the ball well back in your stance with your hands ahead.

Something else you can do when practicing pitch and chip shots is to aim at targets, such as paper cups or little baskets, set out at different distances.

Indoor Practice

If you live in an apartment complex that does not feature a practice putting green, the best thing you can do is practice the old-fashioned way. Simply place some golf balls down on your living-room carpet and putt the ball into the openings of water glasses set out at difference distance. Alternatively, putt to chair legs, pretending that you need to hole the putt to win a big match. This type of practice is less exciting but it works, as the pros prove. They practice in their hotel rooms all of the time.

Keeping Good Records

The simple fact that you purchased this book indicates that you are probably a goal-setting individual who wants to improve his or her short game. If that's the case, I want you to understand that reaching your goal to become better at pitching, chipping, bunker play, and putting requires you to do some homework. Before you can practice at home, you must determine what your shot-making tendencies are.

Because it's extremely difficult to assess the quality of your short game by just looking over your last few scores or going by your overall handicap, you have to track it yourself. In the same way that you keep receipts and organize your records for meals, entertainment, travel expenses, and so on for your tax accountant, you must keep records that reflect how you played short-game shots on the course. Then at the end of the week, month, or year, you can look back and see what you are doing well and not so well. Obviously, you should correct problems in your game at the range or hitting shots in your backyard using the tips I give you in your leisure time at home.

Death Moves

If you practice putting on carpet, be sure the carpet is quite thin and fast running so that it simulates the course experience. Don't practice on a shag or deep thatch rug because it will encourage you to make your stroke too hard and long.

The next time you play, start a new system of scoring. Keep a record of such things as how many full pitches miss the green on the left side or right side, how many fall short of the hole or fly beyond it. Keep records of how many times you get up and down from the fringe and bunkers. Also, note how many of your chip shots finish left, right, short, or long of the hole. Also, record how many putts you take per round, and count the number of times you hit putts short, left, right, or by the hole during the round. This may sound cumbersome, but if you simply record these figures in a small memo pad, it's not so difficult, particularly if you use code markings to identify your shots. For example, say on the first hole you hit your first putt long, left your second putt short, and knocked your third putt in the hole, record it in the book as follows:

Hole # 1: LFP (for long first putt); SSP (for short second putt); HTP (for holed third putt)

At-home putting practice, on a thin carpet, will help you simulate the course experience.

You can dream up whatever system of tracking your putting game you like. The main thing is that you look for trends in your errors.

To help you relearn a specific swing or to fix a specific fault, work on the full array of drills I have presented in this book, particularly those appearing in Chapter 3, "Building Blocks," and Chapter 9, "Fixing Faults," because they were specifically designed to help you improve your pitching, chipping, bunker play, and putting skills. Also refer to the various tips I presented in Chapter 14, "Distance Control," because they deal with ways to control your distance. Rereading this material and applying it during your at-home practice sessions will enable you to alleviate problems you have hitting pitches, chips, bunker shots, or putts short or long of the hole.

Talking to Friends

The words from a Beatles song, "I get by with a little help from my friends," really apply here. If you have a friend or a family member who boasts a low handicap, try talking to him or her about your short-game problems. Most good golfers are very enthusiastic about the game of golf and are only too happy to help. Be sure, however, to choose someone with excellent skills (you can tell by the look of the player's various techniques).

If you choose a golfer with an unorthodox, personalized style, you could end up taking a backward step instead of a forward step. His or her style of pitching, chipping, bunker play, and putting may work fine because this golfer has played that way all his or her golfing life and practiced very hard. If such a golfer is biased toward his or her own method and influences you to totally revamp your shot-making techniques, all you worked for could go for naught. When working with someone whose techniques are fundamentally sound, you will be encouraged to practice the right things common to most low-handicap players and golf professionals.

When asking a friend how he or she hits a particular short-game shot, try to get just one pitching, chipping, bunker play, or putting tip that he or she thinks will turn your game around if you practice. You never want to have numerous swing keys swimming around in your head, because then the tendency is to become confused, freeze over the ball, or make a nonrhythmic disjointed swinging action.

Reading Matter

The next time you are in a bookstore, supermarket, or specialized magazine shop, take a look at how many golf publications there are. You will be amazed at how

Jim's Tips

If you still have problems after determining your shot-making trends and working on corrective drills, seek the help of an established teaching professional. Tell him or her the specific problem you are having—for example, hitting putts left of the hole or leaving chips short of the cup— helps him or her correct your faulty swing and off-target shot-making tendencies.

Death Moves

Don't try out every new tip you read about in golf magazines. Instead, try to single out one that will help you with your problem and then practice it. If you have success, incorporate the key into your pitching, chipping, bunker play, or putting technique. If not, revert to the basic setup and shot-making fundamentals presented in the book you now hold in your hands.

many you have to choose from. Most of these publish instructional cover stories and other articles on all aspects of the game. Flip through publications such as *Golf Digest*, which I write for, as well as *Golf Magazine*, *Golf Tips*, and *Golf Illustrated* and see which one features the best variety of short-game articles. Typically, these articles offer reviews of the basic fundamentals or give you tips on how to hit a short or long pitch, a more sophisticated chip, bunker shot, or putt.

Golf magazines, such as Golf Digest, *are a good source of short game tips.*

Taking the subject of reading matter to a higher level still, there are literally hundreds of instructional books on the market. Most of these books cover the full scope of the game, and include tips on pitching, chipping, bunker play, and putting. At the top of my list are Jack Nicklaus's *Golf My Way*, Harvey Penick's *Little Red Book*, Butch Harmon's *Playing Lessons*, and my own books, including *Golf School*, *The Golf Digest Book of Drills*, and *The Eight-Step Golf Swing*.

There have also been books written specifically about the short game, and these are also readily available in bookstores. One book I highly recommend is *The Short Game Magic of Tiger Woods*, by John Andrisani. In this book, Andrisani, who is the former senior editor of instruction at *Golf Magazine*, analyzes the pitching, chipping, bunker play, and putting techniques of Tiger Woods, golf's hottest player. He also provides you with drills to help enhance your touch around the greens, hit the ball the correct distance for the club in hand, swing with a smooth tempo, relieve tension, and intensify your concentration. In addition, *The Wedge Game Pocket Companion*, by yours truly, is a small book containing easy-to-follow tips on hitting all kinds of wedge shots.

The text contained in golf books is very helpful, but to really understand the instructional message, it is important that you also study the wonderful photographs and illustrations. One reason I enjoyed reading Andrisani's book so much is that it shows Tiger in action, hitting all kinds of short-game shots—everything from the short floating pitch to the three-wood chip, to the bunker shot over a high lip, to the short knee-knocker pressure putt.

Videotapes

Another great source for learning the elements of the short game and finding original pitching, chipping, bunker play, and putting tips is the instructional video. Many of the game's top players have come out with their own videos, and they are available in video stores, golf pro shops, and discount golf shops. Most of these contain sections on the short game, and good ones at that, such as those in Nicklaus's *Golf My Way*. Others contain tips on a specific aspect of the short game, such as putting. On that note, one of my favorites is *Brad Faxon's and Dr. Bob Rotella's Putt to Win*. Faxon, a student of mine, is rated one of the greatest living putters. And two other videos are Ray Floyd's *60 Yards and In* and Jim McLean's *20 Problems, 20 Solutions*.

Jim's Tips

I recommend that you pay a visit to your local library where you'll find many out-of-print books written by the old-time tour professionals. Much of the instruction contained in these books is evergreen, meaning that it still applies. In my mind, two of the best vintage books are Tommy Armour's *How to Play Your Best Golf All the Time*, and *Practical Golf*, by John Jacobs.

Also available are tapes of the major championships showing great shots such as Larry Mize's chip in on the second playoff hole of the 1987 Masters. Look for these, because they give you a bird's-eye view of short game shots being played by the game's best. More important, you can use the freeze-frame button on your video to capture a moment in a particular player's swing or stroke, making it easier for you to learn what to practice.

When choosing material from these tapes, follow the same rules that I recommended you follow when reading magazine articles. Try to pick out one tip for every aspect of the short game that will help you hit more accurate shots the correct distance. Also, look for videos that address faults and fixes. Although I have covered a heck of a lot of material in this book, you may find a little gem hidden on a golf video that works wonders for you. You won't find anything useful without exploring, so start searching out these helpful learning vehicles.

The Least You Need to Know

➤ Building your own at-home short-game station is a very good investment.

➤ Practicing short pitches and chips in your backyard can help you learn how far each club hits the ball in the air, relative to a different length and speed of swing.

➤ It's important that you study your shots and note any trends. If, say, you consistently leave shots short of the hole or pull pitches left of target, you know what to practice at home.

➤ Talking to low-handicap players with fundamentally sound techniques can help you learn how to correct a fault or hit a short-game shot more proficiently.

➤ Reading instructional books and magazine articles and watching videos containing information on the short game can be a helpful exercise, provided you don't flood your head with an overwhelming number of swing keys to try.

Part 6

Perfect Examples

This final part is designed to have you really dig deep to make yourself the best possible short-game player. We all learn from the good examples set by others, and in the category of the short game, the awards go to Tiger Woods for pitching prowess, David Duval for chipping, Sergio Garcia for bunker play, and Justin Leonard for putting. I consider these four players the PGA Tour's supermodels because they exhibit technically correct and creative shot-making skills.

You can learn a lot from reading about how the aforementioned professionals hit short game shots, as you can from studying the methods and attitude of the late Payne Stewart. Payne died tragically in a plane crash in 1999, but what he brought to the game will live on forever.

Chapter 23

Um...That's not what they meant...

The Pitching Supermodel

In This Chapter

➤ Setting up to hit a soft 40- to 60-yard pitch shot

➤ Employing the model backswing and downswing, similar to those of Tiger Woods

➤ Staying smooth

There will always be professionals who win tournaments using unorthodox styles of swing. Having said that, however, your swing should be fundamentally sound, although adding a nuance here and there is perfectly fine if that enables you to feel comfortable and to hit good pitch shots from various distances more times than not. After all, Tiger Woods does.

I love to see juniors copying a tour player's swing to learn a new shot. I think you do yourself a disservice by not taking a serious look at the pitching action used by Tiger Woods to hit high, soft-landing pitch shots from around 40 to 60 yards out from the green. This shot is magical, because the ball seems to stop the moment it hits the green. It doesn't spin back or take several hops forward. To quote a former golf commentator whose name escapes me, "it sits down like a hound dog in front of a fire-place."

Tiger Woods: the pitching supermodel.

(Phil Sheldon, Golf Picture Library)

Tiger is a short-game wizard, although most fans know him for his power-driving skills that allow him to drive par-four holes and reach par-five holes in two shots, instead of the regulation three. It's no wonder that Tiger won the 1999 PGA, his second major championship, and finished the year off at the top of the PGA Tour's money standing list.

I give Tiger and Butch Harmon, his coach, a heck of a lot of credit for their hard practice and perseverance. There was a time when Tiger was criticized for not being able to control his wedge shots, with Butch taking much of the heat. They both had a plan a couple of years ago, and nobody can doubt it's been executed. Tiger has evolved into such a great wedge player that I consider him a supermodel.

Super Setup

When watching Tiger set up to play a 40- to 60-yard wedge shot under normal conditions of lie and weather I have noticed that he's very careful not to position the ball well back in the stance. This is because he knows that such a position promotes a steep backswing action, sharp descending hit, and a shot that spins back. Tiger's priority is to hit the ball all the way to the hole and have it come down so softly you would think it were attached to a miniature parachute. Therefore, he plays the ball closer to his left heel than to the midpoint of his stance. He sets his hands even with the ball or slightly behind it. Ultimately, Tiger wants to come into impact with the clubface going nicely under the ball, not digging into the turf, so he is careful not to set his hands well ahead of the ball, which takes bounce off the wedge. I have noticed too that quite recently Tiger has widened his pitching stance some to prevent an overly steep swing and those *shooters* he was criticized for hitting early in his career. Don't get me wrong, Tiger's stance is still narrow, with the distance between his feet measuring around 10 inches.

Here, I imitate Tiger's setup position for the short wedge shot, making sure to play the ball forward in the stance, set the hands even with the ball, and open the feet slightly.

Swing Lingo

A **shooter** is a shot synonymous with flyer. Due to an overly steep swing, or moisture or grass intervening between the ball and the clubface at impact, the shot flies much farther than normal and is not as controlled.

Death Moves

You will never hit the high, soft lob if you position the ball back in your stance with the shaft leaning forward and toward the target. This setup also leads to a steep angle of attack, which is exactly what you do not want for this shot.

Tiger's stance is slightly open, too, with the left foot a few inches farther from the target line than the right foot. His hips are also slightly open, pointing slightly left of target. This setup provides Tiger with a heightened sense of freedom. Because his hips are in a cleared, or open, position, he prevents an inside takeaway and too much action on the backswing. The added bonus of setting up this way is that he feels more confident about making square and solid contact with the ball. So will you.

Although Tiger opens his feet and hips, he's very careful to set his shoulders fairly square or just the slightest bit open to the target line.

This pitching setup is much different from the one Tiger uses to launch the long ball on the golf course. When driving, he closes his feet as Ben Hogan did and opens his shoulders as Jack Nicklaus still does. This combination of closed feet, open shoulders was used by another great player: Sam Snead, also a super powerful driver of the ball.

When hitting the soft pitch, Tiger is not interested in generating power. He is looking to finesse the ball to the hole. This is why he sets up the way he does and tracks a line from the ball to the target with his eyes. This tracking work helps him sense or feel the distance in his hands. Incidentally, like Jack Nicklaus, Tiger uses an interlock grip rather than the overlap grip used by most PGA Tour players. The interlock grip should be considered simply because it provides you with a sense of unity in the hands. Further, and more important, when hitting this particular shot the way Tiger does, you must keep the clubface open through impact. Gripping like Tiger may help you avoid slippage in the hitting area. It certainly doesn't hurt.

When you feel you are comfortably correct at address, be sure to follow Tiger's other fundamentals to success: taking a nice fluid practice swing that matches the action he intends to employ when actually hitting the shot; and visualizing the perfect shot in his mind's eye before swinging.

Super Backswing

The wonderful thing about Tiger's backswing action is that it is relaxed, with the wrists hinging freely. It is very different from his full-power swing in which he has a late wrist set. There is no effort on his part to make a one-piece takeaway— that is, with the club straight back along the target line, low to the ground, and directed by the triangle formed by the shoulders and arms. Many high handicappers make this mistake, thinking that all shots require this type of one-piece action.

Going back, Tiger's arms swing on a much more upright plane than his turning shoulders, while the club moves slightly outside the target line. As for the weight-shifting action, it is more of a mini-shift. I say that because Tiger leaves much more of his weight on his left foot and leg when hitting this shot than any full shot.

Tiger usually swings the club back to the three-quarter point, for this length shot. This helps him stay relaxed and maintain a certain good personal feel for the club head.

Jim's Tips

When playing a 40- to 60-yard pitch, you might find it very helpful to concentrate on swinging the club back to a specific position. Look at the target, then swing the club and pace off that distance. When you play, have a good sense of how much length you need on your backswing. Many amateurs make the mistake of taking too long a backswing and then decelerating through impact.

Bet You Didn't Know

Compared to the pro golfers of past eras, many pro golfers today are setting the club earlier, particularly when hitting short wedge shots. The reason is that, on these shots, they are not looking to create width in the swing. Make no mistake, the pitch shot is a finesse shot requiring a certain degree of acceleration through impact. However, it does not require you to make a big coil of the body or a wide swing arc.

Tiger swings the club to the three-quarter point, as I do here, no matter how short a pitch he's hitting.

Super Downswing

Indeed, Tiger employs perfect shifting and rotating action of the lower body, but the action is far less powerful or forceful. Another reason the shifting and rotating action is not so brisk and full is that Tiger is controlling the pace of his swing with the pace of his rotation.

A lot of the speed Tiger generates on the downswing comes from the turn of his body. While he nudges the majority of his weight over to his left side, his upper body stays well behind the ball. As the shifting action continues, Tiger's arms accelerate faster. His arms bring the club through the ball, rather than down into it on a sharp angle, while his wrists unhinge.

Here, I demonstrate Tiger's through-impact position. Notice how the upper body tilts away from the target while the lower body drives toward it.

Butch Harmon has worked with Tiger to maintain a firm pressure in his left hand to keep his left wrist stable in the hitting area. If the left wrist breaks down, the right hand and forearm tend to rotate rapidly in a counterclockwise direction, causing the clubface to close. The result is a low shot that runs upon landing. You want to keep the clubface of the sand wedge or lob wedge open when playing this shot so that you loft the ball nicely into the air and land it super softly onto the green, next to the hole.

Super Smooth

As you may recall from Chapter 18, "You Got That Swing," I covered the vital elements of tempo, timing, and rhythm in detail. Still, I want to make a few comments about Tiger's pitching technique, concentrating on why he now is able to do such a good job of controlling distance when, several years ago, he had more difficulty.

Jim's Tips

If you want to hit a pitch that lands super softly but you have difficulty keeping the clubface open through impact, try weakening your grip. This is exactly what many top tour players do to keep the clubface from closing. When you turn or rotate your lead arm toward the target, you place it in a released position. Therefore, it is difficult to release it any further, which explains why the clubface can stay open easily.

The following are the elements to Tiger Woods's pitching technique:

1. In his address, Tiger stands comfortably away from the ball without crowding it. This position helps Tiger relax his arms, hands, and wrists, making for a tension-free swing and more consistency. You know you are the right distance from the ball when you can extend your left arm without feeling the least bit of tension in it. If you do, move a tad closer. If there is too much bend in your left arm, stand farther away.

2. Tiger points the toe of his right foot outward just slightly. When he had a problem hitting flyers, he pointed it perpendicular to the target line, or even a little inward, which made him swing back on an overly steep plane and hit down too sharply. This position is okay if you are looking to impart backspin on the ball, but not when you want to hit a soft-landing pitch.

3. Tiger opens his stance rather than take a square stance. This stance suppresses the feeling that he has to clear his hips quickly at the start of the downswing to open a passageway to swing the club along.

4. Tiger lengthens his backswing to three-quarter length, by incorporating some added wrist action into his technique. There was a time that his backswing action was too short and his arms and wrists were much too tense. Consequently, he felt the need to overwork the lower body on the downswing to generate power. Now, as I said earlier, he generates the power he needs to propel the ball a particular distance largely by accelerating both his rotation and his arms, as the great Johnny Miller did during his heyday of the 1970s.

5. Tiger is a lot steadier over the ball. He realizes that his head has a swing all its own and that it should be allowed to rotate on both the backswing and downswing. However, he also realizes that swaying off the ball and swaying back

toward the target is very hazardous to the health of his wedge game (and it would be to yours, too!).

6. Most important, Tiger's improved wedge play has a lot to do with his footwork. Tiger's right foot stays down longer during the downswing. Butch wants Tiger's right heel to lift only slightly off the ground on these pitch shots and stay well ahead of the toe of the right foot, just as Ben Hogan's used to do.

While on the subject of footwork, let me talk about the left foot. Many recreational golfers let it lift well off the ground on the backswing and even on a short pitch. On short wedge shots, don't lift your heel.

The Least You Need to Know

➤ To hit a short pitch shot like Tiger Woods, it's critical that you play the ball farther forward in your stance than normal. This position enables you to make a more level strike of club to ball, rather than a sharp downward hit.

➤ Good pitching artists, like Tiger Woods, allow their wrists to hinge on the backswing.

➤ To hit a soft landing pitch in the 40- to 60-yard range, it's vitally important that your head stay behind the ball in the hitting area.

➤ To maintain good tempo, timing, and rhythm, on short pitch shots, leave your right foot flat on the ground in the hitting area as long as possible. Only a little of your heel should be allowed to come up after impact.

Chapter 24

The Chipping Supermodel

In This Chapter

➤ Setting up for success around the greens, Duval-style

➤ Using your wrists to promote feel

➤ Nipping the ball off the fringe

➤ Making a rhythmic chipping stroke

➤ Using chipping swing cues

David Duval is likely the greatest player who has yet to win a major tournament. But, I guarantee he will, owing to his complete golf game. This tremendously talented player is really good around the greens, especially when it comes to chip shots. Duval is sometimes criticized for lacking charisma, but he doesn't pay much attention. He just gets on with the show during tournaments and lets his clubs do the talking.

I consider Duval's chipping stroke a good model for anyone because it is a natural action that often differs greatly from the typical high-handicapper's robot stroke. Let's take a closer look at what is so special about this creative short game player who is always looking to hole out from the fringe, not just hit the ball close to the cup.

David Duval: the chipping supermodel.

(Phil Sheldon, Golf Picture Library)

Setup Duval Style

Duval flexes his knees just slightly and bends over slightly from the ball-and-socket joints of his hips so that he's in full balance. When a player stands up too straight, the tendency is to tense the arms, hands, and wrists and make a robotic stroke that greatly hinders distance control. The shot this stroke produces is often a mishit, such as a top or a skull. When the player stoops over at address, he or she tends to pick up the club abruptly on the backswing and hit down using a faulty chopping action. The result can mean a fat shot that falls well short of the pin—or green!

Bet You Didn't Know

There are many great chippers who use a brisk stroke with a very short finish. One player who made an exaggerated, choppy, up-and-down chipping action work for him is Isao Aoki. Aoki is an unorthodox player in general who practices short chips and pitches an average of two hours a day. He has worked hard on his short game since he was a young boy playing golf in Japan. Additionally, he has superb feel for the club head and superior eye-hand coordination. Using this chop stroke, nobody ever chipped or pitched the ball better than Aoki. I far prefer this method to some other long fallen methods that I see taught.

When chipping, Duval assumes a narrow open stance because this setup gives him a good visual picture of the line to the hole and provides him with the freedom he needs to swing the club fluidly through the ball. For a normal chip, he plays the ball just to the right of midpoint in his stance with his hands slightly ahead of it to promote a slightly upward backswing and a descending hit.

Duval's Wrist Action

To nip thea ball cleanly and crisply off the turf so that it carries the fringe and rolls to the hole like a purely struck putt, Duval incorporates a bit of wrist action into his backswing. Some teachers advise amateurs against using their wrists when chipping, arguing that the least number of moving parts produces the best stroke and makes it easier to repeat. Furthermore, they argue that a no-wrists stroke causes the player to swing the club on a shallower plane and to hit chips that aren't influenced by bounce and spin.

There is a time and a place for that style, but I prefer the style I see used by the better players that promotes better feel, touch, and naturalness. I'm with Duval, who knows that because the lie of the ball changes from hole to hole, as do the slopes and speeds of the green, you usually need a stroke that is adaptable to any situation. Besides, trying to employ a wrist-free stroke brings the club into the ball on a very shallow angle, requiring better conditions. More important, an all-arms stroke can create tension in the shoulders, arms, hands, and wrists, thereby hindering feel. You need some wrist action to get the club to create the correct angle for contacting the ball with a slight descending blow.

Here, I demonstrate Duval's narrow open stance, which allows him to better visualize the tar- get line and make a more free swinging action.

Not only does wrist action give you more feel for the club head, it enables you to hit the ball slightly on the descent and to pop it gently into the air. However, be careful. Too much wrist action is destructive. Duval realizes this. Consequently, he arches his wrists slightly. This same setup position will enable you to keep your wrist action to a minimum. Moreover, because it causes the heel of the club to rise up off the ground slightly, it will help you swing with less resistance from the grass.

Which Hand Does What?

Like all good chippers, Duval's left hand serves as the guide and his right hand provides the power once his right wrist unhinges on the downswing. Therefore, he grips the club more firmly with his left hand. To some extent, the pressure applied to the club is personal. Therefore, I highly recommend that you practice hitting shots and determine what degree of grip pressure works best for you when playing different types of chips with different clubs.

The Right Club

Duval hits most of his chips with a sand wedge. However, he sometimes must play another club when the lie or situation calls for it. For example, if the pin is located on the top tier of a green and Duval is on the fringe in front of the green some 75 feet away, there is no way he is going to play a sand wedge. Neither should you, because the percentages are not in your favor. Nine out of ten times you will leave the ball short of the hole. You want to use a less lofted club in this situation, a 7 iron, for example, because the idea is to get the ball rolling on the green as soon as possible.

Bet You Didn't Know

The great Bobby Jones, who won the Grand Slam (comprised of the U.S. Open, U.S. Amateur, British Open, and British Amateur championships) in 1930, used to hit many chips with a 5 iron. Of course, you must appreciate that the greens were much slower in his time than they are today. Most golfers would chip the ball closer to the hole more often if they would use lower lofted clubs.

Pro Backswing

Unless the chip is very long, Duval swings the chipping club straight back and through along the target line. Initially, the club head rises slightly above the ball once as he hinges his right wrist. There is no turning action of his shoulders or hips involved in the backstroke. That's because he doesn't need to generate much power, even to hit long chips. His arms, hands, and wrists control the swing, while his lower body stays quiet. Only Duval's left knee works inward slightly to add rhythm to the backswing as he pushes the club back and then upward. On long chips, his knees are a little more active, but still his hips stay virtually still, as does his head, with his eyes staying focused on the back of the ball. Also, on very long chips, the club swings inside the target line slightly, because of the minimal rotation of the shoulders.

Here, I demonstrate Duval's simple backswing action that involves swinging the club back with the arms, hands, and wrists while the lower body stays still.

Pro Downswing

When swinging down and into the impact zone, Duval gently kicks his right toward the target, again to keep the stroke rhythmic. Although Duval keeps his eyes focused on the back of the ball, he lets his head rotate toward the target immediately after striking the ball. Recreational golfers usually keep their heads down too long, which is one of the main reasons that they get stuck in the impact position and hit the ball fat.) At impact, Duval's club hits the ball cleanly and leaves only a little scrape on the grass.

If you are a new golfer, when you think logically about hitting a longer chip you probably think that you need a longer swing. The fact is you may not. Longer chips are normally hit with less lofted clubs, so you can afford to make a short backswing, swing at a slower speed, and shorten the follow-through action like Duval does. I am suggesting that you keep the follow-through action very short, meaning that just after impact, when the club head is just the ball that you do hold that position with the clubface held square. Don't worry; the ball will carry the fringe, land on the green, and roll to the hole like a putt.

Jim's Tips

If you discover that you are hitting chip shots fat or even slightly behind the ball, your wrists could be too active. Try chipping with the 10-finger baseball grip. You will find that this grip (or a reverse overlap putting hold) enables you to make a wrist hinge without overdoing things and to hit the ball less abruptly on the descent.

Here, I demonstrate how Duval works his lower body and rotates his head toward the target, just like he does on full shots.

Jim's Tips

An aspect of Duval's short shot action that never seems to be mentioned is how his left arm works after impact. David allows his left elbow to bend and even pull up slightly. This subtle move helps him to keep the clubface absolutely dead square because his left wrist stays absolutely solid. This little move produces easy power while providing fantastic accuracy. Watch David and other top tour players use this left arm action and then try it yourself.

Death Moves

Chipping death moves include weight placed on the back foot, shifting weight in the backstroke, dipping or lifting your body, tension, and a low-inside takeaway with the clubface closing.

Super Smooth

Duval's stroke exhibits good rhythm—that is, he has a smooth coordination between the movement of his body and the movement of the club. As I mentioned earlier, Duval's gentle knee action and subtle wrist action allows the backswing and downswing to act like an old grandfather clock. Just as the pendulum goes ticktock, so does the backward and forward actions of Duval's chipping stroke. Even though there are two pieces to the swing, the action blends together nicely into one flowing motion.

Chip Preparation

Duval's smooth tempo, timing, and rhythm do not revolve around only the stroke itself. Good swing preparation has a lot to do with his smooth chipping stroke.

Before Duval chips, he looks carefully at the lay of the land, paying attention to the grain of the grass and the slopes in the green. Normally, he looks at the shot he faces from behind the ball, from behind the cup, and from one side. He moves about quietly, knowing that by staying relaxed he will encourage a smooth stroke when the time comes to hit the ball. In assessing the chipping situation, what he concentrates on most is determining the area of green where he must land the ball.

Visualizing the Chip

Once he comes to a conclusion about where best to have the ball hit the green, he stands near the ball staring at the spot or circle he intends to hit. He then visualizes himself playing a particular club. If the shot is executed perfectly in his mind, he knows that the club he thinks will work is probably the best one for the job.

Bet You Didn't Know

According to mental game guru, Dr. Fran Pirozzolo, when the swing rehearsal session is done quietly but thoroughly, the player is more apt to make a smooth and relaxed rhythmic stroke. Pirozzolo teaches that the process removes anxiety about playing the shot and replaces it with a sense of confidence. In turn, this added sense of confidence encourages the player to make a freer swing.

If Duval has trouble visualizing a good chip, he will switch clubs and let that new scenario play out in his mind. Duval continues this process until he believes his choice of club and the image of what swing to make fit the situation. But that's not the end of the process. To be extra sure that the club he chooses and the swing he has visualized are the right ones, he takes two or three practice swings and, at least once, looks at the target to get a better feel for the stroke.

Super Attitude

Another reason Duval is such a good chipper is his overall attitude. When he first started playing golf on the PGA Tour, he took the game perhaps a little too seriously and sometimes lost his temper during competition. He soon discovered that this attitude lead only to backward steps. Maturing as a player and accepting bad shots and bad breaks has enabled Duval to waltz into the winner's circle numerous times. Now, when he hits a bad shot or has a bad hole, instead of slamming a club down he moves on, giving his next shot 100-percent concentration.

It's his concentration, free of any distractions from the crowd, that enables him to enter a mental cocoon and gather his thoughts about the chip shot he's about to hit. While in this zone, he plans out the chip and visualizes the landing spot and swing, as I have mentioned. Something I have not mentioned is how Duval works his right arm back and forth, first away then toward the target, without a club in his hand. This pre-swing gesturing helps

Jim's Tips

I advise all my students to take several practice swings near and around the green. That's because every shot is always at least slightly different. This always requires special touch to pull off the perfect shot. So get that feel by rehearsing the perfect shot.

285

him feel the distance and strength of stroke necessary for propelling the ball the proper distance. It is something David may have watched Seve Ballesteros do as he grew up watching the great players on television.

If you lose your concentration when you chip, find some gesture or phrase that will be your cue to enter the zone. Tug on your shirt, pull on your glove, or say "Go!" or "Ready!" to trigger a sense of calm concentration. Do whatever it takes, but find a way to get into the right state. I have never asked Duval what he does. Maybe he gets into his cocoon just by immersing himself in the chipping situation. Or maybe blinking is his cue. Don't laugh. Tiger Woods triggers the zone mentality by slowing opening and closing his eyes.

The Least You Need to Know

➤ Good posture, like that exhibited by David Duval at address, is essential for making a controlled on-plane chipping swing.

➤ On short chip shots, Duval lets his head rotate toward the target after hitting through the ball, sometimes even slightly before.

➤ When playing a very long chip shot, use a less lofted club than a sand wedge, just like Duval does.

➤ When chipping the ball, incorporate a little knee action into your swing to help you make a more rhythmic swing. Simply rotate the left knee inward on the backswing and the right knee inward on the downswing, in the same fashion as Duval.

➤ The secret to getting the chipping club to swing upward slightly on the backswing and to hitting the ball with a slight descending blow at impact is slightly hinging the right wrist, as Duval proves.

➤ Being a good chipper takes more than just a sound technique. Like Duval, you must take time to assess the lie and situation so that you pick the right club and play the right shot.

The Bunker Play Supermodel

In the world of professional golf, there are tour players who swing by the book, meaning that they stick entirely to the fundamentals for setting up and swinging. Jeff Maggert of the PGA Tour, Hale Irwin of the Senior PGA Tour, and Karrie Webb of the LPGA Tour are classic examples. There are also supercreative players who play totally by feel. At the top of that list is Seve Ballesteros, followed by Chi Chi Rodriguez and Laura Davies. Next, there is most notably Tiger Woods, who depends on fundamentals but also plays a lot of shots by feel.

Sergio Garcia, the Spanish shot-making genius, is also a super creative player. In the category of bunker play, Garcia is an ideal model, because his technique allows him to play aggressively and thus fight off any anxiety that revolves around hitting the perfect finesse shot. Garcia has a unique way of playing bunker shots that's worth trying. It allows you to go down after the ball and take more sand, just like the great Claude Harmon used to do.

Sergio Garcia: the bunker play supermodel.

(Phil Sheldon, Golf Picture Library)

Super Setup

To appreciate Garcia's technique, you must first know how most PGA Tour players set up to the ball when playing bunker shots. The typical pro ...

➤ Stands open, with the left foot slightly farther from the target line than the right.

➤ Plays the ball just ahead of the midpoint in the stance.

➤ Inclines the body's center of gravity forward, establishing this position by leaning his or her hips toward the target (left hip higher than right) and putting about 60 percent of his or her weight on the left foot.

➤ Wriggles his or her feet into the sand just a little bit to build a solid foundation for swinging the club.

➤ Grips the club fairly lightly, uses a weak grip, and chokes down very little.

➤ Lets his or her arms hang down comfortably to relieve tension and promote a relaxed backswing and downswing.

➤ Opens the clubface just a little and focuses on a spot in the sand about two inches behind the ball. (This spot is where the club will contact the sand.)

➤ Endeavors to take a thin cut of sand.

Garcia is a bit different. He assumes an exaggerated open stance, and plays the ball opposite his left heel. He wriggles his feet quite deeply in the sand to firmly anchor himself and promote an all-arms, -hands, and -wrist swing. He holds the club very lightly and takes a strong grip, with both hands turned away from the target. He chokes well down on the club to encourage a very upright swing. He lays the club very open and usually concentrates on hitting an area of sand about 3 to 4 inches behind the ball. The closer he is to the hole, the more he bends over from the ball-and-socket joints of his hips and flexes his knees, the more he opens the clubface, the more he chokes down on the club, and the farther behind the ball he makes contact with the sand.

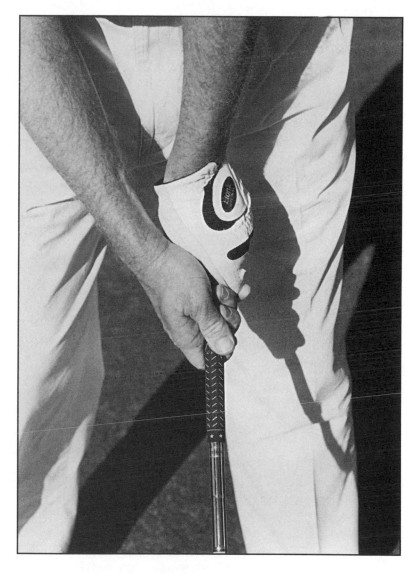

Here, I demonstrate Gurcia's strong grip, a unique feature of his setup that better allows him to slide the club through the sand.

Super Backswing

Garcia's backswing action is also slightly different from that employed by the typical PGA Tour player. He hinges his wrists sooner and he swings the club back on a much steeper plane. Many American tour players, such as Mark O'Meara, who take very little sand, actually swing the club along quite a shallow path and look like they are playing a shot off fairway grass. Garcia will never be accused of doing that.

Here, I demonstrate Garcia's early wrist hinge action.

Garcia's light grip and superrelaxed arms allow him to make a very long and lazy backswing with the club looking like it is swinging outside the target line. But, in fact, it swings parallel to his bodyline. During his entire backswing action, his head and lower body stay rock steady.

Super Downswing

Whereas the tempo of the typical PGA Tour player's downswing is very smooth and syrupy, Garcia's is very aggressive. The typical tour player's swing is slower because he or she is going to take far less sand, and thus hit the ball on a lower flight with more roll. In a way, the tour player hits a bunker shot much like a short pitch off grass. If you don't believe me, watch tour players hitting bunker shots, and you will see the small amount of sand they extract from the bunker.

I think amateurs perform much better in bunkers if they make a swing similar to Garcia. In swinging down, Garcia concentrates on unhinging his wrists the moment he reaches the top of his swing, keeping the club in front of his body, accelerating his arms at a rapid pace, and hitting an area of sand behind the ball. I believe wholeheartedly that focusing on an area of sand rather than a specific spot takes the pressure off and gives an added margin for error. Amateurs make a much freer swinging action. They are also then less apt to simply pull the club into the sand and stop,

Death Moves

When swinging back to play a bunker shot, the worst thing you can do is move the club along a flat plane. You will never be able to hit the proper distance behind the ball to dig out enough sand to lift the ball up over the lip and onto the green. The sand wedge is your heaviest club and is designed specifically for sand shots. But to use it properly, you must get the club head elevated so that you are able to thump the sand.

and instead, accelerate the club into the sand, down under the ball and through the sand, just like my friend and mentor Claude Harmon used to do. (Harmon hit the sand as far as 6 inches behind the ball, and taught students at New York's Winged Foot Golf Club to aim three or four inches behind the ball knowing that with his method, anything between 1 and 6 inches would work fine.)

If you are a weak bunker player who panics when seeing your ball in a bunker because you are afraid that you will not be able to hit the ball over a high lip, Garcia's method could very well be for you. It requires more club head speed but far less finesse and precision. Consequently, you do not have to devote hours and hours to practicing this shot. What makes this shot so wonderful is that you have a wide margin of error. The way you control distance is by opening the clubface more or less and controlling the length of your finish. I touched on this earlier, but to reiterate, the closer you are to the hole, the more you open the face and take a deeper the cut of sand. The farther you are from the hole, the less you open the face and the shallower the cut of sand you take.

Here, I show you how Garcia accelerates his arms downward early in the forward swing, which is a key technique that is especially helpful on long bunker shots.

Zip in the Bunker

Sergio Garcia a fast moving young man, so it makes sense that the tempo of his bunker-play swing is quite fast. As I have said before, the personality of a player often matches the tempo of his or her swing. Although you want some zip in the impact zone when you thump the sand, you can get too quick in the bunker. Do not get fast and short with your backswing. Remember to relax your grip pressure and to soften your arms and shoulders.

Bet You Didn't Know

1982 PGA Champion Lanny Wadkins is one of the best bunker players in the world. Wadkins, a fast and aggressive player, swings just like Garcia, accelerating the club quite rapidly through impact.

Wadkins is another top player who has benefited indirectly from Claude Harmon. Dick Harmon, the pro at the prestigious River Oaks in Houston, Texas has worked extensively with Wadkins. Dick Harmon is one of the finest short-game teachers I have ever seen and is, without a doubt, one of the very best club professionals in the United States.

What's so good about Garcia is that, although his tempo is upbeat, the rhythm of his swinging action is smooth. That's because he times the movement of his body, particularly the hinging and unhinging of his wrists, with the movement of the club. It's one thing to swing aggressively and lose your timing. Its another thing to swing aggressively and to take just the right amount of sand so that your distance control is superb, which is how Garcia takes his swing.

At a young age, Garcia learned how the bounce of the club reacts in different types of sand, such as *powder*, and how deeply to hit down to propel the ball a certain distance. You must educate yourself as well, using the practice bunker as your one-room schoolhouse whenever you get the opportunity. This type of homework teaches you how to adjust your sand wedge when dealing with different length shots and how the sand wedge reacts.

If you are lucky enough to watch Garcia hit a bunker shot at a tournament, listen carefully to the sounds made when he sets up and swings. If you stand close to him, you can hear his feet wriggle into the sand, his shirt rustle as he swings back, and the club thump the sand behind the ball when he comes into impact. Everything about Garcia's pre-swing routine and execution of shot has a rhythm to it. On the first bunker shot he plays during a round of a tournament, he listens very carefully to the sounds made when he digs his feet into the sand and when the club hits the sand. These sounds give

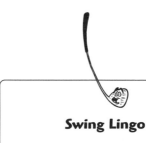

Swing Lingo

Powder is the term veteran golfers use to describe soft, pure white, light sand.

him an indication of the sand's texture, and tell him how deeply he will need to dig the club into the sand to hit the ball to his target.

Deeper and Deeper: The Plugged Lie

In Chapter 5, "Common Trouble Shots," you learned that the secrets to playing this shot are ...

➤ Setting up slightly open, with more of your weight on your left or front foot.

➤ Hooding the face of a sand wedge.

➤ Placing your hands well ahead of the ball.

➤ Making an upright backswing.

➤ Making a smooth downswing.

➤ Slapping the sand about one inch behind the ball.

➤ Burying the club in the sand and stopping.

If you recall too, I told you that this is one of the few times that I suggested you aim for a precise spot behind the ball. When playing bunker shots any other time I told you to aim for an area of sand. I instructed you to hit close to the ball to extract the ball out of the plugged lie. I also told you not to swing down too fast because when you hit down with the face hooded the ball comes out hot. Garcia proves that there are other ways to play this shot. However, it takes much more practice, a lot of talent, and of course, good nerves.

When playing this shot, Garcia sets up very open with the ball played opposite the midpoint in his stance and his head behind the ball. He sets about 60 percent of his weight on his right foot. He lays the clubface open as wide as he can and raises the club behind an area of sand about three inches behind the ball. He sets his hands even with the ball.

On the backswing, Garcia hinges his wrists immediately in the takeaway and picks the club straight up so that its shaft faces the sky. He then pounds the sand several inches behind the ball. When done properly, this extracts the ball very softly. However, remember that this is a highly advanced shot. You'll see the tour pros play this on television, but believe me it is an extremely difficult shot—not recommended for the average golfer.

Coming down, still keeping his weight on his right foot, he pulls the club straight down into the sand. The powerful thrusting he achieves comes from hinging his wrists the moment he reaches the top of the swing. The club enters the sand about three inches behind the ball and digs out a crater under it. Just like my recommended swing technique, there is no follow-through. Garcia just sticks the club into the sand. The ball pops up and floats fairly softly in the air. This is a great shot to play if the sand is powdery and if you have practiced this shot long and hard.

Bet You Didn't Know

Sergio Garcia plays the plugged lie bunker shot over a high lip the same way Seve Ballesteros has his entire career. This is certainly no coincidence when you consider that Ballesteros is one of Garcia's chief swing mentors, particularly on matters of the short game.

The Least You Need to Know

➤ On a bunker shot, hinge your wrists very soon on the backswing, the way Garcia does.

➤ To generate added club head speed on a bunker shot, unhinge your wrists early in the forward swing.

➤ To become a versatile bunker player like Garcia, practice hitting shots out of a many different textures of sand on different courses.

➤ When playing the plugged-lie shot Garcia-style, lay the clubface wide open and thrust the club deeply into the sand about several inches behind the ball.

Chapter 26

The Putting Supermodel

In This Chapter

➤ Learning to clone Justin Leonard's superlative putting setup

➤ Copying Leonard's super backstroke and forward stroke

➤ Leonard's secrets to employing a rhythmic stroke

If there's one thing that golf history proves, it's that putting is the most individualistic part of the game. Recalling the putting strokes of past and present PGA Tour players, I'm always amazed at the large number of varying styles. Two of the most unique styles of days long ago belonged to American Walter Travis and South African Bobby Locke. Travis putted with his arms bent and his elbows pointing straight out, sideways, like a chicken's. Locke stood very closed and actually hooked putts.

Of today's living golfers, Gary Player still uses a jab stroke copied in large part from Bobby Locke, while Billy Casper uses a pop stroke. Arnold Palmer still stands pigeon-toed to putt, although not as often as he did when he first played the PGA Tour. Brad Faxon, like Ben Crenshaw, uses a flowing stroke with some wrist play, while fellow PGA Tour player Jim Furyk putts cross-handed. LPGA player Nancy Lopez putts very aggressively, while 1999 Ryder Cup captain and two-time Masters Champion Ben Crenshaw swings the putter clearly on an inside-square-inside track or path.

Folks, the list is too long to review, so I will stop once I tell you that of today's PGA Tour players, there is a superlative putter with a style I wish more amateurs would model their strokes after, because to me it is as flawless as flawless gets. It belongs to a young Texan who pulled the 1999 Ryder Cup from the hands of the Europeans by sinking a 45-foot winning putt against Spaniard José Maria Olazabal. Let's now review his putting stroke and analyze the putting style of Justin Leonard.

Justin Leonard: the putting supermodel.

(Phil Sheridon, Golf Picture Library)

Superaddress Position

Throughout the history of the game, there have been many great putters who crouched over to putt—most notably Jack Nicklaus. During his winning days on the PGA Tour, Nicklaus set up somewhat like Travis did and used a piston-type arm action that really got the job done on the greens. He used a slight wrist set, a short stroke, and preferred to *die* the ball into the hole. Johnny Miller is another golfer who played out of a crouched address position and incorporated wrist action into his stroke. Miller won so many tournaments during the 1970s in California and Arizona that he was called the Desert Fox.

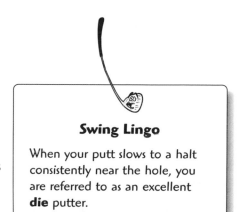

Swing Lingo

When your putt slows to a halt consistently near the hole, you are referred to as an excellent **die** putter.

Leonard Stands Tall

There have also been great putters who set up standing tall to the ball. Ray Floyd, former winner of the Masters, PGA, and U.S. Open championships, comes to mind as one of the best. However, you must appreciate the fact that Floyd uses a longer, 38-inch, putter.

Justin Leonard, on the other hand, uses a standard 35-inch putter, and also stands very tall when setting up to putt, which is somewhat unusual for someone of his short stature. Leonard, who is five feet, nine inches tall, feels that standing up to putt helps him to see the line to the hole more clearly and to employ a more fluid stroke.

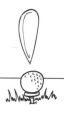

Bet You Didn't Know

Although there is no set rule, I find that the majority of tall players, such as Tiger Woods, Davis Love III, and Ernie Els, stand fairly erect when putting. In contrast, shorter players tend to crouch when they address a putt. As a matter of interest, Woods is 6 feet, 2 inches tall and both Love and Els are 6 feet, 3 inches.

Like many other fine putters, Leonard does the following:

➤ Plays the ball slightly inside his left heel.

➤ Positions his hands in line with the ball.

➤ Sets the putter face perpendicular to the hole or on the line he chooses for breaking putts.

➤ Grips the club comfortably, assuming a reverse overlap grip.

Leonard's Weight, Head, and Arms

As fundamentally sound as Leonard is, he is his own man too, doing some things just a little different from what most of his fellow PGA Tour players do.

First, instead of placing slightly more weight on his left foot, he balances his weight evenly on the central portions of his feet when taking his address. Leonard believes this enables him to make a more level stroke and roll the ball more purely with the *flat stick*. If you put too much weight on your left foot, the tendency can be to lift the putter up abruptly during the backstroke and then chop down on the ball. If you set most of weight on your right foot, you tend to hit the ball too much on the upswing.

As a novice golfer you may not realize that the ball comes off the putter skidding before rolling. Depending on the length of putt, the skid is shorter or longer. You do not want the ball to become airborne nor, conversely, to dig and hop. Leonard's level back-and-through stroke minimizes any negative effect.

Second, instead of setting his head directly over the ball or his eyes behind the ball but over the target line, as Nicklaus does, Leonard sets his eyes slightly inside the target line just like Brad Faxon and Ben Crenshaw, two superior putters. This address position promotes an inside-square-inside path. Leonard prefers swinging the club along this path because it feels more natural and it matches the same path along which other clubs swing when he plays standard shots from the tee or fairway.

Before moving on to the third unique element of Leonard's setup, I would advise you against ever setting your eyes outside the target line. I know only one successful player who does this: Scott Hoch. But then he has an uncanny ability to manipulate the movement of the putter. However, he will be the first to admit that sometimes, especially in a pressure situation, this setup position causes him to take the putter back outside the target line, then across the ball through impact. Hoch will never forget his miscue

Swing Lingo

Pro golfers and hip amateurs refer to the putter as the **flat stick.** I believe Senior PGA Tour player Lee Trevino was the first to popularize this lingo.

in the 1989 Masters. On the first playoff hole, he missed a putt of two feet that would have won him this prestigious major championship.

Here, I demonstrate Leonard's setup position. Notice how my head and eyes are positioned inside the target line and how I stand tall to the ball with both arms comfortably extended.

Third, Leonard lets his arms extend straight down, with just the slightest slack in them. While taking this position, Leonard is very conscious of an imaginary triangle formed by the arms and shoulders, which controls the movement of the putter. When the arms hang straight down as his do, the left wrist flattens, meaning that it lines up perfectly with the back of the left forearm. There is no indentation in the crease between the back of the left hand and the left wrist. By taking the play out of

Jim's Tips

To help you promote a relaxed putting address position like Leonard's, here's a tip I received from a top professional Al Mengert, my first golf instructor. When setting up, imagine that you are a balloon that's just been deflated. Let your arms and shoulders go absolutely limp. This one image will encourage you to breathe more easily and assume a tension-free setup position with your arms hanging down naturally.

Death Moves

If you overuse your wrists rather than your hands, arms, and shoulders to control the backstroke, you will have great difficulty swinging the club low to the ground and controlling distance. You will tend to lift the putter up too high off the ground, chop down on the ball, and mishit the putt.

the left wrist, the left hand can better perform its job of guiding the putter back and through. If you recall, I have taught you already that the left hand and arm guide is a tremendous way to build a repetitive stroke.

Although Leonard stands up straight and extends his arms downward, there is no tension in his body. He ensures comfort by bending slightly at the knees and from the waist, and by gripping the club with a medium degree of pressure—approximately 5 on my scale of 1 to 10.

Super Backstroke

When Leonard makes a short-length stroke, the putter head swings straight back and through along the target line virtually automatically. On longer putts, the putter swings back slightly inside the target line on the backstroke, returns to square at impact, and then returns to the inside after the ball is struck.

What makes Leonard's stroke so special is that he keeps the putter head moving very low to the ground on the backswing keeping the putter in perfect synchronization with his arms and shoulders (the triangle). The longer the putt, the longer the distance the putter head travels. Keeping the putter low to the ground makes for a pure roll of the ball and consistent control.

The left arm is Leonard's dominant force on the backstroke. He depends on it to push the putter back while getting help from the shoulders. And while discussing the shoulders, let me make it clear that, on short putts, Leonard's shoulders rock more than they rotate, much like the action of a teeter-totter. This is another reason he keeps the putter moving straight back along the target line with the greatest of ease. Again, his flat left-wrist position helps, too. On longer putts, Leonard rotates his shoulders in a clockwise direction on the backstroke, causing the putter to swing slightly inside the target line.

In swinging back like Leonard, I use my left arm to push the putter away from the hole.

Super Forward Stroke

Leonard has a very simple, yet calculated, system of employing the forward stroke. On short putts, he simply rocks his left shoulder slightly upward and his right shoulder slightly downward. On longer putts, he simply rotates his shoulders counterclockwise.

Leonard stays in control of the putter head and returns it to a square impact position time after time because he doesn't use the small muscles of the hands and wrists to control the action. He uses the big muscles of the arms and shoulders to control the forward stroke, which is a huge advantage. For most golfers, any time you can keep

303

the small muscles out of the stroke, you should. Tension or pressure during competition often filters into the small muscles and cause alignment problems, which can throw off your stroke.

This extended follow-through, similar to Leonard's, indicates that the big muscles of the body control the forward stroke. When the hands and wrists control the stroke, the tendency is to chop down on the ball at impact then stop.

On both short and long putts Leonard keeps his head and lower body perfectly still as he swings through impact and propels the ball nicely toward the hole.

Supersilky Stroke

Because Leonard keeps his wrists out of the stroke, he does not have to worry about hinging and unhinging them at the right time. His big-muscle controlled stroke enables him to swing the club back and through smoothly while maintaining an even tempo from start to finish.

Whether the putt is long or short, Leonard swings the putter back at the same speed. What does change is the length of his stroke. The longer the putt and the more aggressively he chooses to putt, the longer the stroke action. The shorter the putt and the less aggressive or defensive he wants to be, the shorter the stroke. He knows that if the backstroke is stunted, the tendency will be to quicken the forward stroke and mishit the ball. We are talking about a game of inches here, folks, so you cannot afford to be off by much. Of course, there will be times when you stroke the ball perfectly, yet the ball bounces off line. And other times when you make a not-so-good stroke and a blade of grass pushes the ball into the cup. Overall, though, the better the stroke and the more square the contact, the better the result.

When you watch in awe as Leonard hits long and short putts into the hole, understand that Leonard worked for hours on end putting. He has worked very hard since he was a boy and throughout his amateur and pro careers with the help of teacher Randy Smith. You must practice hard yourself, until you find a length of stroke and tempo that enables you to return the putter face squarely to the ball and control the distance. You must make solid contact with the ball every time if you expect to control the speed consistently.

If your backstroke is too short, practice with a longer putter. The extra length putter promotes a flowing arms-and-shoulders-controlled stroke. If you are just picking up the game, you may want to practice with one until you get a feel for the right pendulum-type motion. Conversely, to practice the feel of Justin Leonard's extended-arms style, try

Jim's Tips

If you feel that your stroke is jerky and see that your distance control is off, try using a double-reverse overlap grip to take the wrists out of your stroke. To assume this grip, place the little finger of your right hand over the middle finger of your left hand, and let the left forefinger overlap the first three fingers of your right hand. This helps you to feel your hands as a single unit.

Jim's Tips

One of the many things short-game guru Carl Welty taught me about clubface-to-ball contact is that this fundamental to great putting is usually overlooked. In studying putting greats, Welty noticed that even though players such as Leonard keep the putter head low on the forward stroke, they keep it high enough off the ground for its face to contact the equator of the ball. So should you, to promote the purest possible roll of the ball.

using an extra short putter of 32 to 33 inches in length. More and more pros are going to this length putter.

Putting can cause you to feel exhilaration or frustration, depending on whether you hole out or miss by a hair. It looks like the simplest part of the game, but it really is not. There have been many great ball strikers who have not made it to the PGA Tour because they couldn't sink putts. If you pay more attention to practicing this part of the game than trying to hit the ball a country mile, you will benefit greatly.

The Least You Need to Know

➤ To promote a level putting stroke like Justin Leonard's, let your arms extend downward at address, making sure that the left wrist is flat.

➤ Let the big muscles of the body control the putting stroke, Leonard-style.

➤ To hit solid and accurate short putts like Leonard, rock your left shoulder downward slightly on the backstroke and upward slightly on the forward stroke.

➤ To hit long putts the way Leonard does, rotate your shoulders clockwise on the backstroke and counterclockwise on the forward stroke.

➤ Control distance as well as Leonard does by shortening or lengthening your stroke, not by changing your tempo.

Chapter 27

R.I.P.

Ode to Payne Stewart

In This Chapter

➤ Payne Stewart's most influential teacher

➤ Payne's pitching prowess

➤ Payne's chipping prowess

➤ Payne's bunker-play prowess

➤ Payne's putting prowess

I had always planned to include Payne Stewart in this book, because he had such a fine short game. However, I did not plan to devote the final chapter to this highly dedicated and talented pro golfer until I started thinking more about his shot-making prowess after his tragic death in a plane crash in late 1999. Payne was very gifted, but most people never realized just how gifted this great golfer was until reviewing his career.

Payne's exceptionally smooth tempo, dedicated work ethic, mental fortitude, and array of short-game shots helped him win numerous tournaments around the world. His victories included three major championships: the 1989 PGA played at the Kemper Lakes Golf Club in Illinois, the 1991 U.S. Open at Hazeltine National Golf Club in Minnesota, and the 1999 U.S. Open contested at Pinehurst Country Club in North Carolina. These three courses are normally very demanding, but are made even more difficult for a major championship. The fairways are cut down very low, the rough and fringe grass is allowed to grow long, and the greens are trimmed down so tight that players feel like they are putting on table tops. What I am telling you is that

Payne could never have won these prestigious championships without being able to hit superb pitch shots, chips, bunker shots, and putts. In his honor, I would like to teach you what I learned from this great champion.

Payne's Personal Coach

Growing up in Springfield, Missouri, Payne had one advantage. His father, Bill Stewart, was a scratch player with a tremendous short game, and he passed many tips on to his son. Payne listened up when he father spoke. After all, his father won the club championship at Missouri's Hickory Hills Golf Club 10 times. He also won the 1953 Missouri State Amateur, qualified for the U.S. Open at California's Olympic Club in 1955, and won the 1957 Missouri State Amateur and the 1979 Missouri Senior Amateur.

Payne's guidance from his father helped greatly. He encouraged Payne to hit different length pitch shots off the fairway and out of rough; chip shots out of good and bad lies with a variety of clubs; practice standard and not so standard bunker shots; and hit putts for hours at a time—and not just level putts, but sloping left-to-right and right-to-left putts as well.

The lesson to be drawn here is to find your own short-game mentor and practice creatively.

Payne's Early Struggles

Payne's road to greatness took time and effort. After playing on the golf team at Southern Methodist University, he tried four times to earn a PGA Tour card that would enable him to play with the big boys, and endured three years of struggling before he won his first tour event: the 1982 Quad Cities Open. He could have easily given up, but he didn't.

Bet You Didn't Know

It's ironic that when Payne Stewart first played on the PGA Tour, he earned the nickname "Avis," because he finished second so many times. Years later, his success erased that moniker. He became a highly respected champion that knew how to win under the intense pressure of competition. Payne Stewart, the man who wore knickers to preserve the game's tradition, will be forever remembered as a winner.

The lesson to be drawn here is to accept the fact that golf is a difficult game but never give up. Learn the fundamentals and check your setup regularly, because the starting position for playing any short-game shot has a lot to do with the type of swing you make—good or bad. The work you put into perfecting the various setup positions required for hitting pitch shots, chips, bunker shots, and putts will help you develop a strong sense of confidence and allow your handicap to drop steadily.

Payne's Pitching Prowess

When setting up and swinging, Payne followed the same fundamental rules I laid out for pitching in Chapter 2, "How to Get Started," and Chapter 3, "Building Blocks." I was particularly impressed with the freedom, tempo, timing, and rhythm of his pitching action. Setting the wrists early and freely, making a long relaxed backswing, and maintaining the commitment to hit through the shot with good acceleration is what I will remember him for. You would be smart to follow in his footsteps.

Payne Stewart's pitching backswing was syrupy. But, on the downswing, he accelerated the club nicely into the ball.

(Phil Sheldon, Golf Picture Library)

Death Moves

I have no objection to playing a variety of chip shots with your sand wedge. But, you must know where to draw the line. Payne Stewart would never have dreamed of playing a long chip off a tight lie in the fringe to a hole, say 90 feet away, with a sand wedge. You should avoid this, too, or you will probably hit the ball well short of your target. Learn to use a variety of clubs to simplify your chipping technique.

Payne's Chipping Prowess

I really liked the way Payne hit chip shots. The fact that his technique stood up during the heat of a major championship proved how fundamentally sound it was. Like most pros, he chipped with a variety of clubs, rather than hitting most shots with a sand wedge. He was against the one-club philosophy because he did not like to depend on any manipulation with the hands and wrists to make one club do another's job. He carefully assessed the lie and hole placement, visualized himself hitting the perfect shot with a particular club, and then used that same club to hit the shot after making two very fluid practice swings. I especially liked the way Payne incorporated some wrist and knee action into his stroke to make it more rhythmic. Also, I admired the way his hands led the club into the ball, which helped him nip it crisply and cleanly off the fringe grass.

Because Payne let his hands lead the club into the ball, he was always guaranteed to hit a solid chip.

(Phil Sheldon, Golf Picture Library)

Payne's Bunker-Play Prowess

I am happy to report that Payne set up and swung according to the fundamentals I laid out for you in Chapters 2 and 3. The shot that he really made look easy was one of the toughest in golf: the long bunker shot.

The most interesting element of Payne's setup was his stance. For the long shot, he closed his stance by dropping his right foot back farther from the target line, which made him swing the club on a slightly flatter backswing plane. This flatter plane enabled him to take a thinner slice of sand and carry the ball a longer distance. He also wriggled his feet into the sand only slightly, knowing this allowed him to work his lower body more freely.

Jim's Tips

When playing long bunker shots, Payne Stewart knew what you should know: If you strive for a long finish, practice using a pitching wedge or nine iron. You might surprise yourself with much improved results.

On the backswing, he turned his left shoulder behind the ball, and made a full-shoulder turn. You never want to let the club get as elevated as it does on short bunker shots, or else you will swing down at too steep an angle, take too much sand, and fail to hit the ball to the hole.

When Payne swung down, he looked like he was playing a pitch off the fairway. In fact, he sometimes used the pitching wedge to play exceptionally long bunker shots. I used to love to watch him swing fluidly through the sand. He truly was poetry in motion.

Payne used a fluid down-swing action to slide the club into the sand under the ball and hit a floating shot over the lip onto the green.

(Phil Sheldon, Golf Picture Library)

Jim's Tips

To sink more pressure putts, no matter what style setup you use, hold the club head very lightly on the ground or even slightly above the putting surface. Many golfers actually press down with the putter head forming a tripod with their feet and the putter head. Don't make that mistake.

Payne used a trusty center-shafted putter to stroke the ball across the green.

(Phil Sheldon, Golf Picture Library)

Changing Putting Styles

Always be prepared to make a slight change or upgrade to your present style when it isn't working. Even the greatest putters make slight adjustments periodically with their putting. Payne Stewart was a prime example. He won major championships with totally different putting styles.

At one time, Stewart putted with a bulls-eye blade putter and held the heel of the putter far off the ground (only the toe—the end of the putter—touched the ground). To do this, Stewart arched his wrists dramatically. Interestingly, however, he won one of his U.S. Opens at Hazeltine doing just the opposite. On this occasion, using a ping cavity back putter, he putted with the toe of the putter off the ground, and only the heal portion of the putter touched the ground at address (similar to the flat style of putter used by tour great Fuzzy Zoeller).

Payne's Tension-Free Secrets

During the course of playing a hole, the recreational golfer often becomes more and more tense when hitting a pitch, chip, bunker shot, or putt. One reason is a lack of confidence because he or she has devoted little time to practicing these shots. The typical player becomes lost over the ball, trying to figure out just what to do. Consequently, the player grips the club too tightly, and becomes so tense that he or she has trouble getting the club back.

Payne never looked tense over the ball, because he did everything possible to stay calm and unhurried. Because of excellent practice habits and knowledge of what it took to hit each shot, he was very relaxed over the ball. He hit many short game shots with such relaxed arms and hands that it looked as if the club was going to come out of his hand.

Jim's Tips

Since most short-game shots require finesse, not power, you must be prepared to vary the strength of your grip depending on the type of shot you need to play, depth of rough, texture of sand, and all the variables involved. Also, take a couple of gentle breaths to help yourself relax and make a tension-free swinging action.

Feel Over Mechanics

During the Doral Ryder Open, played every year at the Doral Resort and Country Club in Miami, Florida, which is my home base, I used to always make a point of watching Payne hit short shots. Whether he was hitting a ball out of a typical position or tough lie, he never seemed to be going through a mechanical checklist in his head to figure out how to play a shot. His practice swings gave the impression that he was searching for the right feel—the length and speed of swing that would propel the ball to the target. You too should be more target and feel oriented, or you stand a good chance of experiencing what is known in golf circles as "paralysis by analysis."

Supreme Confidence

On occasion, Payne was accused of being cocky. I never looked at him that way. I thought that he was simply confident because he knew what he was doing. If I had a junior player who seemed to doubt him- or herself, I would have my student watch Payne play at Doral. Payne never appeared to doubt himself the least bit on the course, particularly when hitting shots around the green and putts on it. The same believe-in-yourself attitude can help you play better golf.

Bet You Didn't Know

Dr. Fran Pirozzolo, who helps athletes gain more confidence—including members of the New York Yankees baseball team—explains that you can choose to be confident. To a large degree, a positive approach is a conscious decision you make. If you stick to shots you have practiced and stay away from shots you are not proficient with, your confidence level will rise.

Golf Is Only a Game

No matter how big the event, Payne always gave the impression that he was having fun on the course. Sure, there was a time early on in his amateur career when he threw clubs and cursed when things didn't go well. But as he matured, he realized that golf was a game that could never be mastered and that there were other things more important in his life, like family and religion. Starting in early 1989, Payne admitted to telling himself before each round how lucky he was just to be able to play golf, let alone play winning-tour golf. It's obvious his new attitude helped. He went on to win three major championships and become a golfing hero. And the lesson we can all take from Payne Stewart is that whatever level you reach, getting your priorities right will make you both a better person and a better golfer.

The Least You Need to Know

➤ To hit pitch shots like Payne Stewart, allow your wrists to hinge on the backswing, and accelerate the club through the ball.

➤ When chipping, let your hands lead the club into the ball, like Stewart.

➤ When hitting long bunker shots, follow Stewart's example of swinging on a slightly flatter plane than normal and taking a thin slice of sand.

➤ To sink more pressure putts, hold the putter head slightly off the surface of the green.

➤ To develop a feel for the shot you're about to play, concentrate on employing technically sound practice swings, just like Stewart used to do.

Glossary

address   The starting position for employing a swing.

alignment marking   Dot, arrow, or line on the top of the putter head that designates the sweet spot of the putter face.

apron   The first cut of grass around a green.

armchair analysis   The golfer sits in a chair and reviews the round he or she has just played.

arms-and-shoulders stroke   Using the triangle formed by the arms and shoulders to control the movement of the putter.

away   A player is away when he or she is farthest from the hole and it's his or her turn to play.

backspin   The ball lands on the green and then spins back, ideally toward the hole. Backspin is imparted on the ball when the golfer makes solid contact striking the ball on a downward blow.

backswing   The movement of the club away from the ball.

ball marker   A small rounded object, about the size of a dime, and flat on one side. The flat side features a tiny pointed prong that enables the player to stick it into the putting green. A ball marker is placed down behind the ball to mark a player's ball on the green. A player marks his or her ball to clean it or to clear the way for a fellow golfer who is farther away and putting on the same line.

baseball grip   All 10 fingers of the player's hands are on the handle when he or she holds the club.

beach   The sand is sometimes referred to as the beach. If a player's ball is in the beach, it is in a sand bunker.

birdie   A score of one below par.

bite   A ball that stops quickly when it hits the green has bite.

blade putter   A putter featuring a streamlined, low, and thin-head design.

blind shot   The player cannot see the green from where he or she is hitting the shot.

bogie   A score of one over par.

bounce   The angled area of flange under the club head. Bounce allows the club to slide through the sand more easily.

break   The degree of slope in a green that causes the ball to turn left or right toward the hole.

brollie   The nickname given by British golfers to an umbrella.

brush stroke   A player makes a brush stroke when employing a low-back, low-through, pendulum-type chipping stroke and the club head brushes the grass somewhat like a paintbrush stroke.

bump   A low shot nudged along the ground that hops onto a green.

bunker   A sand or grass surface that is in a pit or hollowed-out area.

bunker shot   A shot played from a bunker. To hit this shot the club contacts the sand behind the ball, and the sand lifts the ball out.

carry   The distance the ball travels between impact and landing. Also refers to an area you want your ball to go over, as in "I need to carry the bunker."

change of direction   You change direction when you complete the backswing and start swinging the club down toward the ball.

check   When your ball skids, slows, and eventually stops.

"chili dip"   When the club strikes the ground before the ball causing a heavy chip shot that falls well short of the green, landing spot, or hole. Also referred to as laying the sod, chunking, or sticking your pick.

chip   A shot that spends more time rolling along the ground than flying through the air. For example, a chip hit with a 7 iron may carry one-fifth of the total distance to the hole and then roll the remaining four-fifths of the way.

choke down   To grip down an inch or more on the club's handle.

closed stance   When setting up, the player's back foot is a few inches farther than his or her front foot is from the target line.

club head speed   The degree of the club's acceleration during the swing, measured in miles per hour.

club selection   Deciding which club to play a shot with.

cross-handed grip   When holding the club, usually a putter, the right-handed player's left hand is closer to the ball than the right hand. In this instance, it may also be called left hand low.

"Dairy Queen" shot   Named by Claude Harmon, winner of the 1948 Masters tournament. Harmon developed a supersoft bunker shot. It landed so softly that he compared it to dropping Dairy Queen ice cream on the ground.

death move   A very serious swing fault.

divot   A piece of turf extracted from the ground by a swinging club, hopefully, after contact with the ball.

divot hole   An area of dirt usually surrounded by fairway grass. The grass was removed when a former player hit a shot, most likely an iron.

double bogie   A score of two over par (not good).

doughnut   A heavy weighted circular object that is attached to the neck of the club. A golfer swings a club featuring a doughnut to stretch his muscles or to increase swing speed.

downswing   The club starts swinging toward the ball.

drill   An exercise done during practice that helps a player drum a specific swing movement into the muscle memory.

eye-hand coordination   The ability of a player to look at a target, for example a hole, and after judging how far away it is, feel the distance with his or her hands. According to medical experts, the eyes see the target while the brain processes the data and tells the hands the right speed to swing the club to propel the ball to the target.

face   The part of the club head that strikes the ball.

fat   Describes a heavily hit shot. A shot in which the ground is struck before the ball is.

feel   A good sense for judging distance and hitting the ball to the hole.

flagstick   A metal pole that is put into a hole to show the golfer where the hole is situated on the green.

flange   The bottom of an iron club.

flat left wrist   This means that the left wrist stays stable and lines up with the top of the left forearm.

flat stick   Savvy golfers refer to the putter as a flat stick.

flat swing   The club is directed well inside the target line, often behind the body, on a flat or rounded angle or plane.

flex   The amount of play in the shaft of a club. Clubs usually feature shafts with a whippy flex, medium flex, stiff flex, or superstiff flex, also known as an X-shaft. In modern golf club fitting, there are many flexes that can be fit exactly to your swing speed or your feel.

flyer   A shot that flies longer than normal because grass or moisture intervened between the ball and clubface at impact. The result is less spin, often causing a shot with much less control.

"fried egg"   The ball sits down in the center of a crater of sand. The ball looks like the yolk of a fried egg.

fringe   Synonymous with *apron*.

gap wedge   A wedge usually featuring 52 degrees of loft. (Prior to 1990, a pitching wedge had approximately 52 degrees of loft. Newer clubs have been designed with less loft, and now the normal pitching wedge has 47 to 48 degrees of loft. Because a sand wedge usually has 56 degrees of loft, golfers have found the need for a club to bridge this large gap in their set—thus the gap wedge.)

grain   The direction grass grows on a green.

grass bunker   A bunker filled with grass instead of sand.

green-light situation   A course situation that allows the player to hit an aggressive shot.

grip pressure   The amount of pressure in the fingers when a player holds the club.

hacker   A high-handicap golfer.

handsy action   The player uses his or her hands actively during the swing.

hinge   The setting or cocking of the wrists.

hole   A round receptacle in the green, $4\frac{1}{4}$ inches in diameter, at least 4 inches deep, and usually metal-lined.

hole out   The term used to describe the process of knocking the ball into the hole—holing out a pitch.

hole placement   The position of the hole on a green.

holing a putt   Sinking a putt or knocking it into the hole.

hood   When you lean the shaft of your club forward toward the hole, you subtract loft from the clubface.

hook spin   The ball turns quite dramatically from right to left when hook spin is imparted on it by a right-handed golfer.

hot   A shot hit with extra force and minimum speed.

interlock grip   When a right-handed player holds the club, the pinky finger of the right hand intertwines with the left forefinger.

knockdown   A low shot usually played into the wind.

lag   A long putt hit close to the hole.

left-hand-low   Synonymous with *cross-handed grip* for a right-handed golfer.

lie   How the ball sits on the fairway, in rough, or on the green.

lie of club   The angle of the club head at address. The 14 different clubs used in golf each have a different lie angle by design.

line   This is short for target line. The path from the ball to the hole or your target is called the line.

lip   The rim of the hole. "Hanging on the lip" refers to a ball next to or half over the rim.

lob   A high shot that lands softly on the green, usually played with the sand wedge but more recently with the lob wedge.

lob wedge   A short club featuring 60 degrees of loft or more with very little bounce.

loft   The angle on the clubface. Low loft has a straighter face while more loft indicates more angle on the face.

lofted club   The more lofted the club, the higher and shorter the distance the ball travels, when hit properly.

maintaining your level   The player maintains the same height of the body from address through impact.

mallet   A semicircular-shaped putter head.

match play   A competition by holes. For example, Player A wins hole number one against Player B by scoring a par four to Player B's score of five. Players A and B tie the remaining holes. Therefore, Player A wins the match one up.

medal play   Competition where the player who takes the least number of strokes for a round or rounds is the winner.

narrow stance   The player's feet are relatively close together when he or she sets up to the ball.

nip the ball   To hit the ball crisply and cleanly off the turf.

one less club   The player takes a higher numbered, weaker club. One less club is taken to hit the ball a shorter distance.

one more club   The player takes a lower numbered, stronger club. A stronger club is taken when more distance is required.

open stance   Setting up to the ball with the front foot a few inches farther back from the target line than the other foot.

over the top   For a right-handed golfer, the right shoulder juts outward at the start of the downswing, so the player swings the club over the top of the plane line and delivers an across-the-target-line swing path.

overlap grip   When a right-handed player grips the club, the right pinky is draped atop the left forefinger.

overspin   When overspin is imparted on the ball, you have hit above the equator of the ball.

par   The number of strokes a skilled player should take on a hole. The rules of golf state that par is the score an expert player should make on a given hole.

"paralysis by analysis"   The player thinks so much about technique that he or she freezes over the ball.

partially plugged lie   The ball is less than half-buried in sand.

pin   Synonymous with *flagstick*.

pin high   When the ball lies even with the pin—to the side of the green or hole—it is considered to be pin high, and the shot was hit the correct distance.

pin placement   The position of the pin on the green tells the golfer where the hole is. For example, the pin is placed left.

pitch   A lofted shot that spends more time in the air than on the ground.

pitch-and-run shot   A low pitch shot that lands short of the green and then bounces before rolling toward the hole.

pitching wedge   A lofted club featuring 46 to 49 degrees of loft. (Degrees vary from manufacturer to manufacturer.)

plane   The lie angle of the club combined with the angle of the ground the golfer stands on equals the plane angle.

plugged lie   The ball is buried halfway or more in the sand, with little or no crater of sand around it.

pop shot   When playing this shot, the golfer makes a very short, wristy backswing, hits down sharply on the ball, and stops at impact. The golfer gives the ball a stab or pop with the club. The ball pops out of the lie.

powder   Soft, pure-white sand.

preshot routine   The process of preparing for a shot by setting oneself into the address position, in a certain way every time. A good preshot routine features relaxation, visualization, and a repetitive synchronized ritual.

pull   A shot hit on a straight line but left of target (for a right-handed golfer).

putt   The player uses a putter to roll the ball across a green.

putter   A club used to hit a putt, usually having 2 to 5 degrees of loft.

red-light situation   A course situation that encourages you to hit a defensive shot.

reverse overlap grip   When holding the club, the right-handed player's left forefinger overlaps the pinky of his or her right hand.

rhythm   Coordinating the movement of the body with the movement of the club.

sand trap   Synonymous with *bunker*. Sand trap is a term despised by the United States Golf Association (USGA), who insist on calling sand traps bunkers for no apparent reason.

sand wedge   The club used to play a bunker shot, having approximately 56 degrees of loft and a wide bottom called a flange.

setup   Synonymous with *address*.

shank   A shot hit off the neck of the club. A shank can become chronic and a nightmare for anyone getting a "case of the shanks."

shooter   Synonymous with *flyer*.

short game   Shots hit from inside 75 yards.

sink   You hole out a putt. When a shot goes in the hole from any distance and from anywhere, it is called a sink.

skull   The golfer skulls a shot when he or she hits the top half of the ball with the bottom of the club. A skull from a bunker is the worst mistake that can happen, usually worse than a whiff.

slice spin   Imparting dramatic left-to-right spin on the ball.

snake   Usually a putt with a double break over a long distance.

socket   The neck or shank of the club. Hitting a shank is sometimes called a socket job.

soft cut   A controlled shot that flies slightly from left to right.

sole   The bottom of the club head.

square clubface alignment   Setting the leading edge of the clubface at a right angle to the target.

square stance   When a player takes the address, his or her feet are parallel to the target line and equidistant from it.

squeeze the ball   Pure contact on short shots around the green that impart maximum backspin for that length of shot.

stroke   The backward and forward motions of the swing. Stroke usually refers to putting.

stroke play   Synonymous with *medal play*.

strong grip   The player takes a strong grip when the Vs formed by the thumbs and forefingers point up at the right shoulder, or even farther right for the right-handed golfer. The hands are turned right on the grip. Also called a hook or closed-face grip.

sucker pin   A hole featuring a pin or a flagstick in it that is located behind a cavernous bunker or water hazard—you have to be a sucker to attack the hole.

sweet spot   The part of the clubface that imparts the best contact with the ball.

swing weight   The relationship between the clubhead and the grip of the club. Measured from a fulcrum point and registered in golf terms such as C-9 or D-1. C weights are lighter, D weights are heavier.

tapin   An extremely short putt; also called a *gimme*. So close that most golfers just pick them up. This type of putt that is made virtually every time because it is so close to the hole.

tempo   The speed of the swing.

tight pin   A hole located very near to the edge of a green.

timing   Smoothly blending the back and through motions of the swing.

touch   Synonymous with *feel*.

tough track   A very difficult golf course.

tucked left   The pin is located on the left side of the green, often at the back, and often behind a bunker.

tweener   A term used to describe a situation where a player is in between clubs. For example, a player faces a tweener when he or she can't decide whether to hit a smooth pitching wedge or a hard sand wedge.

up and in   An expression used to describe the art of hitting a chip or bunker shot up onto the green and then putting the ball into the hole. Also referred to as up and down.

Vardon grip   Synonymous with overlap grip. Named after the great English champion Harry Vardon, who first popularized this grip.

visualizing a shot   Seeing a shot come to life in your mind's eye before actually playing it.

waggles   The small preparatory movements of the club. These motions often preview the type of shot to be played and also relax the hands, arms, and shoulders.

weak grip   A grip in which the Vs formed by the thumbs and forefingers of the player's hands point at the chin. For a right-handed golfer, the hands are turned to the left.

whiff   Totally missing the ball with the club.

wide stance   At address, the distance between the player's feet is greater than the width of the shoulders for a full swing. Also any stance in which the feet are spread more than is considered normal for that particular shot.

wristy   Very active hand action or loose wrist action.

yip stroke   A nervous-type stroke that causes a putt to be far too short, far too long, or off line. The hands jerk or spasm during the stroke. A yip usually occurs on shorter length putts and is almost always the result of feeling too much pressure.

Golf Schools

Besides myself, Fred Griffin, Butch Harmon, David Leadbetter, Phil Rodgers, Rick Smith, and other top teachers would be happy to arrange for you to visit us or our staff at an instructional site around the country so that you can learn how to improve your pitching, chipping, bunker play, and putting skills. You can take lessons on a one-to-one basis either in a practice area setting or on the course during a playing lesson, or be part of a small group of students at one of our schools.

Dave Pelz is the only golf instructor who teaches the short game exclusively. He has helped many high-handicap golfers, top professionals, and fine amateurs hit more precise pitches, chips, bunker shots, and putts.

Jim McLean Golf Schools

www.golfspan.com

The main bases for my schools are

➤ Doral Golf Resort in Miami, Florida

➤ PGA West in LaQuinta, California

➤ LaQuinta School at the LaQuinta Resort

➤ Grand Traverse Resort in Traverse City, Michigan

You can arrange for lessons by calling 1-800-723-6725.

I also have golf academies in which the instructors use my teaching system and I help train the staff along with other designated master instructors. The academies are

➤ Mariners Point, Foster City, California (located just south of the San Francisco Airport in the center of Silicon Valley)

➤ Weston Hills County Club, Ft. Lauderdale, Florida

➤ Legend Trail, Scottsdale, Arizona

Jim McLean is also part of GolfSpan.com, an Internet teaching team that is part of the *Go Network* and *ESPN*.

Each of my instructional sites has a private teaching area and a superstation featuring state-of-the-art, multiple-angle, and digital video technology. I pride myself in being able to pass on to students the wonderful shot-making secrets I have learned from such talented short-game players as Ken Venturi, Jack Burke, Paul Runyan, and others. I also am proud of my staff, who are all fine players with a tremendous knowledge of what it takes to improve your pitching, chipping, bunker-play, and putting games. My short-game teaching experts include the world-renown Carl Welty, Jeff Warne, Debbie Doniger, and Debra Spain, Christopher Toulson (Director of Instruction at Doral), Marie Salter, and Kevin Sprecher. These teachers are totally focused on our short game schools and, I believe, run the best program in the world. These seven master instructors make up our special short game team.

Grand Cypress Academy of Golf

Fred Griffin is the director of this academy in Orlando, Florida, where golfers learn how to improve their entire game. You can book lessons by calling 1-800-790-7377 or get a feel for what's offered by logging on to www.grandcypress.com.

The 21-acre practice facility, where specialized short-game instruction is conducted by pitching and chipping guru Phil Rodgers, includes three practice holes, an indoor classroom, and computer analysis.

Butch Harmon Golf Schools

Harmon, based at the Rio Secco Golf Club in Henderson, Nevada, offers a one-day short-game school. He can be reached at 1-888-867-3226, or on the Web at www.butchharmongolfschools.com.

Harmon is considered by most to be a swing specialist, rather than a short-game specialist. Still, you certainly will learn some new techniques because Butch learned practically everything he knows about pitching, chipping, bunker play, and putting from his dad, the late Claude Harmon, who not only won the 1948 Masters but was one of the best short-game wizards.

David Leadbetter Golf Academy

David Leadbetter, who has numerous academy locations, including one in Palm Desert, California, three in Florida, and one in Nevada, can be reached by telephone at 1-800-424-3542, or on the Web at www.leadbetter.com.

Leadbetter, who is best known for his work with Nick Faldo, works mainly with touring professionals. David teaches his Eleven Links teaching method worldwide and instructs on all aspects of the game.

Dave Pelz Scoring Game School

This is the only school that offers just short-game instruction for shots within 100 yards of the hole. You can visit Pelz or one of his fellow teachers at the Boca Raton Resort and Club in Boca Raton, Florida, PGA West in LaQuinta, California, and The Club at Cordillera in Vail, Colorado. According to *Golf Magazine*, Pelz also offers one-day clinics in major cities around the country. Pelz can be reached at 800-833-7370 or on the Web at www.pelzgolf.com.

Pelz, who is a former NASA scientist, is best known for testing and studying the techniques of top professionals and then passing on his data to amateurs like you.

Rick Smith Golf Academy

Smith, who is based at the Treetops Resort in Gaylord, Michigan, can be reached at 1-800-444-6711. If you sign up for one of Smith's schools, be prepared to work hard on drills that are specially designed to help you learn a variety of short-game shots very quickly.

Index